ALSO BY ANDREW A. ROONEY

A Few Minutes with Andy Rooney   *1981*
The Fortunes of War   *1962*
Conqueror's Peace   *1947* (with Bud Hutton)
The Story of The Stars and Stripes   *1946* (with Bud Hutton)
Air Gunner   *1944* (with Bud Hutton)

And More by Andy Rooney

And More by

ANDY ROONEY

Andrew A. Rooney

ATHENEUM NEW YORK 1982

Jane Bradford and Neil Nyren helped with the editing of this book and the things wrong with it are partly their fault.

Library of Congress Cataloging in Publication Data

Rooney, Andrew A.
And more by Andy Rooney.

Essays taken from the author's syndicated newspaper columns.
1. American wit and humor.   I. Title.
PN6162.R628   1982   814'.54   82-45183
ISBN 0-689-11316-1

Published simultaneously in Canada by McClelland and Stewart Ltd.
Composed by American–Stratford Graphic Services, Brattleboro, Vermont
Manufactured by Fairfield Graphics, Fairfield, Pennsylvania
Designed by Mary Cregan
First Edition

Contents

Introducing Andy Rooney

To begin with, here are some clues to my character. It seems only fair that if you're going to read what I write, I ought to tell you how I stand:

—I prefer sitting but when I stand, I stand in size 8½ EEE shoes. There have been periods in my life when wide feet were my most distinguishing characteristic.

—When it comes to politics, I don't know whether I'm a Democrat or a Republican. When I was young I was under the mistaken impression that all Democrats were Catholic and all Republicans were Protestant. This turns out to be untrue, of course, and I've never decided which I am. Those of us who don't have a party affiliation ought to be able to register under the heading "Confused."

—I like cold better than hot, rice better than potatoes, football better than baseball, Coke better than Pepsi. I've been to Moscow three times and don't like that at all.

—This morning the scale balanced at 203 pounds. I'm 5'9". My mother always called me "sturdy" and said I have big bones. A little fat is what I am.

—I have an American Express card but often leave home without it and pay cash.

—The following are among the famous people I have met: Richard Nixon, George McGovern, Arthur Godfrey, Frank Gifford, Barry Goldwater, Art Buchwald, Jimmy Stewart and Carol Burnett. I have never met Teddy Kennedy although I've seen a lot of pictures of him.

—I have been arrested for speeding.

—I speak French, but Frenchmen always pretend they don't understand what I'm saying.

—It is my opinion that prejudice saves us all a great deal of time. I have a great many well-founded prejudices, and I have no intention of giving up any of them except for very good reasons. I don't like turnips and I don't like liver. Call it prejudice if you wish, but I have no intention of ever trying either again just to make sure I don't like them. I *am* sure.

—I don't like anything loud.

—Fiction doesn't interest me at all. I haven't read a novel since *Lorna Doone*. I meant to read Hemingway's *The Old Man and the Sea* when it came out, but I didn't. Fiction takes too long for the ideas contained in it. I'm not interested in being diverted from my own life.

—Good ideas are overrated. It makes more difference how a writer handles an idea than what the idea was in the first place. The world is filled with people with good ideas and very short of people who can even rake a leaf. I'm tired of good ideas.

—When I write, I use an Underwood #5 made in 1920. Someone gave me an electric typewriter, but there's no use pretending you can use machinery that thinks faster than you do. An electric typewriter is ready to go before I have anything to say.

—I know a lot about wood, ice cream, the English language and Harry Reasoner. In other areas I have some serious gaps.

—Writers don't often say anything that readers don't already know, unless it's a news story. A writer's greatest pleasure is revealing to people things they knew but did not know they knew. Or did not realize everyone else knew, too. This produces a warm sense of fellow feeling and is the best a writer can do.

—There's nothing mystical or magic about being a writer. A writer is just a person who writes something. There are almost no people who are not dentists who can fix teeth, but there are a lot of people who aren't professional writers who write very well. This is one of the reasons why being a writer is tougher than being a dentist.

—I admire people who don't care what anyone else thinks about what they do, but I'm not one of them. I care what people think and would not want you to know how much I hope you like what I write.

I:

MADE BY HAND

The Old Violin

I'M always on the lookout for something good about people. Often months go by.

There was a story last week about Roman Totenberg, a violinist whose violin was stolen last May after a concert. When he was young he'd lived on almost nothing to save enough to buy it, and it was not only of great sentimental value to him, but he'd used it to play for almost forty years. The musician was quoted as saying it was like having a child kidnapped, and he didn't know whether he'd ever play again with another instrument.

If the story ended happily and added to the flimsy proof we have that people are basically good, the thief would have read about the musician's grief and returned the violin. If he did, I never read about it, but even if he didn't, the story isn't all bad for people. Our affection for the tools we use is one of our nicest characteristics.

If you're a concert violinist, you like your violin, but it doesn't have to be that special. If you're a carpenter, I suspect you have one saw you have a special feeling for. If you do a lot of cooking, you probably have one pan you wouldn't trade for all the others.

Years ago I knew an elderly man who had whittled birds for a hobby most of his life. He had a knife his father had given him when he was fifteen and it was sharpened down to almost nothing, but it was still sharp and he was happiest when he had it in his hand. I suppose that knife was one of the most enduring things in his life. It was always there, always dependable, and there is no way to estimate the total pleasure it had given him over the years.

We all need some of the material things that provide continuity to our lives by always being there and always being the same. As a writer, I type a lot. The English language is often slippery, evasive and complex but my typewriter is simple, easy and dependable. It doesn't care how poorly I may be using the language. It knocks the words on the paper with a loud, comforting clack. I'm very fond of my typewriter, and if someone stole it I'd never write again.

Oh, I suppose I'd write again, because actually I have seventeen more like it. I buy every old Underwood #5 I find. I can write only on this model typewriter, and I don't want to run out of them before I run out of time or things to say.

Most of us tend to be more sentimental about some of the tools we use than is absolutely necessary, but it's a charming fault. I even like the trait in myself. I have a shaving brush in the medicine cabinet in the bathroom that I carried with me through four years in the Army. It's spent time in Ft. Bragg, England, Normandy, Germany, and it has been to Berlin and Moscow. I've been shaving with an electric razor for twenty years now, but I wouldn't think of discarding that tired-looking old shaving brush. It served me well and every once in a while, when I've let my beard grow over the weekend, I'll lather up with it and shave with a blade just to let the brush know I haven't forgotten it.

Most of us get attached to our cars if we keep them for a few years. I've owned cars that I liked and felt terribly disloyal to them when I turned them in on a trade for a new one. It seemed so ungrateful of me just to dump them and leave them in the hands of some hardhearted secondhand car dealer. He wouldn't care. He'd sell them to anyone in order to make a buck for himself.

I wouldn't try to defend our attachment to inanimate objects on grounds of reason or logic, but you have to admit caring for the things that serve us is one of the few nice things we do.

Bathtubs

IT seems to me it's time to rethink bathtubs.

All of us seem to like the idea of having a bathtub, but we almost never take a bath in one anymore. We take a shower. A bathtub is, at best, a makeshift place to take a shower. It's hard to get into and out of gracefully, and there's no good way to arrange the curtain so that no water ends up on the floor.

The statistics on how much more water it takes for a bath than for a shower are overwhelming. The average bathtub holds about fifty gallons of water. The average shower spouts out two or three gallons a minute. In other words, if you put the plug in the tub and took a shower, it would take twenty minutes to fill it. That's a long shower, except for one of my kids. It must mean that a tub bath is very expensive to take.

We have two bathtubs in our house. In the past twenty years I suppose there have been fifty baths at the most taken in them by people. I say "by people" because Gifford, our English bulldog, was given hundreds of baths in the tub downstairs. It was known as Giffy's Tub.

It's easy enough to say shower stalls are better to have in a house than bathtubs, but if you have an old house it isn't that easy to switch over. It's probably easier to convert your furnace to coal. A bathtub is usually jammed in a small bathroom, and there's no way to take it out without breaking through a lot of expensive walls. After you get the tub out of its position in the bathroom, it probably won't fit through any of the doors in the house, either. You might as well be moving a piano.

Once you get used to a shower, it's hard to go back to the tub. On the few occasions I've taken a tub bath in the past ten years, I've emerged from the water wondering how much of the dirt and soap residue was left on me. I always have the feeling after a bath that I want to take a shower.

I wouldn't deny there is something luxurious about a tub bath. You feel warm and weightless in there and relatively immune from your problems with the cruel, cold outside world. It feels good to lie there, submerged, with the water just barely rippling over you. When the water begins to cool down, it's fun to see if you can turn on the hot water faucet with your feet without emerging into the cold to do it.

But those good features about a tub bath are outweighed by the bad. Washing a bathtub is no joke, and it's not what you feel like doing right after you get clean anyway. I don't know why they didn't design tubs with the drain at one end and the faucets at the other. With the water cascading in right over the drain hole, you're fighting an uphill battle when you try to wash the tub. The dirty water can't get out because the clean water is forcing it back, and it's hard to distribute the new, clean stream to the areas that need it.

One of the dumbest compromises I've ever seen is one you find everywhere. People want a shower, but they find the tub dangerous to get in and out of. They don't want to get rid of it, so they stick some nonslip strips of a sandpaperlike material to the bottom of the tub. It may make it safer, but it makes it impossible to use as a tub.

Who wants to go to all the trouble to take a tub bath and then sit there on corrugated strips of sandpaper?

Most hotels maintain combination shower-bathtubs. They have those strips in the bottom of the tubs. I'll bet years go by when no one takes a bath in some hotel room tubs. No one wants to *sit* in the same tub where so many others have stood.

If we're going to get rid of bathtubs and replace them with shower stalls, we're going to have to find something to do with a lot of old bathtubs. According to the last census, there are fifty-four million bathtubs in the United States.

Getting rid of fifty-four million tubs is going to be a real challenge, but if I knew fifty years ago what I know now and could have borrowed the money from my father to swing the deal, I'd be a rich man today. I'd have bought up every one of those big old wooden iceboxes that antique dealers are selling today for $800.

Bathtubs may be the wooden iceboxes of tomorrow!

Old Clothes

My clothes are in a terrible mess. The truth of the situation I'm in came home to me last night when I washed a batch of nineteen socks. The laundry does my shirts and my wife does my underwear along with the household stuff, but I have a few pairs of good wool socks and I don't like to have them go through the washing machine, so I let them pile up until my sock drawer is empty, then I wash them all at once.

Last night I hit a new high in unmatched socks. I ended up with seven odd socks. Seven out of a possible nineteen! I'm going to give up trying to wear socks in pairs. If they're both brown or both blue, they're going to be a pair from now on. I'm not going to worry about whether they're exactly the same or not. I've never known anyone who hated me because of my socks. If I was looking for a job, I suppose I'd wear matched socks, but I'm not and that's the end of it.

It isn't just my socks, either. As I look in my closet and my bureau drawers, all I see is disaster. Two weeks ago I had on my good new brown suit, and by mistake I put a felt-tipped pen without the top on it into the inside breast pocket. The cloth of the suit absorbed the ink from the pen, and the first time I knew what I'd done was late in the day when I found a blue spot the size of a fifty-cent piece on the front of the suit just below the outside pocket.

Everyone around the office had a different idea about what I should do. One said soak it in lemon juice. Well, I don't usually carry a lemon around with me, so I couldn't do that. Someone else suggested cold water. They said I should keep it wet until I got it to a cleaners. I did that.

On the way home I stopped in at two cleaners. Both of them said they couldn't do anything with it because it was wet.

The next day I left it at a third cleaners and he got the ink out, but the suit will never be the same. It's no longer my good new brown suit I could go anywhere in.

About half the shirts in my drawer are size sixteen, and I haven't been comfortable in a sixteen for four years. Sixteen-and-a-half is my size. It looks as if I have plenty of shirts, but when I go to pick one out in the morning, I get one with a frayed collar, a missing button or the one with the brown-suit ink on it. If everything else is perfect, it's a sixteen.

This morning, after I found two socks that were reasonably close to looking the same in dim light, I put my shoes on. I'm always aware when a shoelace could go any day, but in all my life I've never had the sense or foresight to change my worn shoelaces before they break just as I'm rushing to get somewhere.

I buy about five new neckties a year. I buy expensive ties at the post-Christmas sales, but I seem to lose or ruin more than five ties a year. There must be eight or nine very good silk ties with little spots on them hanging on the back of my tie rack. I keep ones with spots on them in a special place. I never throw them out and I never wear them. On several occasions I've sprayed them with that cleaner that has chalk powder in it. It often removes the grease spot and leaves a white chalk mark that nothing will take out.

Downstairs in the hall closet I have half a dozen coats. Half a dozen may seem like a lot but it isn't if you've been using the same closet for thirty years and never threw a coat away. This morning I needed a warm raincoat. The prediction was for rain possibly turning to snow, with temperatures ranging in the mid to low thirties. One of my trenchcoat-type coats has two buttons missing and isn't warm enough. The other has a lining that zips in, but the zipper's stuck and I can't get it all the way in or all the way out.

There are days when I wish I was rich enough to throw out every single piece of clothing I own and go out with a couple of thousand dollars and start all over. Just to be safe, I might buy size seventeen shirts.

Hangers

It has always seemed to me that the President, Congress and news people spend too much time worrying about the problems that are here today, gone tomorrow, and too little time on the problems that endure, year after year, life after life.

I'll just give you one example. There aren't enough places to hang things.

If I had my way, the building code would decree that there be at least three doorknobs on every closet door. We all know a doorknob is the best and easiest place to hang something. Why is there only one to a door? Builders act as though the only purpose of a doorknob is to open a door.

A doorknob has a lot of advantages over the standard wire hanger, in addition to its ready availability. For a man, those wire hangers are hopelessly inadequate. Look at the facts:

If a man is going to wear the same pants tomorrow that he wore today, the chances are he'll want to leave the belt through the loops and some loose change and maybe even a few miscellaneous bits of hardware in his pockets.

The weight of these objects invariably causes the trousers to slide from the thin wire crosspiece of the hanger and drop to the floor. (There are wood hangers with various attachments designed to hold pants. They're good but someone takes these.)

The last place people want to hang clothes is their clothes closet. Closets are mean, inconvenient, often dark and always overcrowded. If a person's closet isn't overcrowded, you can bet that person needs a psychiatrist.

On the sagging crossbar of a clothes closet, wire hangers cluster together, wrapping their grubby little hooks around each other in an orgy of togetherness.

Doorknobs are not the only place around a house to hang something, of course. There are lots of other good places before you have to resort to putting something away in a closet.

The one place to hang a pair of loaded pants, far superior to all others, is from the top drawer of a dresser. Place a few inches of the bottom of the pant legs in the drawer and close the drawer on them just above the cuff, thus trapping them for the night. Nothing could be simpler.

Many people don't understand why cuffs were put on pants. Cuffs give a bureau drawer something to grab hold of. To eliminate cuffs on pants is a step in the wrong direction. Cuffless pants may slip from the drawer.

The best place to hang a suit coat is over the back of a chair. This is not only convenient, but there is something dramatic about a coat hung over the back of a chair.

If you are forced, by some unfortunate domestic circumstance like a neat husband or wife, into putting things away, there are still ways to avoid using hangers.

Most closets have a few hooks on either side. The best way to use these to get the most out of them (by getting the most on them) is by starting with the lighter items first. Several short-sleeved sport shirts make a good base. It is much easier to hang a pair of corduroy work pants over two sport shirts than it would be to hang one sport shirt over two pairs of corduroy pants.

Many four-poster beds are still in use, and they provide wonderful hanging space. During the winter, when you plan to put on substantially the same clothes in the morning that you took off at night, the bedpost by your feet is hard to beat as a place to hang them. They're close, convenient and in the middle of the night, who cares how they look?

There's no doubt of the shortage of places to hang things in America today, but with perseverance and ingenuity, and perhaps some help from Washington, we should be able to keep stuff off the floor.

Glue

I SEE where the Air Force is experimenting with a new glue they hope will hold some of their airplanes together. They think they may be able to replace the rivets in the fuselage with glue and save weight and money in the process. I hope the Air Force has more luck with glue than I've ever had.

The trouble most of us have with glue can't be blamed on the gluemakers. It isn't their fault. We just ask too much of glue and, of course, they encourage us to overestimate what it will do by showing us pictures of a drop of it lifting an elephant. I can't get a dish to hold together, and they're lifting elephants with it. Ed White, the football player, can't pull apart two blocks stuck with it.

It's interesting how often sticking things together and making them stay that way comes up in our lives. In my lifetime, I've had a lot to do with glue and the experiences have almost always been disappointing. I was disillusioned by glue early in life. One of the other kids in first grade told me his mother said you could make things stick together with a paste made of flour and water. Mixing flour and water never worked for me as a kid.

Maybe I just have no knack for glue. It's hard to remember a time in my life when the local hardware store wasn't pushing some new miracle bond, but none of them has ever proved to be miraculous for me.

This Air Force story says they glue two surfaces together and then put them in "an ovenlike pressure vessel at 250 degrees for an hour." Well, I just don't happen to have an ovenlike pressure vessel I can heat. Maybe that's why half the stuff I glue together comes apart.

Around the office I use paper cement. It's fun to play with and it works if it's the right consistency. The problem is, I only use it once a month or so, and it keeps getting too thick in the jar. We have a one-gallon can of paper cement thinner, and over the period of a year I use more thinner than I use cement.

In my cellar I glue a lot of wood together. I've tried the catalyst powder glue that you mix with water, I've tried the two-part epoxies, white casein-based glue, contact cement, hyde glue and the new superglues. Glue and I were simply not meant for each other. If I clamp four mortised legs into a tenoned frame and let the glue set, I find one leg is an inch shorter than the other three because the clamps were too tight in one direction. The glue has dripped down the legs and, all in all, I've made a mess of my project. Our Defense Department would be in sorry shape if I was gluing together planes for the Air Force in my basement.

When it comes to fixing things that are broken, I've had even less success with glue. If the rung of a chair is loose, you have to take the chair apart, put glue in all the rung holes and then try to find a way to clamp uneven surfaces together.

Whenever some china treasure is broken in our kitchen and assigned to me to repair in the cellar, I align the parts and apply the glue. There is no way to apply clamps to a plate, so I hold the pieces together for as long as I can. When I relieve the pressure, it always turns out that the two pieces I've glued together are no longer aligned.

The only thing I can do is give the Air Force my best advice. My advice is for them to consider some other way. Elastic bands, for example, are infinitely better than glue. I've seldom asked an elastic band to do something it couldn't handle. String or rope is a possible alternative to glue. If the Air Force wants to lift a one-ton elephant with a drop of something, I suppose they can use glue, but if they want to hold something together, I'd recommend almost anything else.

Wrappings

DEPENDING on what mood I'm in, I find it either irritating, funny or civilized when I think about how we protect protective coverings in this country.

When I come home from the grocery store and start to unpack, I am always unfavorably impressed with the layers of protective or decorative wrappings we cover our food with.

There is hardly anything we buy that doesn't come in at least two wrappings, and then several of them are assembled by the cashier at the checkout counter and put into a small bag. Then several of the small bags are grouped together and put into a big bag. If you have several big bags with small bags in them, they give you a cardboard box to put the-packages-in-the-little-bags-in-the-big-bags in.

A lot of things we buy wouldn't really need any protective wrapping at all. The skin of an orange protects an orange pretty well for most of its natural life, but we aren't satisfied with what nature has given it. We wrap ten of them in plastic or put them in a net bag, and we put the plastic bag in a paper bag. The orange inside the skin, inside the plastic which is in a paper bag, must wonder where it is.

A box of cookies or crackers often has waxed paper next to the cookies, a cardboard box holding the cookies and then waxed paper and a decorative wrapping around the cardboard box. What seems to be called for here is some stiff, decorative waxed paper.

We have always wrapped our cars in an incredible number of protective layers. We put fenders over the wheels to protect ourselves from flying dirt. Then we put bumpers front and back to protect the fenders. We proceed from there to put chrome on the bumpers to protect them from rust, and we undercoat the fenders to protect *them* from the dirt they're protecting us from.

We paint the car to protect the metal, wax the paint to protect that and then we build a two-car garage to protect the whole thing. If it was a child, it would be spoiled.

I'm laughing, but I'm a protector of things myself. I use wood preserver before I paint lumber, and when I buy a raincoat I always spray it with Scotchgard or some other silicone water resister. Over the years, I'll bet I've spent more on Scotchgard than I have on raincoats.

A good book is designed with a hard cover to protect its contents. The hard cover is protected from dirt and abuse by a dust jacket. A lot of people who are very careful with books cover the dust jacket with a plastic cover of its own.

A relative of ours bought a new couch recently because she liked the fabric it was covered with. She liked it so much she didn't want it to get dirty, so she bought a slipcover to put over it and she laid little oblong pieces of cloth over the arms where the wear is heaviest to protect the slipcover. She called them antimacassars.

We may never again see the fabric she's protecting.

Sizes

A T some point we've got to take some time out and rethink sizes. I'm not a person who likes a lot of uniformity in his life, but we could save time, trouble and space if there wasn't so much variation in the size and shape of things.

Suitcases, for example, should be made in standard sizes. There should be just four. For advertising purposes the makers could call them HUGE, GIANT, LARGE and REGULAR. HUGE would be a big suitcase, GIANT would be a normal size, LARGE would be small and REGULAR would be a small bag used for personal items you wanted to keep with you on the trip.

If suitcases were made in only four standard sizes, we could save fifty percent of the space they now take up in airplane luggage compartments. At home we could have whole closets of space and the predictably shaped suitcases would make packing the trunk of a car a pleasure.

Envelopes should come in no more than three sizes. I'm no defender of the U.S. Postal Service, but it's ridiculous to ask them to handle hundreds of different size envelopes. Some envelopes are hardly bigger than the stamps they bear, while other envelopes are too big to fit in the average mailbox.

The Postal Service might start the ball rolling by making their stamps in standard sizes, too. Stamps should be graduated in size according to price. All stamps for first-class letters should be the same size and shape year after year.

Making stamps of the same denomination in different sizes is as foolish as it would be to make some dimes the size of nickels and some the size of quarters just because they had a new picture of someone on them. It would be a convenience to all of us if we could depend on the size and shape of a twenty-cent stamp. I know stamp collectors like it, but I'm not even sure we need all these inventive designs on new issues of commemorative stamps. We ought to know what a stamp is without having to study it to determine what it will send for us.

Car bumpers should all be the same size and the same height above the road. Some steps have been taken in this direction, but too many bumpers still do not meet. It makes it difficult to start a car by pushing it with another in winter, and it makes for a lot of bashed radiators and trunks all year round.

And while car manufacturers are at it, I wish they'd agree that the key with the square end was always the ignition key and the one with the round end was always the trunk key. Regularly, one major manufacturer decides to reverse that. I'd rather see them save their creative drive for some other feature in their cars.

Boxes of cookies and crackers that we keep on our kitchen shelves need not be so inventively different as they are. Like odd-shaped suitcases, it makes them very difficult to store in a limited space.

I suppose it would be wrong to try to impose standardization on them, but I wish bottles, magazines, receipts and ice cube trays came in just a few standard sizes, too. As it is, they take up too much room. You can't stack them, file them neatly or keep them on the same shelf, because they don't fit together.

Too often the shape and size of things is determined not by anyone thinking of how the item will be used, but by someone in the advertising department whose only consideration is how to sell it.

Letter Writing

THERE ought to be a five-cent stamp for personal letters. Letter writing is one of the good things about a civilized society, and it should be encouraged. It's a shame that everything is conspiring against letter writing. Our whole postal system has deteriorated to the point where mail is no fun at all. The excitement we used to feel about the arrival of the mailman is gone.

It costs twenty cents for a regular stamp now. That's a terrible number, and you don't dare buy a roll of twenty-cent stamps because you know it's going to change before you get used to it and certainly before you use up a roll.

I object to the fact that it costs me more to send a letter to a friend than it costs some fly-by-night real estate operator to send me a phony brochure in the mail telling me I'm the provisional winner of a $10,000 sweepstakes. I don't like strangers knocking on my door trying to sell me something, and I don't want my mail cluttered with advertising. If anyone wants to accuse me of feeling that way because I make a living from the advertising found in newspapers and on television, go ahead and accuse me of it. It isn't true.

I don't get five good, genuine, personal letters a year. The time is coming when the letter written with pen and ink and sent as a personal message from one person to another will be as much of a rarity as the gold pocket watch carried on a chain. It's a shame.

There is something special about a personal letter. It's better than a phone call, no matter what the telephone company says. A phone call disappears into the air as soon as the receiver is put back on the hook. A good letter can last a lifetime.

Some of my most precious possessions are letters that have been written to me sometime in the past. I don't have a single memorable phone call stored in a box in my attic or basement. I've never thrown away a good letter and, like any real treasure, I don't even have to look at them to enjoy having them. I *know* I have them.

The telephone calls come and go. They make no permanent impression on me and have no place in my memory.

A personal letter is a good thing because you say things you can't say in a crowd and might not even say to the person face to face. If you feel like it, a letter allows you to take yourself and your thoughts more seriously than you would dare take them in conversation. And you can say things without interruption.

A good letter is, in many ways, the exact opposite of a political speech. A politician addressing a crowd has to talk so broadly and generally about the issues in order not to offend any one of the thousands of people listening that he usually ends up saying nothing. A letter can be specific, and if the writer has some bias or prejudice, he can even reveal his true self by letting this show. Writing a friend, you shouldn't have to be careful. Abraham Lincoln's letter to his stepbrother telling him he wasn't going to loan him the eighty dollars he asked for tells you more about Abraham Lincoln than the Gettysburg Address does.

Some of our best history has come that way, from personal letters of famous people that scholars have dug up. You get a better idea of what someone is really like from a personal letter they weren't expecting you to read than you get from a carefully considered public statement they've made. We say real things in letters.

There are several reasons why we aren't writing many personal letters. We don't write letters with news of the family because we already have that by telephone; we don't write secrets because we're all so aware that they may fall into the wrong hands and end up in print; and we don't write awkward love letters much anymore because we're afraid of sounding silly. Love letters were almost always silly, but only in retrospect. The moment it is opened and read, a love letter is never silly. That's the other good thing about a personal letter. If you know each other well, it doesn't have to make absolute sense to anyone else.

Personal letters should go for a five-cent stamp.

Missing the Newspaper

WHEN I'm on vacation I can go for days without watching television, but I hate to miss my newspaper. I'm spending this part of my vacation thirty miles away from the nearest big city, and it's a major trip to get the papers. I don't want just *any* paper, either. I like my own bed, my own chair in the living room, my own place at the dinner table and my own newspaper. Reading a strange newspaper is like being in the hotel room you're usually in when you're reading it. It may be good but you're not at home with it. In the hotel room you can't find the bathroom in the middle of the night, and in the newspaper you don't know where they hide the sports page.

One way or another, I manage to get the paper on vacation. During the eight days we recently spent in France, I didn't see an American newspaper at all, with the exception of one issue of the Paris *Herald Tribune*. As a result, there's going to be a hole in my information storage system for the rest of my life. I know because I have some others just like it from times past when I've missed the newspaper.

"What do you mean he's dead?" I'll say. "When did he die?"

"Must have been a year ago. Last summer. Sometime in July."

Then it all dawns on me. The movie star, the sports figure or the poet passed away on one of those days I never got to read the newspaper.

There are going to be all sorts of little stories and events about which I'll be ignorant because of having missed those eight days of history. It's okay to say you can go to the library and look at the files of the old papers, but you don't get at doing that any more than you get at reading those parts of the Sunday paper you set aside to read later.

Once you get familiar with your own newspaper, you know how you want to read it. The trouble with a strange newspaper is, you have to read it the way the editor intended you to and *that's* no way to read a paper, as we all know. Fortunately, newspaper editors are too worldwise to have their little hearts broken by readers, but it must hurt them to see what people do with their day's work. Readers ignore stories the editors spent a lot of time and money on, and readers have their own ideas about which are the most important stories.

Editors try to assemble a newspaper in some logical, orderly way for an illogical, disorderly public. We ignore the editors' order. We don't read the stories they think are important first and then proceed to the dessert. We go right for the cake and ice cream first and come back to the meat and potatoes if we have time. A lot of times we don't have time. Each reader reedits the paper his own way.

I often take a train to work when I'm working, and there are important-looking executives going to town to deal with the world who get on, sit down, open the paper to the crossword puzzle or the ball scores and never once look at page one. The world could have come to an end during the night, but they aren't going to know about it until they get to the office and their secretaries tell them.

Editors know this, of course, but there's nothing they can do about it. They can't lead the paper with the crossword puzzle because even the man who is most interested in that wants the news on the front page whether he ever reads it or not. *Buying* the paper gives him the feeling he's read it.

In some ways I'm careful with money, but when it comes to buying newspapers, I'm profligate. Saturday mornings I buy two copies of the same newspaper. It costs me fifty cents instead of a quarter, but may save our marriage. I used to hate it when I had to sit there waiting for my wife to finish one section of the paper so I could read the jump of the story I'd started in the other section. And when I settle down with the paper, it spoils the pleasure of it for me when someone says, "Can I see a section of the paper?" I want the whole thing or none of it.

Now I have to make that damn thirty-mile drive.

Dictionaries

When I look up something in the dictionary, it's never where I look for it first.

The dictionary has been a particular disappointment to me as a basic reference work, and the fact that it's usually more my fault than the dictionary's doesn't make it any easier on me. Sometimes I can't come close enough to knowing how to spell a word to find it; other times the word just doesn't seem to be anywhere in the dictionary. I can't for the life of me figure out where they hide some of the words I want to look up. They must be in there someplace.

Other times I want more information about a word than the dictionary is prepared to give me. I don't want to know how to spell a word or what it means. I want to know how to use it. I want to know how to make it possessive and whether I double the final consonant when I add -ing to it. And as often as I've written it, I always forget what you do to make a word that ends in *s* possessive. "The Detroit *News'* editor"? "The Detroit *Newses* editor"? I suppose the Detroit *News*'s editors know, but I never remember and the dictionary is no help.

I have at least twenty words that I look up ten times a year. I didn't know how to spell them in high school and I still don't. Is it "further" or "farther" if I'm talking about distance? I always go to the dictionary for further details. I have several dictionaries and I avoid the one farthest from me. Furthest from me?

I am even nervous about some words I should have mastered in grade school. I know when to use "compliment" instead of "complement," when to use "stationery" and not "stationary" and "principle" not "principal," but I always pause just an instant to make sure.

You'd think someone who has made a living all his life writing words on paper would know how to spell everything. I'm not a bad enough speller to be interesting, but there are still some words I look up in the dictionary because I'm too embarrassed to ask anyone how they're spelled. I've probably looked up "embarrassed" nine times within the last few years, and I often check to make sure there aren't two *s*'s in "occasion." "Occassion" strikes me as a more natural way to spell the word.

Sometimes people use words that are wrong because they sound better than the right ones. I often do that. I wouldn't think of using the word "data" as a plural word, which it is. You wouldn't catch me saying, "All the data are in" even though it's proper. I often find myself using the word "hard" when I should be writing "difficult." It's hard to stick to the rules when the rules make you sound more formal than you want to be. I seldom use the subjunctive "were" for "was."

I've had several letters this year from literate readers accusing me of using the word "like" as a conjunction when I should be using the word "as," as in the phrase, "I don't know President Reagan like Nancy does."

That's wrong and I know it, but I can't bring myself to do it right, like in the phrase, "I don't know President Reagan as Nancy does." It just seems to weaken the statement.

The dictionary doesn't help much with the word "like" when I look there for some justification for misusing it. My Webster's starts this way: "like *adj* (ME, alter. of *ilich*, fr. OE *gelic* like, alike; akin to OHG *gilih* like, alike; . . . all fr. a prehistoric Gmc compound whose first constituent . . ." Come on, Webster, give us a break. Never mind the ilich, the gelic and the gilih, just tell it like it is.

The trouble with dictionaries is, they tell you more about words than you want to know without answering the question you have.

Design

L AST summer I made a chair. The wood was maple and cherry, and I invented what kind of a chair it was as I went along. When I finished, the chair looked great, but it has one shortcoming. It tips over backwards when anyone sits in it.

My design was better than my engineering.

Most of us are so engrossed in whatever it is we do with our days that we fail to consider what anyone else is doing with theirs. I attended a meeting in Washington D.C. a short time ago and everyone there but me was a designer of things. I never knew there were so many. I came away realizing that designing what a product will look like is a substantial part of any business. There are thousands of people who spend their lives doing it.

Everything we use has been designed, well or poorly . . . your car, your toaster, your watch. When Alexander Graham Bell finished inventing the telephone, all he had was wires. Someone had to decide on the shape of the instrument it would be housed in, and they came up with that great old standup telephone. That was industrial design.

There is usually trouble between engineers and designers. Most designers are creative artists who tend to ignore the practical aspects of a product. Most engineers, on the other hand, don't usually care much what a product looks like as long as it works.

The only time the consumer wins is when design and function blend together in one harmonious unit that looks great and works perfectly. We know it doesn't happen often.

A lot of artists who can't make a living selling their paintings or anything else that is commonly called art often turn to commerce. Sometimes they are apologetic about having to make a living, but they ought not be. If they are bad artists that's one thing, but if they are competent or even talented artists they ought to take a lot of satisfaction from being able to provide the rest of us, who don't have their talent, with some visual niceties. Making the practical, everyday world good-looking is not a job to be embarrassed about.

It may even be that industrial design and commercial art are more important than art for art's sake. Art always appeals to me most when it has had some restrictions placed on it. I like art that solves a problem or says something a new way. Uninhibited, freeform, far-out art never seems very artistic to me. Artists who can do anything in the whole world they want to do don't usually do anything. Even Michelangelo was at his best when he had a ceiling to paint.

The danger industrial designers face is that they'll be turned into salesmen. The first rule of industrial design should be that the product must look like what it is, not like something else. If something looks like what it is and works, it's beautiful and no amount of dolling it up will help it. This accounts for why bridges are so attractive to us. The best bridges are built from plans that come from some basic engineering principle that hasn't been altered by a salesman who thinks he could get more people to cross it by making it a different shape. I always liked the Shredded Wheat box for the same reason.

The best-designed packages are those whose first priority is to contain the product. The ones we are all suspicious of are the packages that are too big and too fancy for what they were built to contain. We are tired of false cardboard bottoms and boxes twice as big as they need to be to hold something.

The original green six-ounce Coca-Cola bottle was one of the great designs of all time. It was perfect in almost every way and has, naturally, been all but abandoned. The salesmen took over the bottle from the designers, and now it's too big or not a bottle at all.

I hope our industrial designers can maintain their artistic integrity, even though they have turned to commerce, because what worries me about all this is the same thing that worries me about that chair I made. Too often we're making things that look better than they are.

Four Cars

My daughter Emily has scraped together enough money to buy herself a new car—which takes some scraping these days—so she's going to get rid of her 1968 Volkswagen.

I've always wanted to own a Volkswagen Bug, so I told her I'd buy it from her for whatever the dealer offered her in trade on her new car. Emily likes the old car and the idea of having it in the family, where she can keep an eye on it, appeals to her.

Now, if you think of me as a homespun type with simple tastes who walks to the store for the paper Sunday morning, you're going to be disappointed to hear that Emily's Volkswagen would give me four cars. And that's just for two of us. I know that sounds rich and wastefully American, but I don't spend a lot of money on cars, and owning more cars than you can drive at any one time has a lot of advantages. It can even save money.

I'd love to be rich enough to have the perfect car for every occasion and forget about ever buying another new one. I probably drive 25,000 miles a year. If I could spread those miles over half a dozen cars, they'd never wear out.

If I get Emily's Volkswagen, it's going to create some confusion in the driveway. My wife now owns a 1978 Saab. She loves it and I hate it. She loves it because it's small, nicely made in many ways and gets her where she's going on very little gas. I hate it because the windows are hard to roll up, it turns like a truck and it can't get out of its own way on the road.

The car I drive the most is a 1977 Ford station wagon. It's a great car if you can afford the gas and find a parking space big enough to take it. I'm always carrying wood or tools or suitcases from here to there, and it's very handy to be able to dump everything in that huge rear area. It's coming up to 70,000 miles on the speedometer though, and I don't know what to do next. If gas goes to two dollars a gallon, I suppose I'll just have to throw it away, because *nobody* will want it.

My third car is a little beauty called a Sunbeam Tiger. I've owned it since 1966. It's one of those small green sports cars you've seen around, but this one is special. It has, packed under its bonnet, a Ford V8 289cc engine. The car is so small and the engine so big that it will, as my son Brian says, "blow the doors off anything on the road."

I'd give the Tiger to Brian, but I feel he's getting a little too old for a toy like that. And I don't drive it very fast anymore myself, because the engine has always been better than the body. I have a nervous feeling the body could fall off the engine at any time. I don't really drive it much at all anymore. It's too cold in winter and too hot in summer, and I won't take it out when there's salt on the road or when it's raining because it leaks. It's not a family car.

If I don't get Emily's Volkswagen, I'll be needing a new car in another year. I'd *like* to buy an American car. I feel about the U.S. auto industry the way you feel about one of your children who has done something really dumb or wrong. You're disappointed and disillusioned, but you still love it. You want to forgive and forget.

It might be practical for a group of friends on a block to get together and form their own car pool. A "hertz," they could call it. If four families owned eight cars, they could have just about everything they'd need for any occasion. Each family would have one basic car that it kept in its own driveway. The other four—or even six—vehicles would be kept in a communal parking lot. There might be a Jeep, a convertible sports car, a pickup truck and a big expensive car for special occasions. It could be a diesel Cadillac for long trips or maybe even an old Rolls-Royce if the group had a sense of humor and money. They might even want one motorcycle. They'd probably want at least one plain ordinary extra utility car.

But that doesn't solve my problem. Emily says there's some body rot in the Volkswagen, so I'm going to look at it. She always was too honest for her own good.

Advertising

My 1977 Ford station wagon has eight cylinders, a wonderfully powerful engine and an insatiable appetite for unleaded gas. It's a great car, if Ford wants a testimonial, and obviously I'll never have another like it.

It has 83,872 miles on it now, and for the past few weeks I've been wondering whether I should have it serviced and fixed up or buy something new and smaller. It costs me twenty dollars to fill the wagon with gas, which it consumes at the rate of something like fifteen miles to the gallon. I say "something like" because I'm not one of those people who figures out exactly how much a car gets to the gallon.

Last Tuesday I decided to call the Ford place. There were two numbers listed in the phone book, one for "Sales," the other for "Service." I was making a big decision right there when I decided which number to call. I called "Service."

Saturday is the best day for me to do something like take a car in, so I asked the service manager if I could bring it in the following Saturday. Service managers always have a way of making you feel unwanted, and he seemed pleased to be able to tell me they were closed Saturday and wouldn't be able to take me until a week from Thursday.

I didn't make a date. Instead I called the other Ford number under "Sales."

"Are you open Saturday?" I asked.

"Yes, sir," the cheery voice said at the other end of the phone. "We're here Saturdays from eight in the morning 'til nine in the evening, and Sundays from noon until six."

Now, if I can *buy* a car on Saturday, why can't I get one *fixed* on Saturday? What's going on here, anyway?

I think I know what's going on, of course. We're selling things better than we're making them, that's what's going on. Fixing things hardly enters into our economy at all anymore. Whatever breaks we discard and buy a new one like it.

I make my living writing for newspapers and television, both of which are sustained by advertising, so I may be taking my economic life in my hands when I say so, but I think advertising has been carried too far.

Too many bright young men and women are turning their talent to packaging and selling things; too few of them are going into the business of *making* anything. The advertising agencies in New York, Chicago and Los Angeles are filled with bright, creative people pushing products on us that they know or care little about. If their agency loses an account for one thing, they can switch to selling a competing brand or another product without missing a beat. Their techniques are the same whether they're selling extra strength horse-feathers or roll-on headache remedies. They don't care what they're selling, they just know how to do it. They could sell us new, improved sawdust if that's what their client wanted to move.

Advertising has been a force for good in the American economy over the years. It has made us all aware of new products and has pointed out the differences in others. It has helped the economy by creating a market and thus jobs. Advertising has helped make the United States what it has been and that's good. It seems now to be making us what we're becoming and that isn't so good.

I sat on a plane next to a man in the small computer business last week. He told me his company spends more on travel and entertainment than they do making their product.

"Our product costs twelve percent of our budget," he said. "The rest goes for packaging, selling, travel, things like that."

I asked him if he thought that was right. He did, but I didn't.

They used to say no amount of advertising could sell an inferior product, but I'm not sure that's true anymore. We're being sold products on every hand that aren't good enough, by clever, persuasive advertising. I'm tired of great television commercials that are better than the programs they're sandwiched into; I'm tired of new products that are here today, by virtue of a big advertising campaign, and gone tomorrow, and if I buy a new car I'd like to buy it from a place where the mechanics work as hard and are as well paid as the salesmen.

Commercials

THE television set is on. Bob Hope is doing a commercial for a local bank in the Los Angeles area.

Why would Bob Hope do a commercial, I wonder to myself. There are three possibilities I can think of: 1) He needs the money. 2) A friend asked him to do it. 3) He owns the bank.

Of the three, only the last seems like a realistic possibility. I just can't figure it out.

Why does any successful person with a good reputation sell his name and that reputation by giving, as though it were his own, a favorable opinion about a product or service that has been written for him by an advertising agency?

The strange thing in my mind about all this is that I resent endorsements by some people and not by others. For instance, it doesn't bother me at all to see Robert Young doing Sanka commercials. Sanka keeps me awake, but their commercials are well done. I never thought of Robert Young as anything but an actor speaking someone else's words anyway.

There are dozens of people who have disappointed me by taking money to say something nice about something. In the past ten years, many of my heroes have been lost to me. I was at the air base in England during World War II when Jimmy Stewart was awarded the DFC for his heroic work as a B-24 bomber pilot. When I watched him in motion picture roles after the war, I knew there was something of honest substance behind that acting facade. And then one evening he suddenly popped up on my television screen and laid it on real heavy for a tire company. For money? Say it ain't so, Jimmy!

American Express has, singlehandedly, removed half a dozen heroes from my list. When their effective don't-leave-home-without-it commercials featured former North Carolina Senator Sam Ervin, what I had remembered as his homey, dry brilliance during the Watergate era turned to dust in my mind.

For years I braved the rain, the snow, the bitter cold to attend every New York Giants home game in hopes that the great Fran

Tarkenton would get enough help from his teammates to win one. Little did I know that while I was fighting the traffic to get back home before my wife left it, Fran was down in the locker room primping with a hair shampoo. Or is he just saying he did that for money?

I worked for John Houseman years ago. The eminent Shakespearean producer, director, actor and star of the TV show "Paper Chase," is now shilling for a brokerage house and a carmaker.

John worked with Orson Welles in their early days in the theater and maybe something rubbed off on each of them, because Orson is now doing those unctuous wine commercials. Welles has always been called a genius, but if those commercials are the work of genius, I don't understand the word. "Lousy" is the word that comes to my mind. If John and Orson needed money, why didn't they come to me?

And if I could ever understand an entertainer or an athlete selling his word for money, I will never understand an ex-astronaut or a former vice-presidential candidate like William E. Miller doing it.

Senator Bill Bradley, who may have been more help to a basketball team than anyone who ever played the game, refused millions of dollars in offers to endorse products when he was with the New York Knickerbockers. If I lived in New Jersey, this alone would be reason enough for me to vote for him.

When a person we respect for knowing how to do something transfers that respect to a product he knows little or nothing about, it is something other than honest.

New Products

Money is not my game, so I don't often read the *Wall Street Journal*, but someone on the train I take got off at the stop before mine the other night and left the paper on the seat next to me, so I looked through it. The *Wall Street Journal* gives you sort of a digest of the news you get on television.

One small story in there said that the companies that make things are coming up with fewer new products this year than last. The paper suggested this was bad, but I thought it was good. You can carry freedom of choice too far in a grocery store, for example. I don't want all the big companies squeezing out all the little upstart companies, but I don't want to be faced with ten different brands of what is substantially the identical product, either.

Our kitchen sink got stopped up last Saturday and I went to the grocery store for a can of Drāno. I don't know why Drāno. I'm just familiar with what the can looks like, and I was surprised to find a whole shelf filled with products that were supposed to free a clogged sink. There were powders, liquids and pellets. They came in cans, tubes, bottles and plastic. All of them said that if they didn't work, call your plumber. That always makes me suspect that they probably won't work on my problem. I found myself wishing the grocer had taken it upon himself to test the products for me so that he could have become expert enough to narrow my choices to just two or three.

I ended up with a can of Drāno, as always. I don't know whether any of those new, improved products were any better or not. I figured they were all more or less the same.

Genuine innovation is something we all like. That's what we mean by the line "Build a better mousetrap and the world will beat a path to your door."

The trouble is, too many big companies have been making the same old mousetrap and trying to get us to come to their door by painting it a different color or calling it the Official Mickey Mousetrap. That's not innovation, but that's what too often passes for a new product.

The automobile manufacturers of America are in trouble because we wanted something genuinely different and they gave us the same old mousetrap with electrically operated windows. The Japanese came up with some really new ideas in cars and people are buying them. When Volkswagen switched from the Bug to the Rabbit, the difference was more than new bumper stickers. You can tell a Saab from a Toyota, but you can't tell a Chevrolet from an Oldsmobile unless you own one.

Too many "new" products are coming from the sales departments of companies rather than from the engineering division. I hope Americans are tired of being tricked. A lot of good U.S. companies spend big money on product development, on good design, on engineering or improved chemistry. They have good, serious professionals working to make real improvements, not cosmetic changes, but for all the effort that is put into making the product better, it is hardly ever as much money as is put into selling it.

It has always seemed to me that, over the long run, we do one thing about as well or as poorly as we do something else in America. We have some national traits that show through our work no matter what our work is. Sometimes it's good, sometimes it isn't.

For instance, take two products as different as those produced by Detroit and the television industry. Our cars and our television, for all my complaints, are in many ways the best in the world, but they both suffer from the same things. They're big, fluffy and tend to imitate the other products in their market. Two situation comedies on competing networks are apt to be as much alike as an Oldsmobile and a Chevrolet.

Putting the same product in a new package isn't what I call a new product. When an advertisement tells me what I'm buying is "new and improved," I always wonder exactly what the improvement is and whether I was a sucker for having bought the product last year before they fixed whatever was wrong with it.

I don't care what the *Wall Street Journal* says, I like the idea of fewer new products on the market. What we ought to do is keep making the old ones until we get them right.

Quality?

I T is unceasingly sickening to see someone make a bad product and run a good one out of business. It happens all the time, and we look around to see whose fault it is. I have a sneaking feeling we aren't looking hard enough. It's *our* fault, all of us.

If it isn't our fault—the fault of the American people—whose fault is it? Who is it that makes so many bad television shows so popular? Why were *Life, Look* and the *Saturday Evening Post* driven out of business in their original forms while our magazine stands are filled with the worst kind of junk? Why are so many good newspapers having a tough time, when the trash "newspapers" in the supermarkets are prospering? No one is forcing any of us to buy them.

Around the office I work in, they changed the paper towels in the men's room several months ago. The new ones are nowhere near as good as the brand they had for years, and it takes three to do what one of the old ones would do. Somebody in the company decided it would look good if they bought cheaper paper towels. It is just incredible that smart people decide to save money in such petty ways.

I had a friend whose father owned a drugstore in a small town in South Carolina. It was beautifully kept and well run. My friend's father was an experienced druggist who knew the whole town's medical history. During the 1950s, one of those big chain drugstores moved in selling umbrellas, plastic beach balls, tote bags and dirty books, and that was the end of the good, honest, little drugstore.

We are fond of repeating familiar old sayings like "It's quality not quantity that matters," but we don't buy as though we believe that very often. We take the jumbo size advertised at twenty percent off—no matter what the quality is. I'm glad I'm not in the business of making anything, because it must be heartbreaking for the individual making something the best way he knows how to see a competitor come in and get rich making the same thing with cheap materials and shoddy workmanship.

America's great contribution to mankind has been the invention of mass production. We showed the world how to make things quickly, inexpensively and in such great numbers that even people who didn't have a lot of money could afford them. Automobiles were our outstanding example for a long time. We made cars that weren't Rolls-Royces but they were good cars, and just about everyone could scrape together the money to buy one.

Somewhere, somehow, we went wrong. One by one, the good carmakers were driven out of business by another company making a cheaper one. I could have cried when Packard went out of business, but there were thirty other automobile makers that went the same way, until all that was left was General Motors, American Motors, Chrysler and Ford. And in a few years we may not have all of them.

We found a way to mass-assemble homes after World War II. We started slapping them up with cinder block and plywood, and it seemed good because a lot of people who never could afford a home before were able to buy them.

They didn't need carpenters who were master craftsmen to build those homes, and young people working on them never really got to know how to do anything but hammer a nail.

We have a lot to be proud of, but there is such a proliferation of inferior products on the market now that it seems as though we have to find a way to go in another direction. The term "Made by hand" is still the classiest stamp you can put on a product and we need more of them. We need things made by people who care more about the quality of what they're making than the money they're going to get selling it.

It's our own fault and no amount of good government, bad government, more government or less government is going to turn us around. The only way we're going to get started in the right direction again is to stop buying junk.

II:

OLD FRIENDS

Neat People

Neat people are small, petty, nit-picking individuals who keep accurate checkbooks, get ahead in life and keep their cellars, their attics and their garages free of treasured possessions. They just don't seem to treasure anything, those neat people. If they can't use it or freeze it, they throw it away. I detest neat people. I was in a neat person's home several weeks ago and he took me down into his cellar. He must be making a dishonest living, because there was nothing down there but a few neatly stored screens and the oil burner.

I feel toward neat people the same way I used to feel toward the brightest kid in our class, who was also a good athlete and handsome.

My dislike for the tidies of the world is particularly strong this week because I realized Sunday that my desk is such a mess I can't find anything, my workshop looks like a triple-decker club sandwich with tools on top of wood on top of plans on top of sandpaper on top of tools on top of wood. If I need a Phillips screwdriver, it's easier to go out and buy a new one than to find any of the three I already own.

How do neat people do it? I hate them so much I don't want any help from them, but I would like to follow one around someday and see how they live. I bet they don't do anything, that's how they keep everything so neat. They probably do all sorts of dumb stuff like putting things back where they belong. They probably know which shelf everything is on in the refrigerator; they could probably put their finger on the nozzle to the garden hose.

What do you do with all that stuff I have cluttering my cellar, Neat People? Did you throw away the hammer with the broken handle? Mine is still down there.

What about the twenty feet of leftover aerial wire and the small empty wooden nail keg? Don't tell me you were so heartless that you tossed that out. You don't even appreciate the fact that you never know when you're going to have a good use for an empty wooden nail keg. That's how dumb you Neat People are. I, on the other hand, have been ready with an empty nail keg for the past twenty years. That's about how long it's been in the cellar, right there in the way if I ever need it.

You probably throw out broken plates and glass pitchers that can't be repaired, don't you? Tell the truth. I don't. I keep broken plates because I can't stand to throw them out. I'm waiting for them to make glue that will really mend china and glass, the way the ads say the glue will now.

Many years ago a man who owned a hairbrush factory gave me a bushel basket of odds and ends of rosewood. They're beautiful little pieces and I've never figured out what to do with them, but I wouldn't neaten up my cellar by throwing them out for anything.

My wife says the old bookcase I took out of the twins' room in 1973 should be thrown out. She gets a little neat every once in a while herself. Thank goodness that never happens to me. That's why I still have that bookcase.

We have four children and I'm not saving much money, but should I ever die, I'd like to leave the kids something. I have nineteen cans of partly used paint, some dating from the late fifties, in the cellar. I don't want them fighting over my estate when I go, so I think I'll make a will and divide the paint among them. I want it to have a good home.

My Closet

I'VE *got* to throw out some clothes.

My clothes closet in the hall outside our bedroom is at capacity. It looks like a New York City subway at rush hour in there. Clothes hang from hangers so tightly packed together that I can't get one out without removing several simultaneously.

You can laugh if you want, but it's no joke. This thing with my clothes is getting serious. I have three suits, five pairs of pants and a dozen sports shirts that would keep a poor person warm all winter, and I haven't worn them in ten years. They're too good to throw out and I don't like them enough to wear them, that's the problem. Or maybe they don't fit. That's another problem. Maybe they'll fit me later in the year. After I lose a little weight? I've been thinking that for more than ten years, and it hasn't happened yet.

I don't think you can hedge on throwing clothes away. I've given some to the Salvation Army, the Goodwill and other charitable organizations and it makes me feel good, but I seriously doubt whether the stuff I give them makes anyone else feel good. Is there someone living on welfare who really wants the jacket to a white tuxedo I bought for a wedding in 1957? Can someone use a double-breasted pinstripe suit with padded shoulders and bell-bottom trousers I thought looked great on me when I looked at myself in the store mirrors seventeen years ago? The press is still good in the pants and there isn't a spot on it. I just don't think there's a place for the suit in the give-away market.

There probably ought to be a law passed saying you can't buy a new piece of clothing without throwing one out. Maybe the law could work like deposit bottles. The store would have to give you something back on an old suit or dress when you brought it back. That way you wouldn't have the awful feeling you get when you throw something out that has a lot of wear left in it.

It isn't the money that keeps me from throwing clothes out. It's sentiment. I remember all the good times I had in that brown sports jacket. It came through at the elbow years ago and I've worn it to a few football games in the last five years, but I really can't go anywhere in it unless I'm wearing an overcoat I'm not going to take off.

I have thirty-four pairs of shoes. That sounds like a Liz Taylor kind of statistic, but I may even be cheating a little, because if I told you forty-three it would sound ridiculous. It isn't hard at all to accumulate forty-three pairs of shoes if you never throw a pair away. As a matter of fact, if you buy two pairs a year for twenty-five years, it isn't hard at all. Would you believe fifty-three?

When I say shoes I mean shoes, sneaks, loafers, moccasins, snow boots, workshoes, ski boots, black dress shoes for New Year's Eve, huaraches I bought in Mexico and the three pairs of shoes I actually wear.

You probably wonder what my clothes closet looks like. Well, it's sad when the kids leave home, but something good comes out of everything, and if Brian hadn't headed out on his own several years ago and, for all practical purposes, abandoned his closet, I don't know what I'd be doing for space. I've taken over. He has half a dozen abandoned pieces of footwear in there himself and at least ten odd jackets, ski pants and high school football jerseys, but they don't bother me much. I push them way to one side, and when he comes back at Christmas I like him to feel at home, so I stuff all my things back in my own closet or put them down cellar and move what he has left in there to the center of the clothes pole so he won't notice anything has changed.

I don't know what to do. I just can't bring myself to heap faithful old clothes on top of the garbage can, and it seems contemptible of me to think I'm doing anyone any good by giving them to the poor. When Brian comes home, I'm always nice to him. I tell him to take whatever he wants.

He never takes anything.

Throwing Things Out

TODAY is a turning point in my life.

From this day forward, I am not adding one single thing to my collection of possessions. If I bring something new in the front door, I'm going to throw something old out the back door.

The simple fact of the matter is, everything's full. My desk drawers are full and the top of my desk is heaped high with paper.

My two-car garage long ago passed the point where I could get one car, let alone two, into it. Now I can't even open the garage door from the driveway side and walk through it to the door leading to the kitchen. I have to go around.

When the oil-burner man came to give the furnace its annual physical, he said I couldn't have all that stuff piled so close to it. That's easy for an oil-burner man to say, but where would he put it? Where would he put the outdoor chair with the broken leg that's too good to throw away and that I'll probably get at fixing someday? There's no space left anywhere in the cellar except too close to the furnace.

The attic isn't any better. The attic is only high enough in the middle, under the peak of the roof, for me to stand up straight in, but I've hoisted boxes of old letters, books and suitcases filled with papers into it and shoved them over to the side where I have to get down on my hands and knees to shove them under the eaves.

The four kids have all left home, but they didn't leave home with much of their stuff. There is evidence of the eighteen or twenty years they spent in the house in closets everywhere. Parents entertain some foolish notion that they're loved and wanted just because children leave clothes behind when they strike out on their own. The kids, for their part, are about as sentimental about their closet at home as they'd be about a locker in a bus station. I love them, but when they come home for Thanksgiving and Christmas, I'm going to sneak out to their cars at night while they're sleeping and fill the trunks with old sneaks, small clothes and school papers of theirs that they've been storing at home. I'm going to stuff the cute, misshapen clay ashtrays they made in Miss Evans' pottery class into the crevices behind the front seats of their cars. I'm going to make Ellen take those 37 books in Russian she brought home from college.

In the kitchen, the drawers are piled so high with knives, forks and kitchen gadgets for cutting carrots into interesting shapes that something often sticks up too high and prevents a drawer from opening.

My life runneth over and I'm going to do something about it. Beginning today, I solemnly swear on a stack of old Garry Moore scripts, I will not bring one single item into the house or office without casting out some equivalent space-taker. If I buy a new tool, I'm going to throw out an old one. If I buy a new shirt, I'm going to throw out an old shirt.

I am no longer going to save the brown bags the groceries come in. I have a lifetime supply of old brown bags. I am going to cast out coffee cans, elastic bands, book matches, broken toasters, old snow tires and perhaps, just perhaps, my stack of old *Life* magazines.

I'm clearing out my life, beginning today . . . tomorrow the very latest.

Pennies

I think I'm finally about to get rich and I want to tell you about it. It may not be too late for you to get in on it.

My secret is pennies . . . one-cent U.S. coins. Very shortly now it looks as if the United States Mint is going to start making a new one-cent coin that will be made of zinc instead of copper. And you know what's going to happen then. Real copper pennies will start disappearing until there are practically none left, and the ones that are left will be very valuable to collectors.

Now for the good part. I am *already* a collector of pennies. Here's a case where I've really got a head start toward cornering the penny market of the future. Someone sold a 1922 Lincoln penny last year for $16,500. There must have been something special about it, but that's the kind of markup I'm looking for in the near future on the pennies I'm holding.

Here's a brief assessment of my net worth in pennies:

—I know for a fact there must be at least eighteen of them on the floor toward the back of my clothes closet in between several pairs of old shoes I don't wear anymore.

—There are two pairs of khaki pants and one pair of corduroy that I haven't been able to get into for the past few years. I'm certain to find another ten to fifteen pennies in the pockets of those.

—Up until now I've been waiting until I decided to turn in my old car before bothering to fish down in there behind the front seat cushion, but I know darn well there's a comb down there and it'll surprise me if there aren't at least twenty pennies.

—We have about ten suitcases among us in the family, and there's certainly a treasure in pennies down inside those little ruffled pockets of the suitcases.

—My real worth is up on my dresser and in a glass jar hidden between the dresser and the wall. I put the pennies from my pocket in an ashtray every night, and when that's full, I dump them in a glass jar. I've been doing that for eight or ten years. I must have three or four hundred genuine copper pennies in the jar.

Beginning today, I'm going to start being even more careful about saving my pennies . . . not that I approve of hoarding, mind you. I hate people who hoard things. Or, at least, I hate everyone but myself who hoards things. If I can save ten dollars' worth of pennies a week for the next six months before they start to disappear, that will give me twenty-six thousand of them, in addition to the stock I already have around the house.

This will be the first time I've ever been rich, although I've come close several times before. If I'd kept some of those old Benny Goodman records I had in high school, they'd be worth a fortune today. But I didn't keep them.

When I was about eight years old I started saving Indianhead pennies. I'm not sure what happened to those. I suspect my mother used them one day to pay for the laundry.

If I'd hung onto that old 1941 Ford phaeton I bought for $150 in 1951, I could get $10,000 for it today from an old-car collector.

The Lionel electric train I practically gave away twenty-five years ago would get me a bundle today.

So, I've been close before and I'm not going to let it slip away from me again. I've learned my lesson about holding onto things that will get valuable with time. I figure that if I can get together thirty thousand pennies now and hold onto them for thirty years, they'll be worth a dollar apiece and I'll sell them to a numismatist for a nice piece of change.

I'll be ninety-one.

Painting

WE had the cellar room painted last week. It's the playroom, but we've never played much of anything but records in it. I do much of my writing in it, and the walls are lined with books and binders with old scripts in them. The slide projector is down there, and there's always some debris left from the last showing we had with that.

What I resent most about the whole painting operation is that we paid to have it done, but I did most of the hard work. I moved my desk, moved two four-drawer files, moved a couch, six chairs and two storage chests and then took roughly five hundred books off the shelves and nineteen paintings and pictures off the walls. The painter came in, threw a drop cloth over the island of stuff I'd piled in the middle of the room, slapped on a coat of paint with a roller and left. There I was with a lot of heavy lifting to do and hundreds of tough decisions to make. This was obviously a time to weed out some of the literary dead wood.

I have won some awards of which I am proud, but do I hang the plaques and citations back on the walls again? Do I put the statuettes back on the bookshelves? They make me reluctant to ask guests to come down there. It must seem to them as though I've lured them to my trophy room with the promise of a slide show. On the other hand, do I bury these artifacts of success if I am really proud of them? I don't know what to do.

And what about the books? Do I keep all these books? I hate to throw one away, but do I really need *How to Cook and Eat in Russian?* The recipes are in both English and Russian. Here's Martha's fourth-grade arithmetic book, with some of her answers penciled into the exercises. It's a legitimate memento, no doubt about that, but if I keep the arithmetic book, do I also save the geography book in which she has written all sorts of nine-year-old-girl remarks?

I had to empty out the closet at the foot of the stairs too. We keep some overflow kitchen things in that. Here's one of those cute, overpriced wood cheese boards with a place for a knife. Someone gave us this for Christmas years ago. We'll never use it, but it's too good to throw away. Someone will throw it away someday, but it won't be me. I wish I hadn't been reminded it's still there. There's other stuff here, too . . . an espresso coffee maker that seemed like a good idea to buy once . . . an electric iron which I'm not going to take the time to check out . . . some cheap pie tins I must have saved from a take-out pizza place . . . several ugly flower vases. I guess I'll just dump all this stuff back in there and sort it out some other day.

I suppose I could get rid of this table . . . except that it's about the first thing I ever made when I started woodworking.

I'm certainly not going to get rid of any of my old typewriters just because the place was painted.

There must be more than one hundred pens and pencils now that I've collected them from drawers, table tops and from underneath couches and chair cushions. I almost never write with anything but a typewriter, but you don't throw away a good pencil.

What I'd like to do is, I'd like to sneak into that painter's house someday, pile all his furniture in the middle of his living room, put a nice fresh coat of paint on his walls and leave. I'd put a note on the kitchen table telling him I was so pleased with the job he did on my playroom that I wanted to do something nice for him in return.

I don't know why I never learn about jobs like this. If I'm going to pay for help I know exactly what I need. I need someone to come in, move all those books and all that furniture. *I'll* slap the coat of paint on the walls, and then the workmen can come back in, put everything back where it belongs and make all those hard decisions for me.

Now, a job like that I'd be willing to pay real money for.

The Refrigerator

WOULD anyone want to buy two lambchops, the front quarter of a cooked chicken, half a package of green beans, a loaf of bread and five plastic containers, the contents of which are unknown to me?

A recent check reveals that we have these items in our freezer. They'd be a good buy for someone. The lambchops are circa 1976. That was a good year for lambchops. Some of the stuff in the plastic containers will probably turn out to be beef cooked with vegetables in a Chinese manner. One or more might be just plain fat, though. We had a roast beef one night a year or so ago. I poured the fat off the pan before making the gravy, and I think I put it in the freezer to make it easier to dispose of and then forgot to dispose of it.

This one-time-only opportunity for some lucky person is available now because my wife and I cleaned out the freezer the other night. These were the things we thought were too good to throw away. In order to make room for this year's Thanksgiving and Christmas leftovers, we had to throw away last year's.

Years ago, I used to think it would be wonderful to buy whole sides of beef and whole boxes of cans of frozen orange juice. In the summer we would pick our garden fresh vegetables, follow directions on how to preserve their garden fresh character and then freeze them and thumb our noses at the supermarket manager all winter as we withdrew what we wanted each day from our laden larder.

When we first got a refrigerator that was half freezer, I had dreams of instant gourmet dinners. When the best foods were cheapest, we'd buy heavily. When it amused me to cook something fancy, I'd do it in my leisure time and then stow it away and amaze guests months later with my instant culinary expertise.

Ha! Ha! to all of that.

What do we use the freezer for? Ice cubes. That's about it. Ice cubes and perhaps a frozen vegetable or a can of frozen orange juice once a month. I'd trade three quarters of the space in the freezer for another burner on the stove any day.

The people who use their freezers the way they were intended are the people who put up pickles, make homemade chili sauce and have a root cellar. When we stow something in the freezer, it's Good-bye Charley. It might as well be up in the attic with the kids' sixth-grade geography books or down in the cellar under the old Christmas tree stand we don't use anymore since I bought a new one.

The people who are organized enough to label every item they put in the freezer and recall it on demand like a book on a library shelf are a marvel to me. There are a few labels on some of the containers in our freezer, but I suspect that some of them are containers we used for something else and never changed the label on when we changed the contents. When you're cleaning up the kitchen, it's easy to stick things in the freezer with plans to label them the next day.

To tell you the truth, the main section of our refrigerator isn't in great shape either. It's cluttered with all kinds of odds and ends too good to throw away but not good enough to make a meal of.

Part of the clutter comes from an uncertainty about what you keep in a refrigerator (which we still tend to call the icebox). Ketchup, mustard, jam and jelly? I think the commercial brands are all preserved for eternity, but once we open a jar, we keep it cold. We keep the opened can of coffee in the icebox.

Next year I'm going to get my finances in better shape, do my Christmas shopping early, keep a diary for tax purposes and keep track of what's in the refrigerator. Ha!

Lazy?

LAZY? I can't make out whether I'm lazy or not. Sometimes I just don't have the ambition to think about it. When my mother used to ask me to go out and get some wood for the fireplace in the cottage at the lake, I'd always come banging back in through the screen door with more than I could comfortably carry because I didn't want to have to go back out for more.

My mother always said, "That's a lazy man's load."

I don't think of myself as being lazy because I get up early every morning and go to work and I work a long day, but there's no doubt about it, certain jobs I'm faced with bring on a feeling I'd rather go lie down than do them.

It doesn't seem to have anything to do with physical labor. Some of those jobs I don't mind getting at. If I had a friendly family psychiatrist, I'd ask him to explain to me exactly what it is about some jobs that turns off my ambition. For instance:

—I don't mind washing the dishes at all, but if the dishes have been put in the dishwasher, I hate the job of emptying it.

—We have screens and storm windows in the garage that haven't been touched in years because I so dislike the job of putting them up and taking them down. Once you've passed through one whole season during which both were needed without getting them up, it's easier to pass through the next one, too.

—I'll tie a broken shoelace together in three places before facing the fact that I have to pull the whole thing out and replace it with a new one.

—I don't mind replacing a light bulb, but I dislike the job of getting the ladder out and putting it away again if it's the fluorescent lights on the kitchen ceiling.

—There's some theme here because, while I don't do it very often, I don't mind vacuum-cleaning a rug. I even enjoy it sometimes, but then I can hardly bring myself to unhitch the vacuum cleaner and put everything back in its place in the closet. If I'm vacuuming upstairs and have to put the vacuum cleaner away *downstairs*, I especially hate it. When my ship comes in, I'm going to buy a second vacuum cleaner so we'll have one on each floor. Of course, then I'll have to buy a bigger house with another closet upstairs to keep it in.

—We have never moved, because I couldn't possibly face the job of packing up my toys. We've lived in the same house since 1952 and I see no prospect of ever leaving it. It would be too hard.

—There is something satisfying about emptying a waste backet or taking out the garbage. Neither is my favorite job, but I don't mind doing those things. What I'm often too lazy to do is take the waste baskets back where they came from.

—After a long weekend when I've played tennis, done some painting or woodworking, gone to a party and just lounged around the house, I've often gone through three or four changes of clothes. By Sunday night the bedroom looks like the counter of the men's department of a clothing store after a half-off sale. My clothes are scattered everywhere, hanging from doorknobs and draped over chairs and tables. When it comes to putting clothes away, I'm incredibly lazy.

—If we return from a trip late Sunday afternoon or evening, I'll bring some of the stuff in out of the car, but then I'll sit down and watch television or start reading something, leaving the car half full in the driveway. Packing a car is just as hard work as unpacking it, but I do one without complaining and often avoid the other for days.

—Writing letters doesn't bother me as a job. It's addressing them and taking them to the mailbox that I find difficult.

—I don't mind writing my column the first time, but if it isn't good enough or if it's too messy to send out, I'm often too lazy to do it over.

Old Friends

The next time we have friends at the house over a weekend, I'm going to make sure it isn't *old* friends. I want our next house guests to be friends we don't know well enough to be perfectly at ease with—not that I didn't enjoy having Barbara and Quintin, mind you. It's just that we all know each other so well that no one holds back.

"Boy, you got a lot of work to do around this place," Quintin said.

Well I *know* I have a lot of work to do and I *know* I'm not going to do a lot of it, and I don't need a good friend telling me about it.

"I drove up to Montreal to get my paint," Quintin said. "They can still make paint with lead in it up there, and it lasts a lot longer. That's why all the paint is peeling on your house. Paint made in the U.S. isn't good anymore."

He thinks perhaps I haven't *noticed* the house needs painting?

"I nearly broke my neck on those stone steps out by the back porch," he said. "That slab of stone on top is rocking. Can't you jam another little stone or something under there so it doesn't rock? Someone's going to get killed."

Quintin thinks perhaps I haven't been meaning to stabilize that stone for four years now since the frost heaved it?

"That's a good aerial you've got on your television set," he said. "Of course, you're on high ground here so you get a good picture.

Why don't you get yourself a decent-sized television set so you can see it?"

Saturday night we had some other friends over for a drink and dinner. Barbara and Quintin wanted to help.

"Sure," I said. "You can put the glasses and the ice and the bottles out on the table on the front lawn."

"Which glasses?" Barbara said.

I told her where the glasses were and she started taking things out.

"There are only seven of these glasses and there are going to be eight of us," Barbara said.

"I know, I know," I said. "We used to have twelve of them. You have to use one jelly glass. I'll drink out of that one."

"Don't fall on that loose stone step as you go out," Quintin said to Barbara. "What about chairs for out front?" he asked me.

I told him there were some old ones up in the garage if he wanted to get a couple of those.

Quintin is a willing helper. He went out to the garage and he was gone for about ten minutes before he returned carrying two aluminum chairs with broken webbing.

"You mean *these?*" he asked incredulously.

Those were the ones I meant. I knew the webbing was broken. If the webbing hadn't been broken they wouldn't have been in the garage in the first place.

"Boy," he said, as he put the chairs down, "I thought my garage was a mess. How do you ever get a car in there? You got stuff hanging all over. You ought to have a garage sale . . . and sell the garage." He laughed. Friends can be so cruel.

"Why don't I make the salad dressing," Barbara said to my wife. "Is this the only vinegar you have?" she asked, holding up a bottle of supermarket house brand, El Cheapo vinegar. "I guess I'll use lemon instead of vinegar," she said.

"Here come the first guests," Quintin said. "There sure isn't much space for them to park in that driveway of yours."

"I'll go greet the guests," Barbara said.

"Don't break your neck on that stone step as you go out," Quintin yelled after her.

Housing Subtractions

O NE of the secrets to getting ahead in the world is to anticipate trends. If you can figure out what a lot of people are going to be doing next, you've got a head start on the future. This is true about things large and small. The knack for looking ahead and seeing what's coming next is as helpful in choosing a line to stand in at the supermarket as it is in investing in the stock market.

I heard the first evidence of what I'll bet is going to be a trend of the future, and I can't wait until I figure out a way to cash in on it and finally get rich. I know there's going to be big money in it, and it's just a matter of my figuring out exactly what business to go into to make a killing.

We were sitting around with some friends when I first realized what the future held for a lot of Americans. One couple mentioned a loan they were trying to get at the bank to make their house smaller. Do you think you read that wrong? You did not. They've talked to a contractor about putting a subtraction on their house. They've lived in it for twenty-two years, and every few years when they had saved enough money they added a room or a wing or a bathroom to the house, and they are tired of it. They had three kids, all of whom are either at college or married and away from home now, and they don't need all those rooms no one ever uses, and the husband says it's foolish to try to heat it. They estimated they spent $571 last winter heating three rooms no one ever went in.

They talked about buying a new, smaller home, but they ran into the classic problem there. They figured they could get $75,000 for their old house and buy a smaller new one for $50,000. It turns out they could have gotten $50,000 for their old house and would have had to pay $75,000 for a smaller new one.

If you look at half the houses in this country with an analytical eye, you can see ugly additions that have been made to them. The classic farmhouse in America extends back into the growing area because when children grew up and married, they didn't want to live with their parents, but they didn't have any place to go. They were still going to be working right there on the farm, so an addition was put on out back the main house.

When their children grew up, the grandparents were still around and enjoying the main house. The grandchildren didn't want to live with their parents either, so another addition was tacked on.

As a matter of fact, "tacked on" is the dominant American architectural school. Most houses have had something added that doesn't really fit the way the house was intended to look originally.

I was thinking what we could do to our house by way of subtractions. We have a playroom we put in about twenty years ago, and I don't offhand ever recall anyone playing down there. That could come out. We could make it a storage room for junk we've collected. That's what we really need the room for these days. If we want to play, we'll go outdoors.

When this new idea of making houses smaller spreads across the country, specialists in house subtractions are going to be springing up everywhere. Plumbers will be advertising: "TAKE THAT UNNECESSARY BATHROOM OUT OF YOUR HOUSE! SAVE HEAT, WATER AND ELECTRICITY. FREE ESTIMATES."

"DO YOU LIVE IN A BIG BARN?" the contractors will advertise. "LET US CUT YOUR HOUSE IN TWO, MAKE IT THAT CUTE, COZY LITTLE HOME YOU'VE ALWAYS LONGED FOR."

The small-house revolution could be a great thing for this country. For a long while now, houses have been taking up more room than they deserve. You drive through the average city or even the average village these days, and the houses are so close together and there are so few empty lots left that there's no place for the kids to play but in the street. They cut down all the trees in the wooded area to build a new housing development, and the lot down the street that used to be vacant has been built on. Not only that, the houses on both sides of the new house added wings, so there's only twelve feet between them. What used to be a vacant lot is just two narrow alleys now.

I think there's a possibility we made the same mistake with our houses that we made with our automobiles. We built them too big and added too much junk to them. The house of the future will be smaller, tighter, more compact. It will be more like a Dodge Omni or a Volkswagen Rabbit than like a Lincoln Continental.

Teaching from the Classifieds

EVERYONE says kids aren't being taught to read and write the way they used to be taught. Maybe the trouble is that they *are* still being taught the way they always have been. The trouble may be that our schools aren't being practical enough. Children still read Shakespeare, Dickens and Ralph Waldo Emerson as their writing role models. If they're going to be successful in our world, maybe young students ought to study more practical examples of English usage.

A course based on the classified advertising section of any newspaper would provide lots of examples of how we actually use the English language in practical situations. A study of the classifieds would also give students the same kind of mind-expanding exercise that translating from French into English gives them now.

One semester could be devoted to studying and translating the Houses for Sale section of the classifieds, and a second semester could be spent studying the Automobiles listings.

I have just made a comprehensive review of the classified pages of twenty newspapers. The single most frequently used word in the car ads is "loaded." I was surprised at this finding, because the last time I looked at classified ads for autos the most frequently used word was "creampuff." I don't see "creampuff" at all anymore. This would be a good lesson for children. Like so many words in our language—words like "whippersnapper," "humdinger," "dreamy," "soused" and "pickled"—"creampuff" served its purpose for a while as a linguistic fad and then disappeared into the never-never land of lost expressions.

The word "loaded" is a good example of how complex the English language can be, and kids might as well understand that at the beginning. Only recently the word was most used not to describe a secondhand car, but as a synonym for "soused" or "pickled." Now "loaded" is a synonym for "many extras," "custom features" and "fully equipped."

Studying the classifieds would help prepare children for the real world, because they'd learn that things are not always what they seem. Here, for instance, are a few translations for phrases from the automobile section:

PHRASE	MEANS
Asking $3,500	Will take $2,700
$3,500 or best offer	Glad to get $2,500
Good station car	Don't try to go far in it
Runs good	Runs
Runs excellent	Runs
Runs well	Runs
Body needs work	Body rotted out
1981 model only 1100 miles	A lemon
Mint condition	Still some paint on it

Here are a few translations children might be taught from the housing ads:

PHRASE	MEANS
Owner willing to sacrifice	For sale
Transferred, must sell	For sale
Wooded area	Tree in front of house
Heavily wooded area	Two trees in front of house
Landscaped	Has a bush on the lawn
Beautifully landscaped	Two bushes out front and one on the side
Cozy, intimate	A really small house
Secluded	Out in the boondocks
30 minutes from downtown	Out beyond the boondocks
2 ½ baths	Includes the birdbath out back
Wall-to-wall carpeting	House has no real flooring

That's the homework for tonight, children.

Che-Wee

Every so often I'm struck with how dumb I am about something, so I buy a book that's going to solve my stupidity problem. They never help much.

Your Income Tax Made Simple is just as hard for me to understand as my income tax was in the first place.

The Handyman's Guide to Electricity doesn't do anything for me. I'm still a little nervous about changing a light bulb.

I'm not much of a bird-watcher, but we have a place in the country and I thought I ought to get to know a little more about the pretty little things flitting around our trees. All birds look like sparrows to me. There are big sparrows, small sparrows and gaily colored sparrows. But they all look like sparrows. Last summer I realized this was a know-nothing attitude, so I bought two bird books. They were filled with every conceivable kind of sparrow.

One pleasant afternoon, I picked a quiet spot near a tree where the birds usually hung out, carried a chair there and sat with the bird books opened on my lap.

You know, of course, what happened. There had never been a time in all the long history of that particular place where I'd chosen to sit when so few birds came by. There were chipmunks and a woodchuck down at the far end of the garden waiting for me to leave so he could go get the vegetables, but for hours there were no birds.

Several days later, I tried again and finally saw a bird circle in for a landing on the limb of the tree. Quickly I started leafing through the first bird book and found something called an American Redstart that I thought looked hopeful. On closer inspection I wasn't so sure. The bird was making some noise, so I went to the section of the book that describes the sound an American Redstart makes.

Listed under SONG, the first book said, "Che-wee, che-wee, che-wee with the final note slurred down . . ."

Hmmm. Under American Redstart the second book said, "VOICE: A series of rich, piping whistled notes."

This bird of mine didn't seem to be putting any commas or hyphens in what he was saying, and if he was singing "Che-wee, che-wee, che-wee," I couldn't tell whether it was rich, piping and slurred down or not. The neighbor's lawnmower was going, for one thing.

I have never been able to identify a bird from a bird book, a fern from a fern book or any star or set of stars, with the exception of the Big Dipper, from a book on astronomy.

My wife likes expensive rugs. She doesn't buy them, she just likes them. I've tried to get to know something about rugs from glancing through a book she has, and although she has dragged me into a thousand rug stores over the years, I still can't tell a Kaftari from a 500-knot Moolagian.

Whereas I know nothing about birds, ferns, shells or electricity,

I know quite a bit about wood. I can usually identify a board and have had a few nasty rows with antique dealers who were calling mahogany veneer solid walnut. But as good as I like to think I am with lumber, I know I'm not at all good identifying a standing tree.

There must be ten tree-identification books on our shelves. I can tell the books apart, but I can't separate the trees. Once I get past a few basic ones like birch, maple, elm and pine, I'm lost. I wouldn't know a sycamore if it fell on me. The bark and leaf samples in my books don't look like the bark and leaves on my trees.

Books on grammar and usage don't help me much either. If I'm looking for correct usage in some specific grammatical situation, I can never find help.

For example, in the first paragraph of this essay I said ". . . so I buy a book that's going to solve my stupidity problem." Then I added "They never help much." I felt that, strictly speaking, I should have said "*It* never helps much," referring to just one book. I was really referring to all the books I'd bought though and, grammatical or not, "they" seemed better. I don't know whether I was right or wrong and can't find any example close to it in any usage book I own, che-wee, che-wee, che-wee.

Loyalty

For years I kept my money in the same bank and filled my car at the same gas station. I liked the idea that I was loyal.

Over the years there's been a big turnover in bank personnel, and it occurred to me that when I went there, no one in the bank knew I was a loyal customer but me. It was the same with the gas station. I flattered myself into thinking they appreciated my business. When they gave me my change and said, "Thank you, have a nice day," I thought they were thankful and wanted me to have a nice day because I was such a good customer. Several years ago I realized I was kidding myself. The gas station had changed hands three times, and they didn't have the vaguest idea that I'd been buying my gas there for seventeen years.

Lately I've been banking and buying gas at my own convenience. I buy gas at the station nearest me when I need it or I drive to one

I know is a penny cheaper. I've changed banks twice recently because they opened a branch a block closer to my office. Give me a toaster or move in next door and you have my allegiance. Loyalty got me nowhere.

I suppose both gas stations and banks would object to being linked together, but they serve the same purpose in my life. When I run out of gas or money, I have to go to a place where I can get more. Gas stations used to compete for my business by offering free air, free water and a battery and oil check. Now you're lucky if the attendant bothers to put the gas cap back on.

Banks used to care about my business. They knew me. I didn't have to bring my birth certificate, a copy of my listing in *Who's Who*, and four other pieces of positive identification to cash a check for twenty-five dollars. If I wrote a check for more money than I had, Mr. Gaffney used to call and sound real angry. But he *did* call. He knew where to find me. No one at the bank knows me anymore. I went in yesterday to pick up a new Master Charge card that was supposed to be there, but they wouldn't give it to me because I hadn't brought the letter with me that they sent saying the card was ready.

If the bank doesn't know me by name, the feeling's mutual, because I don't know my bank's name anymore, either. It usually changes before I've used up all the checks they've sent me with the old name on it. My bank seems to keep acquiring other banks—with my money, I suppose—and they throw the other bank a bone by putting some little part of its name in with their primary name.

My bank's name was originally the Chemical Bank, plain and simple. They changed it to Chemical National Bank, then Chemical Bank and Trust Co., then they acquired the Corn Exchange Bank and my checks said the Chemical Corn Exchange Bank. I always liked that best, but it didn't last. They bought another bank, dropped the "Corn" and called themselves Chemical Bank New York Trust Co. This was unwieldy, and I was pleased several years ago when they renamed the bank once again. The new name? The Chemical Bank.

There is a bank in New York called the Irving Trust Company, and I've always sort of hoped they'd buy my bank and call it Irving's Chemical Bank.

It's too bad everything is as big and impersonal as it is now. I'm sorry to have lost personal touch with the people running the establishments where I do business, but if they don't care, I can't afford to be sentimental. When I was a little boy, we patronized Evans Grocery Store. It had oiled wood floors, and Mr. Evans always gave me a free candy bar when I brought him the check for the month's groceries. The supermarkets were just getting started, and eventually, of course, they ran almost all the little neighborhood grocery stores out of business. My mother kept buying things from Mr. Evans, even though the same loaf of bread was two cents cheaper at the new supermarket. She wanted to help him survive, but apparently the two cents wasn't enough, because he didn't make it for long. He never got to be Evans New York Chemical Corn Grocery Store.

Love Thy Neighbor

IT seems to me that neighbors are going out of style in America. The friend next door from whom you borrowed four eggs or a ladder has moved, and the people in there now are strangers.

Some of the old folklore of neighborliness is impractical or silly, and it may be just as well that our relations with our neighbors are changing. The biblical commandment to "Love Thy Neighbor" was probably a poor translation of what must have originally been "Respect Thy Neighbor." Love can't be called up on order.

Fewer than half the people in the United States live in the same house they lived in five years ago, so there's no reason to love the people who live next door to you just because they happened to wander into a real estate office that listed the place next door to yours. The only thing neighbors have in common to begin with is proximity, and unless something more develops, that isn't reason enough to be best friends. It sometimes happens naturally, but the chances are very small that your neighbors will be your choice as buddies. Or that you will be theirs, either.

The best relationship with neighbors is one of friendly distance. You say hello, you small-talk if you see them in the yard, you discuss problems as they arise and you help each other in an emergency. It's the kind of arrangement where you see more of them in the summer than in the winter. The driveway or the hedge or the fence between you is not really a cold shoulder, but it is a clear boundary. We all like clearly defined boundaries for ourselves.

If neighbors have changed, neighborhoods have not. They still comprise the same elements. If you live in a real neighborhood you can be sure most of the following people will be found there:

—One family with more kids than they can take care of.

—A dog that gets into garbage cans.

—One grand home with a family so rich that they really aren't part of the neighborhood.

—A bad kid who steals or sets fire to things, although no one has ever been able to prove it.

—People who leave their Christmas decorations up until March.

—A grouchy woman who won't let the kids cut through her backyard.

—Someone who doesn't cut their grass more than twice a summer.

—Someone who cuts their grass twice a week and one of the times always seems to be Sunday morning at 7:30.

—One driveway with a junky-looking pickup truck or trailer that's always sitting there.

—A family that never seems to turn off any lights in the house.

—A teenager who plays the radio too loud in summer with the windows open.

—Someone who leaves their barking dog out until 11:30 most nights.

—One mystery couple. They come and go but hardly anyone ever sees them and no one knows what they do.

—A couple that has loud parties all the time with guests that take an hour to leave once they get outside and start shouting good-bye at each other.

—Someone who doesn't pull the shades.

—A house with a big maple tree whose owners don't rake the leaves until most of them have blown into someone else's yard.

It is easier to produce nostalgia about a neighborhood than about a community, but a community is probably a better unit. A neighborhood is just a bunch of individuals who live in proximity, but a community is a group of people who rise above their individual limitations to get some things done in town.

Home

ONE Saturday night we were sitting around our somewhat shop-worn living room with some old friends when one of them started trying to remember how long we'd lived there.

"Since 1952," I said. "We paid off the mortgage eight years ago."

"If you don't have a mortgage," he said, "the house isn't worth as much as if you did have one."

Being in no way clever with money except when it comes to spending it, this irritated me.

"To whom is it not worth as much," I asked him in a voice that was louder than necessary for him to hear what I was saying. "Not to me, and I'm the one who lives here. As a matter of fact, I like it about fifty percent more than I did when the bank owned part of it."

"What did you pay for it?" he asked.

"We paid $29,500 in 1952."

My friend nodded knowingly and thought a minute.

"I'll bet you," he said, "that you could get $85,000 for it today . . . you ought to ask $95,000."

I don't know why this is such a popular topic of conversation these days, but if any real estate dealers are reading this, I'll give them some money-saving advice. Don't waste any stamps on me with your offers to buy. You can take me off your mailing list.

Our house is not an investment. It is not a hastily erected shelter in which to spend the night before we rise in the morning to forge on farther west to locate in another campsite at dusk. Our house is our home. We live there. It is an anchor. It is the place we go to when we don't feel like going anyplace.

We do not plan to move.

The last census indicated that forty million Americans move every year. One out of every five packs up his things and goes to live somewhere else.

Where is everyone moving to? Why are they moving there? Is it really better someplace else?

If people want a better house, why don't they fix the one they have?

If the boss says they're being transferred and have to move, why don't they get another job? Jobs are easier to come by than a home. I can't imagine giving up my home because my job was moving.

I have put up twenty-nine Christmas trees in the bay window of the living room, each a little too tall. There are scars on the ceiling to prove it.

Behind the curtain of the window nearest my wife's desk, there is a vertical strip of wall four inches wide that has missed the last four coats of paint so that the little pencil marks with dates opposite them would not be obliterated. If we moved, someone would certainly paint that patch and how would we ever know again how tall the twins were when they were four?

My son Brian has finished college and is working and no longer lives at home, but his marbles are in the bottom drawer of his dresser if he ever wants them.

There's always been talk of moving. As many as ten times a year we talk about it. The talk was usually brought on by a leaky faucet, some peeling paint or a neighbor we didn't like.

When you own a house you learn to live with its imperfections. You accommodate yourself to them and, like your own shortcomings, you find ways to ignore them.

Our house provides me with a simple pleasure every time I come home to it. I am welcomed by familiar things when I enter, and I'm warmed by some ambience which may merely be dust, but it is our dust and I like it. There are reverberations of the past everywhere, but it is not a sad place, because all the things left undone hold great hope for its future.

The talk of moving came up at dinner one night ten years ago. Brian was only half listening, but at one point he looked up from his plate, gazed around the room and asked idly, "Why would we want to move away from home?"

When anyone asks me how much I think our house is worth, I just smile. They couldn't buy what that house means to me for all the money in both local banks.

The house is not for sale.

III:

EATING AND LIVING

Fresh Fruits and Vegetables Incorporated

It's a funny thing that all of us get up every morning and set out to make progress, because when you think about some of the things progress has brought us, it isn't all that desirable sometimes.

We have a summer vacation place about a hundred fifty miles north of New York City, and to get there we pass through parts of the Hudson Valley that grow some of the best fruit and vegetables the world produces. The season is very limited and the crops are small, but when the strawberries come, there are none better. Shortly after that, the raspberries appear. They are gone in ten days, but when you can get them, they are as subtle and delicate a flavor as anything our taste buds can savor.

There is one roadside vegetable stand we patronized for years. We would stop there on every trip and load up with whatever fruit or vegetable was at its best. After the berries were gone, the corn came and along with it yellow squash, zucchini, green beans and peas. For a brief period every year I could imagine becoming a vegetarian. That's how good they were. These were local fruits and vegetables at their best, nothing imported from elsewhere, nothing frozen.

It is sad for me to report to you that progress has set in at our vegetable stand. We always waited with anticipation for those great, red-ripe, thin-skinned tomatoes. Last week we stopped at the stand, and they had tomatoes all right, but not the tomatoes that took me four miles off course to buy. These were the pink, perfectly formed, tough, tasteless variety. They give the impression that they weren't so much grown as manufactured. The only thing they're good for is as decoration on a salad plate. You can't actually eat them. They're to be used like parsley in a restaurant that serves small portions but wants to fill the blank spaces on the plate.

The virtue of these square tomatoes is that they can be picked by machine and shipped for thousands of miles over a period of months without deteriorating. I suspect it wouldn't hurt one of them much if one of the trucks behind the picking machines ran over it. The driver might think he'd hit a rock, but no real damage would be done to either the truck or the tomato.

My vegetable stand—my *former* vegetable stand now—had also decided to stock oranges from Florida, raspberries from California for $2.79 a half pint, and melons from Arizona. If I'd wanted melons from Arizona or tomatoes from California, I'd have stopped at the supermarket near home before I left for the place in the country.

The same thing has happened to roadside stands everywhere, even in California. Making a living from the good things grown locally is too tough a business so they branch out, and first thing you know, every roadside stand in America will carry the same things. I suppose some conglomerate will come along and buy up a few hundred roadside stands and make a chain out of them. The chain might be called Mom's Roadside Stand or Fresh Fruits and Vegetables Incorporated. They wouldn't bother handling the things the local farmers grew, because it would be too much trouble. Instead they'd be selling prepackaged products from the big commercial growers hundreds or even thousands of miles away.

If I am ever elected to Congress, I think I'll try to get a law passed making tomatoes and melons illegal, except for certain months of the year. I have spent more money on hard, tasteless melons and tomatoes in the last ten years than I've spent on toothpaste, shoelaces and typewriter ribbons combined. I never learn. I look at these things and my memory of how good they used to be in season makes me reach for my money.

My law would also prohibit a roadside stand from calling itself a vegetable or fruit stand if it also sold commercially made candy bars, souvenir ashtrays, gum, canned goods or homemade bread that wasn't made at home.

The federal government has sponsored research that has produced a tomato that is perfect in every respect, except you can't eat it. We should make every effort to make sure this disease, often referred to as "progress," doesn't spread.

Ice Cream

BECAUSE of the seriousness of our national and international situations, I'd like to say some things about ice cream.

The three things I have spent the most time thinking about and working with are words, wood and ice cream. Of those three things, it is possible that I'm best with the last.

Several times a year I fly into a rage as I'm reading a newspaper or magazine article on how to make ice cream. You may notice my hands are shaking this minute. The August issue of a good magazine about food called *Bon Appétit* arrived in the mail, and I've been reading a long feature story in it.

On the cover the story is called "The Best Homemade Ice Cream." Inside, the story is called "Ice Cream Greats." Magazines have gotten in the habit of calling their articles by one name on the cover and by a different name in the table of contents so they're hard to find. But this is not my complaint. My complaint is about their advice on how to make ice cream.

Under the heading "Easy Basic Vanilla Ice Cream," the writer gives this recipe: "2 cups half and half, 2 cups whipping cream, 1 vanilla bean, 8 egg yolks, ⅔ cup sugar, 4 tablespoons unsalted butter."

This recipe is not easy, it's not basic and it is not ice cream, it's frozen custard. The writer gets off to a bad start with me right away when she recommends "half and half." The assumption everyone makes is that it's half milk and half cream, but no one really knows what either half is.

I will tell you right now what easy, basic vanilla ice cream is. It is as much heavy cream as you can afford, enough sugar to make it sweet and enough pure vanilla extract to make it taste like vanilla. That is absolutely all you need to make great vanilla ice cream, and anyone who tells you something different hasn't made as much ice cream at home as I have.

I don't know why advice on how to make ice cream has been so bad over the years. The freezers they're selling have gotten a lot better just recently, but articles on how to make it are as bad as ever. When I was young, there were five kids in my summer group. We often made ice cream on hot evenings and it was no big deal. We'd decide to make it at 8:00, have it made by 8:30 and have the whole freezerful eaten by 8:40. The five of us ate it right out of the can with long spoons. It cut down on the dishwashing.

In the days before homogenized milk, about four inches of cream came to the top of each bottle. The five of us came from three families. We'd go to each icebox and take the top off whatever milk bottles were there, being careful to refill each skimmed bottle to the top with milk from another skimmed bottle. We thought this gave our parents the illusion that we hadn't taken the cream.

We used about a quart and a half of liquid, and if we didn't have enough cream, we filled in with milk or a can of evaporated milk. So, don't tell me about easy, basic vanilla ice cream that has eight egg yolks, half a stick of butter and a vanilla bean in it.

Bad or difficult ice cream recipes anger me for an obvious reason, I guess. We all like other people to enjoy what we enjoy, and these recipes are scaring people off homemade ice cream. I'd like everyone to enjoy making it and eating it as much as I do.

The first recipe in this magazine article after basic vanilla is one for "Prune and Armagnac Ice Cream." What would you serve with that, white clam sauce or ketchup? The magazine doesn't even give a recipe for the best ice cream to make in August, peach. To make peach ice cream, add mashed peaches to cream and sugar. Please don't put a lot of other stuff in it.

Part of the fascination of making ice cream is the physical principle involved. I know so few physical principles I get great satisfaction in knowing this one. The outside container of an ice cream freezer is wood or plastic. The container that holds the mixture is metal. You pack ice mixed with salt around the metal container. Salt converts ice to water without lowering its temperature. Any action like this consumes energy (heat). Neither wood nor plastic conducts heat the way metal does, so the energy to accomplish the conversion of the ice to water is drawn from the mixture inside the metal can, and when its heat is gone, it's frozen.

I'm not as sure about that, of course, as I am about how to make ice cream.

Donuts

When I was about ten years old, my mother went on a donut-making binge. It lasted almost a year. Two or three times a week she'd heat up the oil, make the batter and start dropping them in. I even recall that she also cooked the part she had cut out of the center, as a little round ball, and I liked those best.

We had never had donuts before that and we never had them again afterwards, but for one year, boy! did we have donuts.

I mention this not to tell you about my mother's donuts, but to illustrate something that seems to be true of most of us in relation to food and cooking. We get hooked on a few things we like to eat or know how to prepare, and we have them over and over again until we're sick and tired of them. Americans are creative about most things but not with food.

Our own kids won't have their mother's donuts to kick around when they look back at their childhood, but they're not going to be able to forget those beef stew years, the applesauce cake era or my own popover period.

My most recent kick has been Chinese. For more than a year now I've been stir-frying everything in ginger and garlic and adding soy sauce. My bread-making drive seems to have waned, I'm not making lasagna or Caesar salads the way I used to, but I'm stir-frying up a storm when I get dinner.

I don't know why we get stuck on something that way. There are so many cooking styles open to us with what we have in our refrigerators and on our kitchen shelves that it's a shame we limit our menus as we do.

All you have to do to realize how insular we are about cooking is to consider how different meals taste in other countries, even though they have been prepared from basically the same ingredients we use.

A good Chinese cook could take the ingredients most of us have in our refrigerators and produce half a dozen dishes that would be unrecognizably delicious to our taste buds.

The French can produce gourmet meals out of substantially the same bag of groceries from which both the English and the Germans would cook something tasteless and lead-weight. (I didn't write this to make friends.)

I've often thought it would be fun to have a cooking event in the Olympics. You'd put ten cooks, each from a different country, in similar kitchens stocked with similar food supplies. When the referee said "Go," each cook would look around to see what he could produce for dinner in two hours. We might also have a breakfast and lunch competition. It would be fun to see how different the meals turned out even though they were made from the same ingredients.

During WW II, the U.S. Army was supplied with absolutely first-rate food that was more often than not ruined in preparation. The standard for Army units that were moving around but not actually in combat was something called the Ten-in-One ration. The solidly packed boxes were designed to serve ten men for one day. Each box had all the staples including meat but, of course, no fresh vegetables, milk or eggs. A lot of American soldiers learned that if they could find some friendly French woman to whom they could turn over the ration, both they and the French woman's family could eat better.

It was always best not to ask any questions or count. The French woman added fresh eggs, vegetables and genius, and deducted from the box the things the French couldn't get for themselves under wartime conditions. There was more sugar in the package than most soldiers wanted, for instance, and she would take most of that.

The mystery about all this is, with international travel so common, why there hasn't been more of a coming together of cooking. Why isn't there an international style of cooking that borrows the best from each culture? Why haven't we learned to use more of the Chinese tricks for making food taste good? How come the Germans have lived next door to the French all these years without having acquired any of the magnificent French knack for preparing food?

And, for that matter, how come they never have donuts in Peking, like mother used to make?

Holiday Recipes

My question is this. Does anyone actually *make* those holiday dishes recommended in the home sections of newspapers and magazines?

I don't want to start trouble with the editors of other sections of the newspaper, but aren't some of those recipes a little far out? Leftover turkey in aspic with cherries? Turkey pie with ripe olives flavored with rum? Turkey with oyster sauce?

I suspect I know what you editors over there are doing to us. You're just trying to shake us up a little. You think we're too set in our ways about the holiday meals we have, and you're trying to make it more interesting for us.

It's an unfortunate fact that there is something a little wrong about the meals we have on Thanksgiving and Christmas. They're great but they're the same. I don't know about your house, but at our house on both occasions we have turkey, stuffing, mashed potatoes and gravy, squash, creamed onions, two kinds of cranberry sauce and dessert. The only difference in the two meals is the dessert. At Thanksgiving we have mince and pumpkin pie. At Christmas we have several kinds of cake and homemade peppermint stick ice cream.

Every family has a dish or two of its own or some special variations of the traditional ones, but basically we all have the same feast. We like it that way, too. We enjoy reading about nine new and different ways to stuff a turkey, but we aren't going to stuff ours any one of the new ways. We're going to stuff ours the way we always have.

You editors and recipe writers think we're all dissatisfied with having the same meal twice on two occasions so close together, and you're trying to get us out of our rut. We're not going to budge an inch, though.

The good thing about all those recipes is that they make wonderful reading. A lot of people who are not in what is called the Smart Set enjoy reading about those people who are. A lot of people who aren't out of work get a kick out of the classifieds, and other people who aren't looking for a house wouldn't miss the real estate section. That's what saves it for you home section editors. We love your stuff. All of us who wouldn't think of switching from turkey for Thanksgiving and Christmas enjoy studying the details of how to prepare pheasant with braised endive and black grapes as "a delightful holiday change."

Just this one year alone I have rejected quail with truffles and foie gras, roast goose with haricot beans and guinea hen with juniper berries as an alternative to turkey. My wife is thoroughly familiar with our dinner and Christmas is not a day to get clever in the kitchen.

The fact is that Americans like to ask for advice and they even enjoy being given advice, but they hate to take any of it. We're always asking someone what they think or how we ought to do something, but just as soon as they've gone we do it the same way we always have.

Recipes are difficult to use. I do some cooking, but I don't use recipes much, because there's always something in one that either I don't understand or I question. Do they mean I mix all these ingredients together first and *then* add the other stuff . . . or do I mix this in with that now and put the other stuff aside until later?

Only good cooks should use recipes probably. It's the exact opposite of what you'd think. A good cook can look at a recipe, understand it as you would a sentence in a foreign language, and then put the recipe away and make the dish. The good cook doesn't have to go back and read the recipe line for line, because he understands it.

But keep those exotic recipes coming at us, food editors. Just one thing. If we come over to your house after Christmas, we better not catch you eating plain, cold, sliced turkey.

Diets

Is there anyone left who is confused about which foods are fattening and which foods are not?

Thumb through the papers or the magazines and, nine times out of ten, you'll find a new, improved, easy, foolproof, delicious way to lose weight and still eat all you want of your favorite foods—as long as they're raw carrots, cottage cheese, gelatin and grapefruit without seeds.

"Five Wonderful Ways to Lose Weight!"

"A Diet That Can't Fail!"

"Our Computerized Diet. Lose Weight by the Numbers."

"Take Off Pounds with the Amazing Chicken Fat Diet."

"Why Movie Stars Are Switching to the All-Chocolate Diet."

I've had enough advice myself. As an overweight American, I'd like to give some advice back to the people who write diets: knock it off, will you?

We *know* why we're fat. We eat too much, that's why. Telling us how to lose weight is like telling an alcoholic how to keep from getting drunk. It's like telling a teenage girl what not to do if she doesn't want to get pregnant.

We aren't ignorant of what causes these things. Drunkenness is brought on by alcohol, pregnancy by sex and overweight by food. What kind of any of those is of relative unimportance. That's why I've never been able to take diets seriously.

A typical day's diet will read something like this:

Breakfast:	One prune
	¾ oz crust wholewheat bread
	Black Sanka
Lunch:	*Two* prunes
	¼ cup peanut butter
	6 grams cottage cheese
	2 licks of a lollipop
Dinner:	¾ cups lambchop
	37 calories of rice
	2 tsp chocolate chip ice cream, chips removed

I just don't need to have dinner broken down for me into units of measurement I don't understand. And which the food wouldn't understand either. All I have to do to lose weight is not eat so much.

The best weight-losing story I ever heard came out of a program conducted by a Midwestern university years ago. I've forgotten the university but I remember the story well.

They asked for twenty grossly overweight volunteers who wanted to slim down. When the volunteers came forward, they were asked to go back home and keep careful records of every single thing they ate for the next three weeks.

At the end of three weeks, the volunteers came with their records and were housed at the university under strict supervision. They were allowed no visitors and, to prevent cheating, they couldn't leave the building. For a second period of three weeks, each volunteer was fed everything he or she had put on the record as having eaten in the previous three.

If they said they ate a hamburg and apple pie for lunch, they got a hamburg and apple pie for lunch. If they admitted they snacked on a Hershey bar in midafternoon, they got a Hershey bar in midafternoon.

At the end of the second three-week period, the volunteers, eating under strict supervision, had lost an average of twenty pounds apiece. One woman lost thirty-five eating exactly what she said she'd been eating all along.

The moral is clear. When it comes to overweight and diet, we kid ourselves a little and lie a lot to our friends.

The Andy Rooney Upside-Down Diet

THE two biggest sellers in any bookstore are the cookbooks and the diet books. The cookbooks tell you how to prepare the food and the diet books tell you how not to eat any of it.

The quickest way for a writer to get rich is to write a diet book. A cookbook is more difficult. With a diet book all you need is one bad idea and a lot of statistics on what has how many calories. If you want to make the book thicker, you put in a whole series of typical meals that adhere to your idea.

As someone who's been eating too much all his life, I think I'm as qualified to write a diet book as anyone, and as a writer I'm twice as ready to get rich. Not only that, I have an idea. My book would be called *The Andy Rooney Upside-Down Diet Book.*

My theory is based on the idea that the average overweight person has to change his eating habits drastically. The overweight man or woman has fallen into a pattern of eating that is making him or her fat, and the only way that person is going to lose weight is for him to turn his eating habits upside down.

The appetite itself (I'll say in the Foreword to my book) is a strange mechanism. Our stomach often signals our brain that it's ready to have something sent down when our body doesn't really need anything yet.

As I understand it—and you don't have to understand things very well to write a diet book—the appetite is depressed as the blood sugar level rises. The trouble is that the blood sugar level rises slowly as your digestive processes start taking apart the food you've consumed, so that you can still feel hungry for quite a while after you've had enough because your blood sugar level hasn't caught up to your stomach.

So much for theory. Here, in brief, is my diet. You'll want to buy the book later, I imagine.

Basically, what I'm suggesting you do is reverse the order in which you eat things at a meal, and change the habits you have in regard to what you eat for what meal.

Forget cereal, pancakes or bacon and eggs for breakfast. We're going to start the morning with a bowl of chicken soup. Chicken soup will serve a dual purpose. It's nourishing, not fattening, and because it's a hot drink you won't need coffee. If you don't have coffee, you won't need sugar. No one is going to be tempted to put sugar in chicken soup.

The beauty of my diet—and I want them to make this clear on the jacket of my book—is that you don't have to deny yourself anything. Eat absolutely anything you feel like eating. The magic of my diet is in making sure you don't feel like eating much.

Before dinner many of us consume what we call appetizers. Don't take appetizers off your diet if you like them, just don't eat them first. In our *Upside-Down Diet Book* we'll be laying out more than one hundred weight-losing model meals. A typical breakfast might consist of half a grape, a bowl of chicken soup and plain butter, no toast.

Lunch might consist of ketchup, a Fig Newton, two Oreo Creme Sandwiches and lukewarm Ovaltine. In other words, Eat All You Want, but Change What You Want.

Your main meal will be dinner. Classic cuisine has called for an appetizer first, soup, a fish dish, meat, vegetables and potatoes, followed by cheese and then dessert. We're going to ask you to shake that up if you want to lose weight.

Each of our Upside-Down Diet meals will start with a bowl of ice cream or a chocolate eclair. Follow this with a small fish dish or oysters, clams or shrimp with a chocolate sauce. This will have the effect of raising your blood sugar level abruptly, and by the time the main course of oatmeal, corn flakes or Fruit Loops with buttermilk comes, you may not want any at all.

I don't want to be greedy, but after the book is published I have high hopes that it will be made into a movie.

Living Is Dangerous to Your Health

W<small>E'RE</small> all bombarded from every side with bad news about what's good for us, aren't we?

How often does a day go by that you don't hear about something else you eat or do or don't do or wear or own that's bad for your health? At least once a week they announce another item on our diet that's suspected of causing cancer. If it doesn't cause cancer, it brings on heart attacks.

The fact of the matter is, *life* is bad for you. For one thing, living brings on age, and we know how debilitating age can be. It's something everyone should avoid.

I wouldn't be surprised if the government started making us wear little labels that said CAUTION: THE SURGEON GENERAL HAS DETERMINED THAT LIVING IS DANGEROUS TO YOUR HEALTH.

No matter what we do, they scare us to death for doing it.

We take a little vacation to lie in the sun and get some rest, and what happens? We can't get any rest, because we keep remembering being warned that too much sun produces skin cancer.

In order to lose some weight, because we've been warned of the dangers of being fat, we start using substitutes for sugar. Next thing we know they're warning us that cyclamates, which we never heard of before, are a principal ingredient in some sugar-free food and drink, and because there is evidence that they're bad for mice, we ought to stop using them.

Periodically they issue a report on which cars are the most dangerous to drive. Which cars are you most apt to be killed in if you have an accident? Naturally the answer is that the most dangerous cars are the small, foreign, gas-saving machines we've all been buying to save money. You're safest in the big, fat, expensive gas guzzlers. Would the people in charge of announcing bad news have had it any other way?

There are doctors who say that jogging is so tough on the hip, knee and ankle joints that people ought to find some other way to exercise.

It's almost as though someone was out to get us just as soon as they see us taking pleasure from anything.

The reason I bring this up at all is because I finally read some good news. It was announced at an annual conference of the American Heart Association. A group of doctors attending that conference said that a moderate amount of alcohol every day might help prevent heart attacks.

There were other doctors present who *didn't* think alcohol was good for you and I personally tend to doubt it myself, but what difference does that make? At least it's good news, and if it's good news, who cares whether it's true or not—right, America?

The Scientific Community doesn't think it's loved or understood by the rest of us. If the Scientific Community wants to do something about that, I can think of a lot of announcements it could make that would endear scientists to us.

I was thinking about a few things they could expect to read about themselves if they played their cards right:

DOCTORS REPORT CHOCOLATE CANDY BENEFICIAL TO PROSPECTIVE FATHERS.

SCIENTISTS DETERMINE LARGE QUANTITIES OF MAPLE WALNUT ICE CREAM PREVENT COLD SORES IN MICE.

HIGHWAY STATISTICS SUPPORT PSYCHIATRIST VIEW THAT FASTEST DRIVERS HAVE FEWEST ACCIDENTS.

OVERWEIGHT ELK FOUND TO BE LESS SUSCEPTIBLE TO SNOW BLINDNESS.

These are the kind of encouraging signs we want to have from those people who announce things. We've had enough bad news for a while. If Geritol causes hangnails in women more than fifty, we don't want to hear about it.

Doctors

TODAY I'd like to talk about something I'd rather not talk about, doctors.

What I have in mind is that bit of advice each of us reads or hears fifty times a day. It's just three little words: "See your doctor."

The reason I don't like to think about it is . . . well, maybe you're not going to believe this but, see . . . I don't *have* a doctor.

When I was young, Dr. Traver gave me some shots. When I was fourteen, Dr. Van Loon removed my appendix, and more recently when I broke my collarbone in a skiing accident, it was stuck together at a hospital in Vermont by a competent resident whose name I have lost. In 1978 Dr. Bienfield repaired a rent in my intestinal wall.

So, all in all, I've had good medical attention, but I do not have a doctor I can call my own, and I wish they'd stop telling me to go see him.

Even the yearly physical checkup is a problem. Over the years I've had a few checkups, but never by the same doctor, and I'm always reluctant to make an appointment with one for anything so vague as "a checkup." I have this recurring nightmare of what will happen when I present myself at the doctor's office.

"Good morning, Doctor," I say in this dream.

"Good morning, Patient #17. What seems to be our trouble?"

"We don't have any trouble," I say, falling into the medical "we." "We just thought we ought to have a checkup."

"Don't you know how busy doctors are these days?" the doctor snaps at me. "We heal the sick and mend the wounded. If there's nothing wrong with you, don't waste a busy man's time."

"But, Doctor," I say, "they told me to 'See your doctor.' "

"Nurse!" he shouts. "Give the patient his pants and show him the door. And find out if he wants the bill sent to his home or his office."

A doctor wouldn't say any of those things, of course, but if he did he'd be putting his finger on a universal problem. The day has come when each of us needs a basic medical education of our own just to be smart enough to know what's wrong with us so we can choose the right specialist to go see. If you have a heart attack and rush to see an orthopedic surgeon, you are making a big mistake.

Doctors don't like to admit we know anything about our bodies. They hate having us guess what our trouble is, because we're wrong so often. The fact of the matter is, though, that very often the dumbest patient knows a little something about his condition that the doctor doesn't know. When I broke my collarbone, I knew just a little something about broken collarbones that the resident who fixed it will never know until he breaks his.

I was skiing with a friend who is a psychiatrist when I fell, and he didn't have any idea how to fix the bone, and on the trip to the hospital he worried about how the pain was affecting my psyche.

That's what any specialist does. He interprets syndromes in terms of his own specialty.

If we go to a doctor with a pain in the neck, his approach to our problem depends on what kind of a doctor he is. The thoracic surgeon wants to know whether we smoke, the ophthalmologist inspects the possibility that faulty eyesight, poorly corrected with the wrong glasses, might be the trouble. The orthopedist thinks our bad posture may have led to deterioration of the spinal column which has manifested itself in a neck condition. The brain surgeon is most apt to think that the persistent pain in the neck comes from above, while the internist wants to know if we've been passing blood.

I like doctors. The ones in my class who became doctors were the smartest kids. As much as I respect them though, I still say it's awfully hard to pick the right one. Every time I read that advice "See your doctor," I find myself wishing someone would give me one for Christmas.

Too Many Doctors?

I KEEP reading statistics I don't believe. There was a story out of Washington last week saying that by the year 1990, there will be too many doctors in the United States. Sure. And gas will be back to twenty-seven cents a gallon.

Someone is dreaming if they think there are *ever* going to be too many doctors. A day doesn't go by when I don't have a question or a problem for a doctor, but I haven't been to one in four years now because they're so busy I hate to bother them.

There won't be too many doctors until every one of us, including each doctor, has a doctor of his own. When that time comes, each of us will get the kind of medical attention we'd like to have—the kind the President of the United States gets.

Now, maybe this article meant that there would be too many doctors for the *doctors'* own good, not for *our* own good. Maybe the story was put out by some medical group that figured doctors might make less money if there was a change in the supply of medical services that came closer to meeting the demand for them.

To tell you the truth, I wouldn't feel terrible if business got just a little worse for doctors.

I can't believe anyone really thinks there will ever be too many doctors. Maybe they mean there are going to be so many by 1990 that we won't have to sit around in their waiting rooms for two hours. It could even mean that a good doctor could live a normal life and work a normal day without feeling that he was abandoning a lot of dying patients every time he took a day off.

Here's the way I'd like to have my telephone conversations go when I call a doctor's office.

VOICE: Hello. Dr. Keller's office.

ME: Hello. This is Andy Rooney. I'd like to make an appointment with Dr. Keller sometime this year.

VOICE: Why, certainly. Any time. This is Dr. Keller. What seems to be our trouble?

ME: Sorry to bother you, Doctor. I thought I'd get your nurse's secretary.

VOICE: Oh, gosh, my nurse hasn't had a secretary for more than a year now . . . since about 1989. We aren't too busy anymore, you know. As a matter of fact, I gave my nurse the day off.

ME: Could you see me before Christmas then, Doctor?

VOICE: Sure could. What are you doing right now? I'm just sitting here doing the crossword puzzle myself. I don't have another appointment until two thirty.

Well, I should live so long to have a conversation like that with a doctor. No statistic can convince me there'll ever be too many of them. Science is discovering new things we're dying of faster than they're curing the old ones. They may have licked yellow fever, diphtheria, mumps, smallpox and whooping cough, but now we have a whole new set of things that are killing us. There's plenty for doctors to do until they lick this ugly business of dying.

If by any chance I'm wrong and the time actually comes when there are too many doctors, there are a lot of repairs I'm going to have made on my body. First, I'm going to have that mole removed from behind my ear. I've been meaning to do something about that since I was twenty-four. And I'm certainly going to get some attention for my right foot and ankle from a good orthopedics man. Something's wrong in there with the ligaments.

I often worry about my blood pressure, and years ago I was rejected when I tried to give blood because my white corpuscles were wrong. They either sank or floated when they were supposed to do the opposite. They didn't want my blood. I'd go to a doctor about that.

I've got a dozen little problems that could stand some medical attention, and when the day comes when I can see a doctor without standing in line, I'll have them attended to.

You, I suppose, don't have any problems at all.

Doctors and Doorknobs

Doctors should never talk to ordinary people about anything but medicine. If I were a doctor, I'd never go to another party where there were anything but other doctors present.

When doctors talk politics, economics or sports, they reveal themselves to be ordinary mortals, idiots just like the rest of us. That isn't what any of us wants our doctor to be. We want our doctor to be an intellectual giant who knows all about everything. We don't want him to be someone who has a lot of petty little theories about what's wrong in Washington, or what play the coach should have sent in Sunday when it was third and nine on the twenty-four.

Saturday night, I was talking to a doctor at a party, and he was telling me that the nurses situation is getting desperate.

"Young women just don't want to do that kind of hard work anymore," he said. "A lot of the good ones are quitting," he told me, "because they like nursing but can't take the paperwork." Another thing, he said, was that a lot of nurses resented doctors and often thought they knew as much about a patient as the doctor did.

Well, first thing you know we were arguing about how little a nurse is paid compared to a doctor and how a lot of women ended up as nurses when they should have been doctors and vice versa. I won't tell you which side of the arguments I was on, but neither of us distinguished ourselves. It was the kind of conversation that makes me realize doctors are only mortal men, and it's always a disappointment. I'm looking for a god in my doctor.

Surgeons I meet worry me. When I get talking politics with a surgeon who has done a hundred and fifty open-heart operations, I usually wonder how he ever did it without killing the patients. It turns out he's just as dumb as I am. His opinion of the current Administration is the same as the one I heard from the man who runs the shoeshine stand in the station last week, and I certainly wouldn't want the shoeshine man fooling around with my heart valves through an incision in my chest.

Years ago, my wife and I were spending the weekend in the house of an old college friend of hers whose husband was an orthopedic surgeon. One morning I started out the front door and the knob came loose. It just twisted around in my hand, so the doctor went down cellar to get a few tools. The doorknob was obviously on the critical list.

All I could think, as I watched him attack the problem, was how happy I was to be a houseguest and not a patient. He fussed with that doorknob for more than half an hour before he got an ill-fitting setscrew in there to hold it. I'd give that doorknob another three days. Here was a distinguished surgeon who had replaced the heads of two hundred femurs with stainless steel balls that enabled patients to walk once again free of pain in their hips, but he couldn't figure out how to fix that one lousy doorknob. What do you make of this?

One problem medical men and women have is one we all share with them. To be really expert in our chosen field takes more than one type of skill, and a person who has one doesn't necessarily have others. The young medical student who masters the details of anatomy and gets the best marks in his class is not necessarily manually dexterous. The dentist who has the ability of a good cabinetmaker to put together perfect, tight-fitting parts that hold together in a person's mouth was not always—or probably even usually—the dental student who finished at the top of his class.

A doctor can't help it if he isn't born with dexterous hands, but if he also has a lot of dumb opinions about the world, the least he can do is keep them to himself so we don't get wondering about his hands.

IV:

PREJUDICES

Street Directions

WHERE do streets go in a strange city and where do they come from?

If America wants to save gas, it ought to start over with its street signs and give everyone directions on how to give directions. It would not do this country any harm at all if there were college courses on the subject of direction giving.

Someone will say, "Go down here and turn left at the third traffic light. Keep going until you run into a dead end at Sixteenth Street, then bear right."

Those are simple enough, so you set out to follow directions. Within ten minutes you're at the corner of Broad and 4th streets, hopelessly lost. You never saw a Sixteenth Street. You feel either stupid and frustrated for not being able to follow simple directions or you feel outraged at the person who gave them to you.

I've often wanted to go back, find the guy and grab him by the throat. "All right, fella. You told me to turn left at the third traffic light and then keep going until I hit a dead end at Sixteenth. You were trying to get me lost, weren't you? Confess!"

It wouldn't be any use though. I know what he'd say. He'd say, "That's not counting this light right here. If you count this light, it's four."

Or he'd say, "Maybe it's Eighteenth Street where the dead end is . . ." or "You see, Sixteenth Street turns into Terwilliger Avenue after you cross Summit Boulevard."

Whatever his answer is, it's hopeless. He didn't mean to mislead you and you didn't mean to get lost, but that's what usually happens.

You can't lay all the blame on the people giving directions. People don't *take* them any better than they give them.

My own ability to retain directions in my head ends after the first two turns I'm given. Then I usually say to whomever I'm with, "Did he say right or left at the church on the right?" If there are seven or eight turns, including a couple of "bear rights" and a "jog left" or two, I might as well find a motel room and get a fresh start in the morning.

The superhighways that bisect and trisect our cities now aren't any help at all in finding your way around. Streets that used to lead across town in a direct fashion now end abruptly where the highway cut through. Finding the nearest entrance to the superhighway, so you can drive two miles to the next exit in order to get a block and a half from where you are, is the new way to go.

If they do start college courses in direction giving, I hope they devote a semester to arrow drawing for signmakers. It seems like a simple enough matter, but it is often not clear to a stranger whether an arrow is telling you to veer off to the right or to keep going straight.

Different towns and cities have different systems for identifying their streets with the signs they erect. Some have the name of the street you are crossing facing you as you drive past. Others identify the street with a sign that is parallel to it. This is more accurate, but you can't see it. And if you don't know which system they're using, it's further trouble.

There are cities in America so hard to find your way around that, unless you're going to live there for several years, it isn't worth figuring them out.

Many cities, like Washington, pretend to be better organized than they are. They have numbers and they use the alphabet just as though everything was laid out in an orderly fashion.

New York City, for example, has numbered avenues that run longitudinally up and down the island. What the stranger would never know is that in midtown the names go from Third Avenue to Lexington, to Park, and then to Madison before the numbers start again with Fifth Avenue. Where did Fourth Avenue go? Sorry about that, that's what we call "Park."

And then "Sixth Avenue" is next? Well, not actually. New Yorkers call it "Sixth," but the official name and the name on the signs is "Avenue of the Americas." No one calls it that but the post office.

I have long since given up asking for directions or reading maps. I am one of that large number of lost souls who finds that, in the long run, it's better simply to blunder on until you find where you're going on your own.

The 55 MPH Speed Limit

Y OU'LL all be pleased to read that I'm not going to give you an opinion on (1) gun control, (2) abortion or (3) the Equal Rights Amendment. Just trust me that I'm in one hundred percent agreement with you on these issues. I can't imagine how any right-thinking person could possibly believe other than we do. I trust, in turn, that if you're for one, you're for them all. If you're against one, you're *against* them all.

The fourth most controversial issue is the matter of the fifty-five mph speed limit. I'm going to comment on that because, while it gets people yelling and hollering at each other a lot, it doesn't bring out quite the same dirty, bitter, low-down kind of viciousness in nice people that those other issues do.

I stand unequivocally equivocal about it. I'm firmly of two minds. It's a law I hate and break all the time, but if I had been in Congress when it passed into law, I'd have voted in favor of it. To be honest with you, I think everyone *but me* should be limited to driving fifty-five mph.

Even though I'd have voted for it, it seems to me the law is too general to cover every driving situation. It ought to be more flexible. I know people who are safer driving seventy-five than my sister is driving thirty-five. She's basically a good person, but she's a lousy driver. She could never roller skate, either. Does my sister get to drive as fast on the highway as Richard Petty or Mario Andretti?

If fifty-five is safe for a competent driver, we ought to have a lower limit for incompetent ones. It's ridiculous to suggest that all of us have equal skill at the wheel of a car. There's no reason to think there's any less difference between a great skier and a bad one than there is between a good driver and my sister. The two skiers shouldn't have to come down the mountain at the same speed.

Besides the difference in the competence of drivers, there's the difference in road conditions. The fifty-five mph speed limit is too fast on a narrow, winding macadam road with traffic, even if it's legal. It isn't fast enough on a six-lane highway that stretches for a hundred straight miles in Wyoming. Why should the speed limit be the same in both places?

There's some evidence that the speed limit has saved both lives and gas. The National Safety Council estimates eight thousand lives were saved last year. If it's true, that's a persuasive argument. The trouble with the statistic is that people are driving a lot less than they were five years ago because of the cost of gas. If people drive less, fewer of them die driving. If no one ever drove at all, of course, no one would ever die in an auto accident, but the government isn't prepared to go that far. Where it stops and starts protecting us from each other is a very difficult decision for the government to make. It would be safer if no one ever crossed a street, too. That would make some life-saving statistic if we all avoided crossing a street for one year.

I've always objected to any law making it compulsory for me to wear a seat belt for my own safety. Passing a law to keep me from going too fast in order to protect *other* people's lives is one thing, but when the government passes a law making something mandatory *for my own good*, the government has gone too far. My life is none of the government's damn business. I'll save it or spend it as I please.

If Congress was serious about the fifty-five mph speed limit, it would have taken one effective step years ago. It would have made it illegal for anyone to sell a car that can *go* faster than fifty-five. What sense does it make to be producing cars that will go a hundred thirty miles an hour when there isn't a road in the country you can legally drive them on that fast?

And that's where I stand on the speed limit, straddling the solid white line.

Prejudices

W E are all warned that prejudice is a bad thing, but it is very hard to separate prejudice from experience. If the same experience produces the same result for you time after time, you get so you know what to expect. You prejudge what the results will be. There are a million little prejudices I have, and I have no intention of giving them up. For instance, it has been my experience that:

—It's not much of a sale if the sign says EVERYTHING MUST GO!

—He doesn't want to talk to you if the secretary says, "Just a minute. I'll see if he's in."

—If you haven't already seen the movie on television tonight, it probably isn't anything you want to watch.

—When the phone rings after ten at night, it's usually a wrong number.

—No envelope with one of those little windows in it ever contains anything as good as you'd hoped for.

—If the literature in your hotel room can name all the places of interest in the city, it isn't a very big city.

—If it takes longer to ride than to walk, you're in New York City. If it's too far to walk, you're in Los Angeles. If it's too steep to walk, you're in San Francisco.

—The person conducting the interview on television is in trouble if he starts a question by saying, "Tell me, exactly how did you get started?"

—You'd better rinse the soap off quickly if you're in the shower and the water is only warm and the cold water faucet is all the way around to off.

—Television shows with what are advertised as "All Star" casts are no better than movies with "All Star" casts used to be.

—If you can see the bottom of the cup in a cup of black coffee, the coffee isn't worth drinking.

—The older the paper money is, the farther you are from a big city.

—When you get a piece of mail saying you've won something, you haven't won anything.

—The gas station that doesn't have a big sign up saying how much it's getting per gallon is charging more than the station down the street.

—There's no sense thinking a ballpoint pen will start to write again once it runs out of ink and starts to skip.

—Most of the people in the cafeteria between 2 and 3 PM are overweight.

—If the announcer on the television show you're watching says "Stay tuned for more of our show" at eight minutes to the hour, it means the show is over and you're about to see eight minutes of commercials and promotions for other shows and the credits for the program you just watched.

—When a government official announces the price of something may go up "by as much as four to six cents in the next five months," the price of whatever it is will rise ten cents in the next two weeks.

—If the restaurant isn't overcrowded, there's probably a better one in town.

Sound and Noise

THEY'RE tearing down a nine-story building just outside my office window. It doesn't look as though it's going to be a short job either, because when they finish jackhammering this to the ground, they're going to start riveting up a new one. Obviously I've either got to get used to it or move.

I think the trick is to get thinking of it as a sound instead of a noise. The difference is hard to define, but a noise is mindless and irritating, while a sound can be soothing. I've known people who live in the city who can't sleep when they go to the country because of the crashing silence.

I like the sound of someone whistling on his walk to work, but if someone starts whistling around the office, my mind comes to a halt and I can think about nothing except how irritating the noise is. I start psychoanalyzing the whistler, trying to think why it is he or she feels compelled to make this noise by forcing a stream of air through pursed lips.

On the other hand, I've worked in newspaper city rooms filled with people moving, yelling and typing and I can continue to work, absolutely oblivious to the pandemonium around me.

A horn honked unnecessarily or more than once for any reason is noise. Every time someone behind me blows his horn the instant the light turns green, I turn red.

A ringing telephone can be a welcome sound or an irritating noise, depending on the circumstances. I've gotten over that feeling that it may be someone wonderful calling me every time the phone rings, but there is still a sense of anticipation we're all programmed to have when we hear the phone. Even when I know it's not for me, I can't stand to have a phone ring without answering it.

A barking dog is a noise, not a sound. There are almost no times of day when I can stand to hear a dog bark. Part of it is that you have the feeling the dog wants something it isn't getting and if you like dogs, that bothers you. It's like a crying child.

One of the most inexplicable noises is a soft one. It's the one each of us hears when we're staying alone in a house at night. Who *are* those people we always hear creeping up the stairs to our bedroom? The house never makes a noise when there's someone else in it with us.

There are good sounds and bad noises everywhere. Bullfrogs in the distance down by the pond are a great sound; so is Dave Brubeck, Segovia, Pavarotti or Horowitz. Even Frank Sinatra is a good sound if you're in the mood for him. The most intrusive sound being inflicted on most of us by a few of us these days is the loud radio or stereo tape player blaring out rock music.

Sounds are important in a war. In 1944 the 1st Infantry Division, the Big Red One, was our most warwise fighting force. It didn't panic. It did what it had to do. At one point in the move across France, a green infantry division was moved in on the 1st Division's flank. One company of that division ran across an arsenal of German weapons. When the 1st Division found German weapons, they destroyed them. These inexperienced soldiers were intrigued with the handy little German Schmeisser machine guns and, during a brief fire fight in the middle of the night, started using them against their former owners. Hearing that familiar sound on their flank and assuming the presence there of the enemy, a mortar unit from the 1st Division calmly turned its weapons in that direction and dropped shells until there was silence. Tragedy of war.

Everyone should think twice before making a noise.

The Theater

IT seems like some kind of cultural shortcoming on my part, but I've never liked the Theater. By "the Theater," I mean plays acted out on stage before a live audience. There is a mystique about it for people who love the Theater that I've never understood.

You might as well know right now that I don't care whether I ever see *Hamlet* again or not. I hate going to a Shakespeare play, and I feel terrible about myself because of it. I simply think Shakespeare reads better than he plays now. If I have time to do it carefully, I enjoy reading Shakespeare from time to time, but I'm not smart enough to take much from it when the words are being spoken by an actor on stage. I just sit there, amazed that he could memorize all that, but I'm not really hearing what he says. I've been to the Theater when I wanted to stand up and yell, "Hey, wait a minute, will ya! I don't get it. Say that over again, slowly this time."

If you live in or near New York, which I do, you are very aware of the Broadway Theater. It's the Big League and I like having it there, but I seldom attend anymore. I have two rules about the Theater, and they have kept me away from it for most of the last five years.

My first rule is "If you can buy tickets, don't go." The hit shows are always sold out, and while there may be an occasional gem being ignored, most of what's left is third rate. Most of the hits are second rate.

The second rule that keeps me away from the Theater concerns the reviews. If the reviewer spends most of his column telling me how good the acting is, I know the play is a dog. When the critic starts his review by saying something like "Coleen Handley is an absolutely marvelous Darcy in Wambly Frobisher's production of *Winterthorne*," I know I don't want to see it.

The problem for me is, I don't *like* good acting. Good acting annoys me even more than bad acting. If I'm aware of how good the acting is, it's bad for me. It is my opinion that the audience should not notice how good the acting is and as soon as it does, something's wrong with it. The actors are overacting.

It seems to me there are too many actors and not enough writers. There are thousands of actors standing around New York and Hollywood, ready to grab any part that's written. Why are there so many actors and so few writers? I have a sneaking suspicion it's because acting is easier and more lucrative than writing. (You, of course, have a right to have a sneaking suspicion that I think writers ought to get more money and attention because I'm one of them.) The actor's name is up there in lights. The actor gets the big contract. All the writer gets is trouble from the producer and the director who want to change his work.

There's no doubt, I suppose, that my complaint about the Theater is a personal one. They do not give much importance to writing, and if writing isn't important, and I'm a writer, then I'm not important.

There is no doubt either that the writer has been considered of little relative importance to Broadway plays recently. Of the thirty-five current productions listed in the newspapers, only about ten display the writer's name. Three of them are usually Neil Simon. The writer in most cases is anonymous. The hottest thing on Broadway recently was something called *42nd Street.* Everyone knows it was produced by David Merrick because they've seen dozens of television and newspaper interviews with him, but I have no idea who wrote it or whether, as a matter of fact, it was written at all.

If I could turn off a bad play and go to sleep, the way I do with bad television, I'd go to the theater more often.

Bilingual Education

W HEN I listened to President Reagan's denunciation of federal programs designed to support bilingual education in the United States, I would have stood and cheered if I hadn't been a little embarrassed about agreeing with such a conservative, hard-hat opinion.

"It is absolutely wrong," Reagan said, "and against American concept to have a bilingual education program that is now openly, admittedly dedicated to preserving their native language and never getting them adequate in English so they can go out into the job market and participate."

He was referring, of course, to the large number of children in our school system who speak only Spanish and, to a lesser extent, to the large number who speak only "Black English." This may not be much of a problem in your home town, but it is if you live in Los Angeles, Miami or New York.

The very concept of language calls for one system of word use to be spoken and written by everyone interested in communicating with one another. If we're going to understand each other, we all have to agree on what words stand for what ideas. You could suddenly decide to call a chair a franakapan if you wanted to, but no one would know what you meant. In English we call a chair a chair and all English-speaking people understand.

It is wrong for any large number of people to decide they want to speak another language because they already speak it and because it's part of their heritage. It's part of what Spanish-speaking people should have been willing to give up when they came here.

Language is an emotional issue, which is why a lot of people will be irritated by what I just said. Some of us may learn two or three languages in our lifetime, but we're only sentimental about the one we picked up by osmosis from our parents when we were small children.

English-speaking people, especially Americans, have always been accused of being pigheaded in their refusal to do business in anyone else's language. We've been accused of using our economic and military muscle to shove our language down foreign throats. There's been no doubt we were often guilty of some form of national conceit, but as far as the English language goes, we probably have a lot to be conceited about. It is a very good, very useful tool. It is certainly the biggest and probably the most precise language on earth.

If we've been overbearing as soldiers, tourists or businessmen when it came to insisting everyone who wanted to talk to us speak in English, we have been more democratic about accepting foreign words into our language. We've taken in foreign words just as we've taken in immigrants. We don't have the same hang-ups about the purity of our language as the French do, for instance, and as a result, English is a more useful language than French. Evidence that we are not language snobs is the fact that something like seventy-five percent of all the words we use are derived from some other language.

There is a good case to be made for English as the one international language if the day ever comes when we have one. Not only is English the language with the most words, but it seems also to be the language most acceptable to other people.

If a vote were taken among all the people in the world and they were asked to choose five languages in order of preference, each nationality would no doubt rank its own language first, so there wouldn't be any agreement on the first choice, but the majority of people of other nations would beyond doubt make English their second choice.

Spanish is a magnificent language with a great literary tradition and a sound to it that is better than English, and I can understand anyone's reluctance to give it up. "Black English" is not a language at all. Some great words and expressions have come from it, and they'll be taken into standard English along with so many other good words English has adopted. After that it should be rejected and abandoned as soon as possible—just as anything called Black Arithmetic would be if it claimed 2 × 2 equals 5.

Color

THERE are some ideas I stick with even though I'm vaguely aware that I may be wrong.

Last week I was watching a golf match on television and I noticed one of the players was using a yellow ball. For no reason at all, I disliked it. I thought it was out of place. Golf balls, in my little mind, are white.

In this one case I decided to force myself to change my opinion. Why should golf balls be white? I remember seeing the results of a study made years ago that proved that the color yellow was easiest to see. That alone is reason enough to make golf balls yellow. Tennis balls have been yellow for about ten years. You can hardly buy a white tennis ball now.

I don't know how we get our feelings about color. Why does blue stand for melancholy? How come we "see red" when we're angry? Yellow has always been a synonym for cowardice. That's an awful thing for a nice color like yellow to have associated with it.

I remember how slow I was coming around to calling Negroes blacks. About twelve years ago I was asked to write a television documentary and the producer, a friend named Perry Wolff, was calling his series "Of Black America." I remember telling him I thought using the word black for Negro was a passing fashion and wouldn't last. I was wrong, of course. Now the word Negro seems old-fashioned and I wouldn't think of using it.

I have a lot of color prejudices to get over. I dislike seeing women wear anything but red lipstick; I'm not keen on any color for underwear except white; I don't want to offend a lot of publishers who have spent a lot of money on color presses, but I like my newspapers black and white.

The color of something is probably not a very important feature of it, but our first impression of anything comes more from its color than its shape. We've been propagandized to react to colors. We've used the color red so often for danger or as a signal to stop that we don't pay much attention to it anymore. The backs of some cars show a string of red lights that brighten up a hundred times in a ten-mile drive, and we become so inured to their signal of danger that they're meaningless. Red has become meaningless because all the roadside signs trying to attract our attention use it, too. We just can't pay attention to all the reds we see vying for our eye's attention, so we ignore some we shouldn't. Maybe there ought to be a law limiting the use of red.

My favorite color is dark green, but I forget why. I think I may have been in love with a girl who said her favorite color was dark green when I was about ten. My wife grows a lot of flowers, and my taste for color is a little more sophisticated than it used to be. If I hadn't been saying my favorite color is dark green for so long now, I might say it's something else. I just hate to change. It's one of the few questions in my life I'm settled on.

How flowers come up out of the same ground different colors is certainly one of the ten major mysteries of life. You put two seeds in the ground and they look identical. You put a shovelful of manure in the earth around them and for a few weeks or months everything remains brown. Suddenly two thin green shoots appear. In another few weeks the two shoots have emerged from the manure, both smelling great and both looking great, but one is a red rose and one is yellow. How do they do that? Why do they smell the same and look different?

There are things we all learn in school and then intentionally ignore because, while they may be true, they don't fit our sense about them. I remember being told that white isn't a color because it's the absence of any color. Black, on the other hand, is a mixture of every color of the spectrum. I don't care. I still think of white as a color and it's at its best as snow. If they could only figure out a way to have snow come down on cities black and gradually turn white as it gets driven over, walked on and pushed around.

I only watched that golf game with the player using the yellow ball for about three minutes—and look where it got me.

Snow

THERE are about half a dozen potentially calamitous events I worry about. None of these has ever taken place and may never, but I worry that they might.

I refer to such big events as Earth being bumped into by a star bigger than it is, or Earth gradually getting too hot or too cold to live on. This is the sort of thing I mean. When I worry, I worry big.

The worry that always nags at me at this time of year is the possibility that, little by little, as we run out of ways to heat homes, factories and offices, everyone in the United States will move to someplace warm.

It has happened to a slight degree already, of course, but I'm not talking about retired people going to Florida for the winter months. I'm not talking about the people who decided long before there was an energy shortage that they like it down there. I'm talking about all of us *deserting* the Northeast, the Midwest and the Northwest.

I have these terrible nightmares about great empty cities and suburbs where zoning boards are no longer in cahoots with real estate operators and builders, because there are no people to build or buy. We're all down there huddled together in the Sun Belt. Boston would be inhabited by a few hundred hardy caretakers who slept with their mukluks on through the winter months. There would be no heat or water in the buildings, and the wind would whistle through the empty corridors of the Quincy Market.

Syracuse, Pittsburgh, Cleveland would be ghost towns, and people would migrate back to the Great Plains states for just a few warm weather months in order to plant and harvest quickly before they have to leave again to survive.

Well, fortunately for us all, this great event isn't any more likely to happen than the sun is likely to grow cold soon. Fortunately for Florida, California and Texas, ninety-eight percent of this country's population will *not* be moving there. There will be a trend in that direction, but for the same reason the Eskimos have never abandoned the Arctic Circle for the Virgin Islands, the people of Minneapolis will not be migrating to New Orleans.

There is something perverse in the nature of people who live under difficult weather conditions, and it seems to do good things for their character. This is not to say that the people of Maine are necessarily possessed of more character than the people of Georgia, but they do have an admirable ability to hold their ship to the wind in the worst weather. If this generality were not true, nothing ever would have been accomplished in Buffalo.

It is also strange but true that the farther north you get in the United States, the less attention people pay to bad weather in the winter. If Washington, D.C. gets an inch and a half of snow, the city is paralyzed for days. Commerce and government cease to operate.

In Glens Falls, N.Y., on the other hand, two feet of snow may not make page one of the newspaper. They shovel out and go about their business as usual. Just for fun I called the Board of Education in Glens Falls, and they said that in the 1978–79 school year, their schools were closed for just three days because of snow.

In Philadelphia, two hundred miles south of Glens Falls, where they have substantially less snow and no rural dirt roads to plow, schools were closed for five days because of snow.

It's apparent that the people who have the most snow get good at knowing how to handle it. Many people in the upper North seem actually to enjoy and derive strength from the rollercoaster extremes of the seasons. The rigors imposed by snow and cold weather in the most northerly sections of the country produce something in the body that moves it.

So, I can relax and stop worrying. Everyone in the Snowbelt is not going to abandon it and ruin the warm and lovely South by crowding into it.

Hot Weather

I detest hot weather. That's easy enough for me to say in the middle of a heat wave, but I'll say the same thing on the coldest day of the year.

Somehow we don't worry quite so much about the people subjected to relentless heat as we would if they had been through a flood or a hurricane. There are no pictures of it for television, and millions suffer silently.

Even though there are no pictures of heat and no one dies instantly as they might in a storm, in some ways heat may be worse than other natural disasters. In terms of physical damage to material things like houses and cars, the hurricane and the flood are worse, but when you're talking about the human spirit, a heat wave is worse. People join together and work shoulder to shoulder with a great sense of camaraderie to fight the effects of a flood or a snowstorm, but in oppressive heat all effort is impossible.

Half a dozen memories of the worst heat I've ever experienced come to my mind when it gets hot.

My first month in the Army was spent at Fort Bragg, North Carolina, in August. I will never forget having to stand at attention for hours on the red clay drill field on that one-hundred-degree day. The commanding colonel of our artillery battalion made a maddeningly slow inspection tour of the full field packs we had laid out on the ground, and our company was the one he came to last. Nine men fainted or decided to drop to the ground so they'd be carried off.

Later in World War II, I flew with the 8th Air Force on bombing raids over Germany and I traveled across Europe with the First Army, but I never had that bad a day again.

When I go to bed at night, I often toss and turn without being able to go to sleep for as long as fifteen or twenty seconds. Insomnia has never been one of my problems. I can go to sleep when I'm worried, I can go to sleep with a headache and I can even go to sleep when I have one too few blankets over me on a cold night. There's just one thing that keeps me awake, and that's heat.

Late at night in those early Army days at Fort Bragg, I lay awake in the barracks thinking about ice water. One night I couldn't stand it any longer. I got up, waited for the guard on duty in the company street to pass, then I slipped out the door and crawled under the barracks. The barracks were built on stilts, and there was plenty of room to walk in a low crouch. Underneath, I made my way the length of the barracks to the next company street and waited silently again for the guard to pass. It was as though I was a German infiltrator about to blow up the base, but all I wanted was ice water.

I made my way under three barracks until I came to the post exchange. It was 2 AM by then and the PX had closed at nine. But there was something I knew. Every night as they cleaned up, they dumped all their ice on the ground outside the back door. I finally arrived, undetected, and there it was, just as I had hoped. Cakes of ice that had originally been so big that even in the heat they were still huge chunks glistened. I took two cakes so big I had to hold them braced on either hip. It was cold and wet but wonderful, as the icy water soaked through my pajamas.

It took me ten minutes to get back to the barracks and my friends were glad to see me. As a matter of fact, I do not recall a time in all my life when I was so great a hero to so many people.

We broke the ice into pieces, filled our canteen cups with them and then added water. For more than an hour, ten of us sat silently on our bunks in the sweltering heat, drinking that beautiful ice water.

I'm one of the privileged class who lives and works mostly in air-conditioned buildings. For us, hot weather is like a heavy rainstorm. We get out of our air-conditioned car and rush a short distance to an air-conditioned house. During the workday we move quickly from air-conditioned building to air-conditioned building, as if to keep from getting wet in the rainstorm.

I feel terrible for the people I read about being subjected to awful heat, and I always wish I could bring them ice water.

Weathermen

Unless there's been a flood, a hurricane or three feet of snow, we aren't interested in a weather *report*. What we want is a prediction. We know what the weather has been like. We want to know what's coming next. And we don't want to be told it's raining, either. We want better information than we can get from looking out the window.

I suppose we expect too much of weathermen. We often malign them, but I think they have it coming.

Most newspapers give the weather forecast in just a few lines, but television and radio forecasts aren't usually that direct. If the local secondhand-car dealer wants to sponsor the weatherman, he needs a show that lasts longer than five seconds, so the weatherman has to stretch it out. He has the same information the newspaper has, but he has to make it last longer.

If the weatherman came on, smiled and just said, "Cloudy with showers late this afternoon," the secondhand-car dealer would feel cheated and his one-minute commercial would be out of proportion to his five-second show.

This has led to the extended weather report on local television news broadcasts. Some of them are good some of the time, but usually they are too long. For one thing, it doesn't matter how normal the weather has been today and is going to be again tomorrow, the weather report has to fill the time allotted to it.

Anchormen and weathermen, with nothing much to say about the weather, get involved in a lot of cute small-talk. The weatherman gives us some pseudo-technical talk about high and low pressure areas just to reassure us that he knows more about weather than we do.

All we want to hear is whether we ought to take along a raincoat or not, and he's telling us that something has dropped from 31.2 to 31.1 and is headed our way from Canada. Nothing ever heads our way from Mexico.

I'm suspicious of this, too, because it seems to me weathermen are imprecise with their geography. When they make those sweeping chalk marks to indicate fronts, three or four hundred miles one way or the other never seems to bother them. They'll draw big half circles to show us what the weather's going to be around the Great Lakes area, but it doesn't seem to matter to them if the chalk catches a little bit of Nebraska and a corner of Tennessee.

The necessity for consuming more time than a weather forecast actually takes is the cause of weathermen and women having acquired all sorts of irritating habits on the air. They'll say, for instance, "I'm sorry to have to tell you, ladies and gentlemen, that the weekend doesn't look good. Sunday is going to be a rainy, cold, dismal day."

In the first place, I'm not interested in whether he's sorry to have to tell us or not. I don't mind being told it's going to be cold and I want to know if it's going to rain, but when the weather expert tells me it's going to be a "dismal" day, he's gone too far.

"Dismal" is a state of mind, not a condition of the weather, and there is no way in the world that a weatherman can predict how a cold, rainy day is going to affect my state of mind.

If it's a Sunday and I have a fire in the fireplace and wish to settle down and read the paper instead of doing all those dirty jobs outside that I'd have had to do on a clear day, "rainy" might be just what I want for weather. The house is warm and cheery, and it gives me a good feeling that I am able to protect my family and myself from the elements. There is nothing "dismal" about it. Rainy and cold, yes, but "dismal" is none of the weatherman's business.

Weather reporters feel compelled to predict our reaction to conditions all the time, and they give us a lot of advice, too. "It'll be bitter cold and windy today, folks, so bundle up."

Is he giving us the weather forecast or advice on how to stay warm? Is he afraid we'll leave home in our shirt sleeves if he tells us the temperature is below zero but neglects to advise us to dress warmly?

"There's ice on the roads today and many of the roads are slippery, listeners, so please drive carefully."

Does he think we're idiots? Does he think we don't know ice is slippery? Does he think that if he simply told us the roads were icy without telling us they were slippery, we would ignore conditions and break our necks?

I have nothing against weathermen. I just wish they'd stick to the weather.

Sleeping on My Back

One of the great disappointments of my life is that I can't sleep on my back. I wish I was six feet tall and I wouldn't mind if I was handsome, but I'd trade either for being able to sleep on my back.

I've thought of going to a doctor, but what doctor do you go to for something like that? They're all busy doing heart by-pass operations, fixing broken bones and analyzing our psyches. They don't have time for why I can't sleep on my back. Obviously I'm not going to die of it.

Going to sleep is one of the things I don't have any trouble with at all if I lie on my side. I can drink two cups of strong black coffee after dinner, read, work, watch a little television and sometimes even take a little nap before going to bed, but it still doesn't keep me from falling asleep. I can hit the pillow at 11:14 and be asleep by 11:15. Unless I have to get up to go to the bathroom, I don't wake up until my clock radio goes off at 6:15 the next morning. That's if I don't lie on my back.

If I've been doing a lot of physical work that day or if I've played tennis, it often feels good at night to lie supine and relax every muscle in my body deliberately. That's when I get in trouble. It feels good to my body but terrible to my brain. I can't sleep and I begin thinking evil or depressing thoughts. I begin wondering how long I have to live, whether the furnace will blow up and whether that noise I hear downstairs is someone trying to break in.

Everything goes wrong when I lie on my back.

There doesn't seem to have been any grand plan made for how we're supposed to lie down and sleep. The body is shaped much better for standing or sitting than it is for lying down. Our hips are wider than our legs, and our shoulders stick out so much farther than our head that the head has to be supported by a pillow to keep it from dropping off at an uncomfortably sharp angle. There's nothing good to do with the arms.

Ever since prehistoric man laid himself down on a bundle of branches in his cave, we've been putting something soft under us before we go to sleep. If we lie down on some hard surface that doesn't give at all, our own weight bears down on the parts of us underneath and hurts or cuts off the circulation. It's related to why horses and elephants sleep standing up.

Bedding is pretty good in our country. Mattresses are usually firmer than those you find abroad. I spend quite a few nights away from home every year and I have a lot of complaints with the heating system and the lack of fresh air in hotel and motel rooms, but the beds are almost always fine. Doctors recommend a firm bed for anyone with a bad back. I'm sure it's good advice, but when doctors give it I think they're assuming people sleep on their backs, even though the doctors themselves don't. Most people don't, because they have my problem.

There's nothing much worse than lying awake in the middle of the night, staring at your life. One of the worst things about not sleeping is, you don't get any sympathy. The next morning you may say "I couldn't sleep," but no one feels sorry for you and sometimes they don't even believe you. The strange thing is that the following morning, even though you were sure at the time that you were awake from 2 AM until 5 AM, it's often hard to believe yourself. There's an unreal quality to being awake all night.

I've only had half a dozen sleepless nights in my life, and when I'm having one I always end up on my back. In addition to not sleeping, I have these black thoughts. I've often thought that I'd like to be buried on my side.

Airlines

ALTHOUGH no airline has ever written to me asking for advice, I'm going to give them some while a cross-country flight I just made is fresh in my mind.

The good thing you have going for you, airlines, is that we are all somewhat exhilarated by the thought of going to a distant place. I'm not a chronic airline knocker, but getting there these days is too often an unpleasant experience and, for your own good, I don't want you to take the magic out of it.

You do a lot of things well. You seem to try hard. I like the way one airline will give us information about another over the phone or at the counter, even when there's no business in it for them. Your facilities are usually clean and your employees courteous, but there are some things I want to talk to you about.

You seem to understand that all of us hate standing in line at the ticket counter at the airport, for example, but what you don't seem to realize is that we wouldn't hate it so much if we were absolutely sure we were standing in the right line and that it was necessary for us to stand in it at all. Which line is which? Can we go directly to the gate? Are we really checked in? You aren't going to give our seat away, are you? Which one of all these sheets of paper in this envelope is really the ticket? How many times do we have to show things to people before we get on the plane, and whom do we have to show what to? Help us with these matters.

It's a good feeling once we are actually on board and seated, but it takes too long to get there. It takes too long to get off, too. Couldn't you board and unload through two doors?

One of the reasons it's taking too long is that you're letting people carry too much junk on board. They take junk on board because it is still taking too long to retrieve a bag that's been checked through.

I was in Los Angeles last week and the return flight to New York was one hour and fifty-five minutes late taking off. I don't know why you didn't give us any explanation, but as soon as we got in the air the pilot came on and thanked us for our patience and understanding. I had not been patient and understanding at all, and I resent the pilot's assumption I was. As a matter of fact, I was damned *impatient*, if the pilot wants to know the truth.

There's something else I want to tell you about your pilots, too. Most of us hate the folksy ones. One of the best ways to pass time in flight is by sleeping. Last week, about half an hour out of Los Angeles, I was sound asleep and blissfully unaware of the discomforts of a crowded flight when the pilot blasted me awake over the intercom.

"There's a good view of the crater formed when that meteorite hit the Earth near Winslow, Arizona, over there to our right, ladies and gentlemen. The walls of the crater are 525 feet high."

Thanks a lot, Captain. I happen to be on the *left* side of the plane and can't see a thing. Where were you when we wanted to know why our flight was two hours late? Not only that, you told me to buckle my seat belt for my own comfort and convenience. I happen to think you wanted me to keep it buckled for *your* convenience, so I wouldn't stand up and get in the stewardesses' way. But that's another story. So what am I supposed to do? Get up and lean over someone on the right side of the plane or try to go back to sleep?

I can't complain much about your stewardesses. They aren't as young or as pretty as they used to be and this seems like a step in the right direction, but I do have one or two suggestions. Will you please tell them to stop making that announcement where they say, "If there's anything we can do to make your flight more enjoyable, please don't hesitate to call on us."

The chances are she's got a planeload of people and we'll all be lucky if she has time to throw lunch at us. We've got about as much chance of getting special attention from a stewardess as we'd have getting the only floor nurse in the middle of the night in a crowded hospital.

And another thing. Stop having her ask us if we want cream in our coffee. I don't know whether you airlines have noticed or not, but none of you serve cream anymore. You serve a white liquid plastic for the coffee.

You notice I haven't complained about your food. Actually I feel sorry for the chefs who design and prepare your meals. It is obvious they start with good ingredients and do well by them in the kitchen, but bricks wouldn't stand up to what happens to airline food between the hangar where it's fixed and the passenger's tray table. So, a last bit of advice. Keep the food simple. Don't try to serve us scrambled eggs on a flaming sword.

Air Fares

IF the airlines don't stop flimflamming us with the kind of numbers we're more used to seeing in secondhand-car lots, they could bring back the railroad train.

It is almost impossible for the average person to find out what the best deal is for him when he wants to fly somewhere. Air fares are so variable that many airlines ticket agents can't keep up with them. There doesn't seem to be any relationship between what it costs an airline to fly a person from one place to another and how much they charge for that service. The airlines are playing some game, but we don't know the rules and they won't tell us what they are. It isn't the sort of thing that gives us any confidence in airlines, and I often find myself hoping their mechanics are more dependable than their prices.

What follows is the transcript of a telephone call I made to an airline, as closely as I can recall it:

AR: Could you tell me how much the fare is from New York to Los Angeles?

VOICE: Thank you for calling Ace Amalgamated Airlines, Your Stairway to the Stars. All our agents are temporarily busy. Please don't hang up. You will now hear Beethoven's Sixth Symphony by the Akron, Ohio, Symphony Orchestra, conducted by Sir Clarence Schimmel. Your call will be placed in our computer and will be answered automatically by one of our agents as soon as one is available. Thank you.

(At this point I held on to the phone through the first two movements of Beethoven until an agent broke in.)

AGENT: Hello, this is Linda, may I serve you?

AR: Yes, how much is the air fare from New York to Los Angeles?

AGENT: When did you wish to depart, sir?

AR: I don't wish to depart at all until I find out whether I can afford it. How much is it?

AGENT: Will we be traveling Economy or First Class?

AR: It's not "we," it's "me." I'd like to go tourist.

AGENT: Ace Amalgamated no longer offers a tourist class, sir. Would you like Coach, Economy, Super Saver, Super Coach, Super Duper Coach, or a seat with room in front of you for your legs?

AR: I read an advertisement that you have a one-way fare for $149.

AGENT: Yes, sir, but that's only available in Los Angeles if you're in New York . . . and vice versa. And you have to have bought your ticket at least three years in advance. And you have to stay at least eight days but not nine.

AR: Well, what's the cheapest fare from New York to Los Angeles that I can get now?

AGENT: If your plans call for an extended visit in California, we offer our Family Plan.

AR: What's the Family Plan?

AGENT: This is reserved for economy-minded travelers who don't mind being in the middle seat when the window seat and the aisle seat are occupied by a family . . . a mother and father and two small children.

AR: How much is first class?

AGENT: Regular or economy first class?

AR: What's the difference?

AGENT: Regular first class features all the champagne you can drink and food you can't eat at all. Our Economy First Class Special is $329 roundtrip. This includes an all-expense-paid trip to Disneyland, lunch with Carol Burnett and a reporter from the *National Enquirer*, and a room at the Y in Beverly Hills.

AR: I'll take that.

AGENT: I'm sorry, sir. Our Economy First Class Special is sold out. Actually we only had one seat allotted to that and the pilot's mother is using it. Are there any other reservations we may make for you while you're in the Los Angeles area?

AR: I think I'm all set.

AGENT: Thank you for calling Ace Amalgamated Airlines. If your future plans call for air travel, please call on us again.

Coaches

THE word "coach" has taken on a new meaning and I don't like what it means anymore.

A coach used to be the person who helped organize a team and then showed the young people how to play the game. Not anymore. Now the coach dominates every aspect of the game. The players are incidental. They have nothing to say about strategy and the coach manipulates them the way a general moves elements of his army at war.

Basketball and football coaches seem to be the most objectionable. In a televised basketball game you can always see the coach stalking up and down the sidelines, waving his arms in wild gestures and screaming at both players and officials.

"Shut up and sit down!" I want to yell at them. As a matter of fact I have yelled that at them, even though we don't have two-way television in our house yet.

Last season the coach of Princeton and the coach of Columbia got into a fight after their basketball games. I'd fire both of them.

There have been two recent cases where coaches have been fired for striking players. You wonder how long it had been going on before someone caught them doing it in public. What kind of a way is this to play a game for fun? The kind of sportsmanship a lot of young athletes are learning from their coaches is going to make them eligible for competition on the pro tennis circuit with such world-famous good sports as John McEnroe and Jimmy Connors.

Baseball is the only game where they face the fact and call the person running the team the manager. He's the one who runs out on the field, sticks his nose up against the umpire's nose and tells him off.

The coaches in other sports have learned how to do that too. They always complain loudly about a referee's decision. No decision by the officials in all the history of sports has ever been changed because a coach or manager complained about it, but they still do it during every game.

The intrusion of the coaches into football is ludicrous. Deciding what play would be most effective at any point in the game is an important part of knowing how to play football. It is a decision that should be made on the field, by one of the players appointed to do that. Traditionally the quarterback called the plays. Now most of the plays in professional football are called by the coach on the sideline, who gets advice from a man at the top of the stadium with whom he's in touch by telephone. High school and college coaches are, more and more, sending in plays.

It was about twenty-five years ago that Cleveland Browns' coach Paul Brown started shuttling two players in and out. After each play was over, the man standing next to him on the sidelines was told what Brown wanted the team to do next. He'd run in and make the announcement in the huddle. After the play, he'd run back out and the second man would run in with more instructions.

It has not been so long ago that it was illegal for anyone on the sideline to give advice to any of the players. When a substitute came into the game, that player couldn't join the others in the huddle for the first play. The teammate next to him whispered into his ear as they went to the line of scrimmage so he'd know what the play was. This seems like the way it ought to be. There is no doubt in the world that the rules of football should be changed to exclude the coach from making decisions about what to do next on the field.

The whole point of sports is fun. It is a diversion from the seriousness of life. We all make decisions every day that make a real difference to our happiness and our prosperity. Sports should provide a relief from that pressure. Sports don't make any difference. Vince Lombardi was absolutely wrong when he said, "Winning isn't everything, it's the only thing."

If a coach sets out to win, with no concessions made to fun or sportsmanship or more important factors in a young person's life, that coach can be a winner. I don't know any way that can be controlled but it always seems to me it's almost like cheating.

And please don't write and tell me there are a lot of good coaches. I know that, and they agree with me.

Tipping

I'D be just as happy if they passed a law tomorrow making tipping illegal.

There are all sorts of things wrong with tipping. It puts both tipper and tippee in a bad position. Why should anyone have to depend on what I choose to give them for their services? Who am I to leave a dollar grandly under my plate for the waiter as if I was doing him a big favor? I hate tipping. Why shouldn't an employer have to pay an employee a decent wage?

The first thing wrong is that most of us don't know who to tip or how much. We don't know what the person we're tipping expects from us. We don't want him to think we're cheapskates, and we don't want to look as though we're from out of town by tipping too much. Most of us tip out of fear more than gratitude. We're not moved to give away money by any sense of being thankful to the person who provided us with service. We just know we're supposed to do it.

I eat in a lot of restaurants during the course of a year, and the tip I leave the waiter or waitress very seldom bears any relationship to the quality of service I get. I leave the same tip for good service as I do for bad. Occasionally when service is really terrible, I'll shave the tip to the socially acceptable minimum but never below that. I'm a coward when it comes to tipping. Dr. Joyce Brothers would certainly point out that I hate tipping because I hate myself for tipping the way I do.

Years ago George Bernard Shaw ate in a restaurant in New York and the service was terrible. The waiter ignored him, got the orders mixed up and was rude. After the meal, Shaw paid the check and as he was leaving he looked the waiter in the eye and dropped a fifty-dollar bill on the table.

"This is what I tip for *bad* service," Shaw said.

The word "TIPS" is supposed to have come from the first letters of the words To Insure Prompt Service. I don't know whether that's true or not. All I know is it doesn't help the service at all and we ought to drop the custom.

There are a lot of small towns in the United States where no one would dream of tipping someone. That's the way it ought to be, but in the big cities you're expected to tip half the people you meet. In a hotel there are always a lot of people doing things for you that you'd rather do yourself, because they're looking for a tip. When there are nine taxicabs in a line outside the hotel, I don't need a doorman whistling his head off to get me one. I resent tipping doormen for doing almost nothing.

A friend of mine spent several days at the fancy Greenbrier Hotel in West Virginia once, and as he was leaving he held out a dollar to a doorman who hadn't done anything for him and said, "Do you have some change?"

The doorman looked at my friend and said, "Sir, at the Greenbrier, a dollar *is* change."

Several times a year, I find myself in an expensive restaurant that has a washroom attendant. I'm perfectly capable of washing and drying my own hands without having an attendant hand me a towel, and I think the establishment should pay someone to keep the place neat and clean without making the clients pay for it with tips. The attendant usually has four or five dollar bills in a dish, as if that's what you're expected to leave.

I don't have my shoes shined anymore because it costs too much with tip. I've never known how much to give the captain in the restaurant with a washroom attendant and if I have to slip a head-waiter ten dollars for a good table, I'm going to eat someplace else.

I'd like to put an end to all tipping, but I don't dare start the movement all by myself.

Gambling

THERE's nothing more satisfying than getting mad. I thoroughly enjoy it once in a while, and I want to thank the New York State Department of Taxation and Finance for getting me off to a great angry start today.

This morning I got up early and turned on the radio to make sure the world hadn't come to an end during the night. (I always do that because if the world does ever come to an end, I think I'll just go back to bed.) As usual, the world hadn't come to an end, and right after the weather report there was a commercial, paid for by New York State taxpayers, saying what a good idea it was for everyone who wants to get rich to gamble on a numbers game, the New York State Lottery. The New York Off Track Betting Commission has comparable advertising telling everyone what a good idea it is to bet on horses.

Well, gambling on numbers or betting on which horse will run fastest is *not* the way to get rich, and New York State ought not to suggest to its citizens that it is.

When these gambling bills were proposed before the state legislature, the argument for them was that people were going to gamble anyway so the state might as well take gambling away from the crime mob, run it honestly and make the profit itself. How come, I'd like to know, if people are going to do all this gambling naturally, the state has to buy radio and newspaper commercials to try to get them to gamble?

Why don't those commercials tell people what chance they have of winning in the state lottery? The state takes forty-five cents of every dollar bet. Does that sound like a good deal to you? Who but the dumbest and most desperate among us would take a chance like that?

The radio stations give the winning numbers every day, giving favorable publicity to big winners. I think the radio stations ought to announce the names of the *losers* every day. That would be some list!

All you have to do to see who this kind of betting appeals to is to stand outside a New York State Off Track Betting parlor any day of the week and watch the people who spend their time hanging around hoping to get lucky. They are the duds, the derelicts and the human disasters. Why does the state prey on these poor devils who can't take care of themselves?

New York State pays millions of dollars a week in welfare to its indigent citizens. Does it make any sense for the state to hand out money for food and lodging one day and take it away the next at the betting window so the state will have money for the welfare payments again the following week? It is absolutely the dumbest thing I ever heard of. This is robbing Peter to pay Peter.

How can we teach kids that hard work is the way to success if they hear radio commercials paid for by their government suggesting that the way to get rich is to bet money on a horse or a number? How can Americans who profess to believe in such classic virtues as honesty, thrift, hard work and intelligent action allow any part of the government they formed to run a gambling operation?

Gambling is a destructive force. People who spend their money on that don't spend it somewhere else. The man who blows twenty dollars at the OTB parlor doesn't have it to buy a new pair of sneaks for his son. What good does that do for the legitimate businessman who runs the shoe store or for the man's son?

I like to gamble. I go to Saratoga once a year and even Las Vegas has a terrible fascination for me. If blackjack was whiskey, I could become an alcoholic. I'm glad no casino is readily available to me because I need to be protected from myself. But for our own government to promote and make money by taking it away from the weakest among us in a gambling operation is the lowest form of taxation.

Now, I've been angry for today. I feel good and I can get at the day's work.

Oil Eaters

Didn't you put gas in the car yesterday, dear?"

"Yes. I had it filled. What's the matter?"

"I can't get it started and the tank says empty."

This is how I envision the beginning of the end of the world.

The Supreme Court has just ruled that a new form of life invented by man can be patented and sold for profit. The scientists at General Electric came up with a new organism that eats gas or oil and turns it into carbon dioxide and protein. When the oil is gone, the inventors say, the new organism dies. Maybe!

The scientist, Ananda Chakrabarty, invented this new microorganism with a great plan in mind. He thought that when there was an oil spill in the ocean, a small colony of these little devils of his could be released in it. They'd start multiplying and eating all the oil they could find in the ocean. When they had licked their plate clean, they'd all die of starvation and that would be the end of them and the oil pollution.

But let's look at another scenario. One sunny day these organisms are gulping down all the oil they can eat when one of them decides they need leadership. He gets himself elected president of the new bacterial group and decides his followers ought to look ahead to the time when the oil spill is gone and they won't have anything more to eat. They develop a long-range plan.

A special task force made up of the youngest and most athletic bacteria gets itself a huge piece of floating debris. It is actually the door off the captain's cabin of the oil tanker that sank and left the oil slick.

They load up the door with a three-week emergency ration of oil to eat and set off exploring for new oil. They drift for weeks and things begin to look grim. Then one night they see the lights of a huge oil tanker bearing down on them. They jump into the water and, with their little feet kicking away, push the door into the path of the oncoming ship. Sure enough the tanker hits the door and all the microorganisms, a little weak now because their eating oil is almost gone, clamber up the sides of the ship and scamper down into the hold. There, in huge holding tanks, is a sight for sore microorganic eyes! Millions of gallons of good eating. The organisms get straws from the ship's galley and have themselves their first square meal in weeks.

When the ship gets to port, its oil is almost gone. The shipping magnate accuses the captain of having sold it en route. The captain insists there must be a leak in the tanks. With barely enough fuel left to get them back to the Middle East, the tankers leaves port to get another load.

By the time the SS *Ayatollah Esso* has reached port again in the Mediterranean, the oil-eating microorganisms are near starvation and the ship itself barely makes it to port. No sooner is it tied up at the docks than the pipes are coupled to its tanks and a new load of oil starts pouring in.

That small hardy band of microorganic green berets who started their trip so long ago on the captain's door are sick of the sea by now. They want a more secure life and a more certain source of eating oil.

Like salmon swimming upstream to multiply, Dr. Ananda Chakrabarty's Supreme Court blessed bacteria fight their way back up through the pipeline until finally, after almost giving up against the tide of oil rushing at them, they make their way down the oil-drilling rig and enter upon a placid, underground ocean of oil from which all oil company blessings flow.

Here in this land of plenty the organisms get religion and are told by their leaders to multiply and grow and go forth and populate the land.

They do this until they have entered into every oily place on the face of the earth and have consumed it all and there is no more to eat and the furnaces grow cold and the oil company profits cease to flow and the cars won't go. And a great silence falls upon the land.

Vacations in Outer Space

WE'RE getting into space none too soon.

There's just no doubt about it, we're running short of everything here on earth and we need some of that room there in outer space. No one knows how big outer space is, of course, nor if it ends, what's just beyond it.

When John Young arrived back on earth after that first space-shuttle mission, he said that interstellar travel was not far off. I certainly hope so, because one of the things we're in most desperate need of is some new place to go on vacation.

We're all looking for some places to go that everyone else hasn't already been to, and they're getting scarce here on earth. There's a mountain behind a cottage we have on a lake in northern New York State, and it used to be a great adventure to climb it. We never went up or down the same way twice, and we were often lost and sometimes scared for short periods during the climb, but it was never dull. Now there are four well-marked trails with color-coded signs pointing the way, and when you reach the top, the rocks at the summit are littered with orange peel, Styrofoam cups and discarded soft-drink cans. The adventure has been taken out of the trip. There are three other parties of climbers up there with you, and one member of one of them has brought a portable radio which is tuned to a rock music station in Albany.

The word "pioneer" in relation to geography can be retired from the language. Every place has been walked on and is not far from the federally funded highway.

All the good and remote places to go have been discovered and ruined. Yellowstone National Park gets so many visitors at times that they have to close the gates as if it was a rock music festival. I remember when it was chic for Americans with money to go to the magnificent crescent-shaped beach at Acapulco and return bragging about this wonderful place they'd found in Mexico. Today you can hardly find the beach if you go to Acapulco because it's hidden from the road by a solid phalanx of hotels.

There are travel agents who will book you a trip down the Amazon through the wilds of South America, but the Jungle Lodge at Iquitos, Peru, provides most of the civilized comforts of a Holiday Inn. I haven't been up there, but I wouldn't be surprised to find an Igloo Hilton at the North Pole. A few years ago we rented a quaint, thatch-roofed cottage on Galway Bay for a week and all our neighbors in adjacent cottages were, as we were, American tourists.

A friend of mine just returned from "a trek" to Mt. Everest. It was complete with Sherpa guides who carried all the heavy stuff and an American doctor who got his trip free in exchange for his services in the event they were necessary.

We can put the word "adventure" away with "pioneer," because there isn't much of it left. The trip down the Colorado in a rubber raft is safe enough to be taken by a President's wife and a quota of Secret Service agents. To fit the definition of the word "adventure," a trip ought to have an element of danger or uncertainty, and there aren't many places left to go that have either.

Travel agents find themselves in a paradoxical situation because people come in wanting something different and exciting, but then they want the travel agent to arrange things so carefully that all the elements of risk and surprise are taken out of the trip. They want to go someplace man has never set foot before, and when they arrive, they want to go up to their room, take a shower and rest a while before going out to some good restaurant that serves American food for dinner.

All we can hope is that the spaceship Columbia is the covered wagon of the future, and that it will open the way for long weekends and summer vacations in the unexplored wilds of outer space where prefab picnic tables have not yet been provided.

On Conservation

M<small>Y</small> grandfather was right and wrong about a lot of things, but he was never undecided. When I was twelve, he told me we were using up all the good things on earth so fast that we'd run out of them.

I've worried about that. I guess we all have, and I wonder whether it's true or not. The real question is, will we run out of the things we need to survive before we find substitutes for them? Of course, we're going to run out of oil. Of course, we're going to run out of coal. And it seems very likely that there will be no substantial forests left in another hundred years.

Argue with me. Say I'm wrong. Give me statistics proving there's more oil left in the ground than we've already used. Tell me there's coal enough in the United States to last seventy-five or a hundred years. Make me read the advertisements saying they're planting more trees than they're cutting.

I've read all those arguments and I'll concede I may be wrong in suggesting impending doom, but if doom is not exactly impending, it's somewhere down the line of years if we don't find replacements for the basic materials we're taking from the earth. What about five hundred years from now if one hundred doesn't worry you? What about a thousand years from now? Will there be an oak tree left two feet in diameter? How much will it cost in a hundred years to buy an oak plank eight feet long, two inches thick and a foot wide? My guess is it will cost the equivalent in today's money of a thousand dollars. A piece of oak like that will be treasured as diamonds are treasured today because of its rarity.

I don't think there is a more difficult question we're faced with than that of preservation. A large number of Americans feel we should use everything we have because things will work out. They are not necessarily selfish. They just don't believe you can worry about the future much past your own grandchildren's foreseeable life expectancy. They feel someone will find the answer. Pump the oil, mine the coal, cut the trees and take from the earth anything you can find there. There may not be more where that came from, but we'll find something else, somewhere else, that will be a good substitute.

The preservationists, on the other hand, would set aside a lot of everything. They'd save the forests and reduce our dependency on coal and oil in order to conserve them as though no satisfactory substitutes would ever be found.

It's too bad the argument between these groups is as bitter as it is, because neither wants to do, intentionally, what is wrong. The preservationists think business interests who want to use what they can find are greedy and short-sighted. Businessmen think the preservationists are, in their own way, short-sighted. (One of the strange things that has happened to our language is that people like the ones who run the oil companies are called "conservatives," although they do not approve of conserving at all.)

All this comes to me now because I have just returned from Hawaii and seen what havoc unrestricted use can bring to an area. To my grandfather, Honolulu would probably look like the end of the world if he could see it now.

We have just about used up the island of Oahu. Now we're starting on Maui. Is it right or wrong? Do the hotels crowded along the beach not give great pleasure to large numbers of us? Would it be better to preserve the beauty of Hawaii by limiting the number of people allowed to be there? Would it be better if we saved the forests, the oil and the coal in the world and did without the things they provide? If there is middle ground, where is it?

The answer will have to come from someone smarter than I am. I want to save oil and drive a big car fast. I want to cut smoke pollution but burn coal to save oil, and I want to pursue my woodworking hobby without cutting down any trees.

V:

QUESTIONS FOR THE PRESIDENT

What About a King?

EVERYONE complains so much about the political campaign for the presidency that I was wondering if it might not be a good idea for us to consider another form of government, one that would allow us to have some kind of leader other than a President.

What about a king?

It seems to me a king might be good. For one thing, no one takes a king very seriously anymore. We need a leader we don't take so seriously.

A king would sure save us a lot of trouble every four years. Once you've got yourself a king or a queen, you're all set for life. His or her life, that is. And when something *does* happen to a king, there isn't a lot of worrying about whether they were careful enough when they elected the Vice President. There is no vice-king. They just give the crown to his oldest kid or his next closest relative.

There was actually some talk of having a king here when Franklin Roosevelt was elected for a fourth term, although most of that talk came from his enemies, who said it as a bitter joke. If we had made Roosevelt king, King Franklin, we would have saved ourselves nine long, nasty political campaigns since then. When Roosevelt died in 1945, the throne would have been turned over to his son James. That is, if his mother, Eleanor, had allowed him to have it. King James would still be reigning now at age seventy-four.

It would also have been easy for us to switch over to a monarchy right after World War II. Eisenhower would have made a logical king. Had we made that change, we would now have King David. Julie Nixon Eisenhower would be a princess by marriage—although if Eisenhower had become king, Nixon never would have been President, and Julie and David might never have met and married.

We wouldn't have to make a lot of expensive changes to install a king. He could live in the same quarters the President lives in. We'd simply call it the White Palace. The changing of the guard might give a boost to tourism in Washington.

It just seems to me that a king or queen doesn't give you the same kind of trouble a President gives you. For one thing, a king doesn't really do much, and we're all agreed that one of the things we need is people in Washington who do less.

A king isn't the only alternative to our President. If we're really tired of these political campaigns every four years, we might look into a dictatorship. Dictatorships have acquired a bad name because we've had some bad dictators in recent history. What we'd have to have, of course, is a *good* dictator.

Dictatorships are an old concept. During the great years of the Roman republic, they used to get themselves a dictator every once in a while when things weren't going too good. They'd give this fellow complete control over everything for six months. He'd straighten out the country and then the Romans would return to their democracy. It's people like Hitler, Mussolini and Franco who ruined the image of the wise and benevolent dictator. What we could use is a real Mr. Nice Guy.

In the Soviet Union they've done several clever things that have largely blunted criticism of the management often found in dictatorships. First, young Russians are taught from birth that theirs is the best system, so when little Russians grow up, it doesn't occur to many of them that it stinks. Second, the Soviet dictatorship is no longer personified; it is a dictatorship by committee. A committee is harder to really hate than one man.

The only other alternative I can think of to a presidency is a junta and I don't think any of us would want a junta. For one thing, we don't know how to pronounce it.

Presidential Candidates

Presidential candidates act as though there was a lot of difference of opinion among us as to what we wanted to hear from them. I don't think there is. I know what I'd like to hear one of them say, and I suspect a lot of the rest of you would like to hear some of the same things.

First, a presidential candidate ought to be a man or woman who doesn't really want the job, who knows he isn't smart enough to do it and says so.

If a candidate is so conceited as to think he's got the brains it takes to solve this country's problems, I don't want to have anything to do with him. Of course he can't solve our problems. If he's honest, he'll tell us he's just going to do the best he can to keep everything from going to hell.

He ought to admit he's never going to be able to balance the budget and that he'll have to find some sneaky ways to raise taxes while he's talking about lowering them.

I don't mind if the candidate has an attractive wife (or husband), but I hope she's the kind of woman who doesn't want to get into the act all the time. If we wanted a wife (or a husband) for President, we'd have elected one.

To be perfectly honest, I'd be happy if my candidate didn't have any children, brothers or sisters. I know this makes me sound as though I hate dogs, but I just don't think we need kids or brothers of the President confusing us about what we think of him.

I wouldn't mind hearing my man admit that one of the reasons he's running for office is that he needs work. The job pays $200,000 a year plus a lot of fringe benefits. He gets a nice house to live in and someone to do the dishes.

When my candidate comes on television just before Election Day, I know just what I'd like to hear him say:

"Good evening, voters.

"Hope I look okay. I don't usually have my hair this slicked down, but I just took a shower and this is the way they told me I ought to look. This is a new suit I'm wearing, too. Sure hope I got all the tags off.

"There are a few things I want to say right off. If I'm elected, there are a lot of idiots who contributed money to my campaign and the chances are, I'm going to have to give jobs to some of them. You ever been in that kind of spot? I don't know what else to do. I'll try to put them in jobs that won't hurt much. Ambassador to Liechtenstein, that sort of thing. I mean, what's $40,000? Am I right or am I wrong?

"If I get in tomorrow, I'm going to knock off with those tours of the White House, too. Who wants people with muddy feet tramping through their house all day? It isn't like they were going to buy the place from me, you know.

"One more thing, before I get to some of the good stuff. I got this friend who'd do anything for me, you know what I mean? He may not be the smartest guy in the world and he's been involved in a few . . . well, nothing dishonest really but a little, like, well, shady deals.

"But what I want to say about him is, he's my friend and he can help me and I'd appreciate it if the press would stay off his back.

"I don't know a damn thing about foreign policy. I hate Mexican food, and I don't know how to use chopsticks. The only time I've been out of the country is ten days I spent in Puerto Rico on vacation. If you call that out of the country.

"There are two more things I want to tell you. First, I hadn't been to church in nine years before I started running for this office and, second, if elected I don't want the Secret Service around all the time.

"I have a pretty good wig and a false nose and about once a week my wife and I would like to slip out the back door of the White House and eat dinner alone at a little bistro we like over in Georgetown.

"Who knows, I might even tie one on once in a while."

Now, this is a candidate I could vote for with confidence.

Republican or Democrat

I F I say I am neither a Republican nor a Democrat, it seems to me it shouldn't make anyone angry. It does, though. What seems to happen is that when I say that, *everyone* gets mad at me. My Republican friends think I've lost my marbles and my Democratic friends think I've sold out to the enemy.

The fact is, though, I am neither. I have absolutely no inclination to sign up with any party or to vote their ticket right down the line, either. I'm against whoever is in office. That's not a party.

I can usually spot a liberal Democrat or a conservative Republican at one hundred feet, and I have no trouble at all when they come close enough so I can hear them talk. It doesn't matter whether the subject is sports, fashion, oil, politics, religion or breakfast food. I know one when I hear one. I credit my perception to my neutrality. I'm neutral against both extremes.

Most Democrats are considered to be liberals and most Republicans are thought of as conservative, but a strange thing has happened in relation to the word "conservative." In the first place, liberals are more conservative in matters of the land and our total environment. They want to save it. The traditional political conservatives, on the other hand, are not for conserving much of anything. They think all the trees and oil should be used.

The second paradox in relation to the word "conservative" is that most Republicans no longer fit the classic definition. "Conservatism," Thorstein Veblen said, "is the maintenance of conventions now in force."

In the 1930s, when Franklin Roosevelt was trying to curb our free enterprise system by imposing government on capitalism, Republican conservatives fought him. They wanted to maintain the status quo. They lost, though, and things did change. We no longer have that same free enterprise system. Government is in on the distribution of money at every level. Republicans want to get the government out. They are the revolutionaries who want change. Liberal Democrats wish to maintain things the way they are. *They* are, by definition, the conservatives.

Not knowing whether I'm a Democrat or a Republican sometimes gives me an insecure feeling of inferiority, and I've often tried to lay out in a clear way what I think Republicans believe and what I think Democrats believe. If I could do that, I might be able to take sides. I like liberals better than conservatives, but conservatives make more sense.

Democrats (I think to myself) are liberals who believe that people are basically good, but that they need government help to organize their lives. They believe in freedom so fervently that they think it should be compulsory. They believe that the poor and ignorant are victims of an unfair system and that their circumstances can be improved if we give them help.

Republicans (I think to myself) are conservatives who think it would be best if we faced the fact that people are no damned good. They think that if we admit that we have selfish, acquisitive natures and then set out to get all we can for ourselves by working hard for it, that things will be better for everyone. They are not insensitive to the poor, but tend to think the poor are impoverished because they won't work. They think there would be fewer of them to feel sorry for if the government did not encourage the proliferation of the least fit among us with welfare programs.

The President and the Press

THIS is not so much about Ronald Reagan as it is about journalism. President Reagan told a reporter for the *New York Times* that he was always amazed at people who spent half an hour or less with him and then went away and psychoanalyzed him and drew negative conclusions about his ability to be President.

It's easy to understand the outrage most people in politics feel toward the press and television news. The media are always badgering them, prying into private matters, emphasizing things they wish they'd never said and even making misstatements of fact about them.

Fortunately for the nation, the press works a lot like our democracy. People vote for various candidates for various reasons, many of them wrong. Some of their reasoning is faulty or is based on misinformation or on no information at all, but the funny thing is that for a lot of wrong reasons, we elect a lot of right people.

The news media work somewhat the same way. No one reporter has all the story or has it all right. Most stories are inaccurate, but in different ways. In total, the public ends up with a somewhat confused picture of the candidate, but one that is close to the truth.

I don't think there is much difference between the public perception of Ronald Reagan and the whole truth of what he's like. Most of us don't swallow the real nasty stuff or the stuff that endows him with greatness. The same could be said for Jimmy Carter. He didn't like what was said about him, but I think the public got an accurate picture of what he was like.

Our Presidents don't seem to appreciate the public's ability to take in, sort out and then spit back about ninety-eight percent of everything it is told. If one reporter spends half an hour with Reagan and concludes that he is incompetent, not many readers are going to accept that as the last word. Some other reporter will be presenting evidence that suggests Reagan might make the best President since George Washington. The public isn't going to swallow that either. The public gets a picture that is a composite drawing. It sees in the picture what it wants to see and doesn't see anything else. How else do you account for the deification of Ted Kennedy by some people and the vilification of him by others exposed to the same information?

Years ago I was the writer of a one-hour documentary about Frank Sinatra. Several of us went to his home in Palm Springs to film and for two days saw quite a bit of him. Exposed to his charm firsthand, it was easy to understand his popularity.

When Walter Cronkite interviewed Sinatra for the report, he asked some hard questions about incidents in his past. He asked about mob associations, women and attacks Sinatra was reported to have made on newsmen or photographers. Sinatra was angry in response. He went point by point down a long list of things that had been said about him. He claimed, in quite a convincing way, that every one of those stories was untrue.

I always believed him. I suspected that the events had not taken place precisely as the public had been led to believe they had; but I also came away with an even stronger conviction about the journalistic process.

The public has a more accurate idea of what Frank Sinatra is really like than Frank Sinatra has of himself.

I think the public also knows almost exactly what Ronald Reagan is like. Under the same circumstances, that's the sort of thing that would make any one of us nervous and irritable.

Reagan's Gray Hair

CLOSE observers reported that Reagan's thick black hair showed definite patches of gray during his West Coast vacation." That's how a paragraph read in the *U.S. News and World Report.*

Shame on you, *U.S. News and World Report.* You're a good magazine with an important-sounding name and you ought not to dabble in drivel. What's going on in California, Poland, Afghanistan? That's what we sent you out to report back on, not the color of the President's hair.

President Reagan is seventy-one years old, he's got one of the hardest, most important jobs in the world, and he's got all that brush to clean out at the ranch. Of *course* he's getting gray.

What about George Washington, *U.S. News?* I don't see you

taking pot shots at the Father of our country and his hair was not only gray, it was white. I believe there were formal occasions when he wore a powdered wig. You'd have some time with Ronald Reagan if he showed up for a press conference with a powdered wig, wouldn't you? And did you get on President Eisenhower's back because he was bald? I don't know what's got into you.

The trouble is, you're playing into the hands of the people who are making a big deal about the color of a man's hair. If you keep talking about the President getting gray as if this was some kind of awful thing, Mobil Oil will be taking over Grecian Formula for its growth potential.

The American public already thinks the press does too much negative reporting and the press ought to save it for important things, not derogatory chitchat.

How would you like it, *U.S. News and World Report*, if I started criticizing your magazine for its petty faults? Just let me ask you a few questions:

—What's with your title, *U.S. News and World Report?* Is there any reason you didn't name your magazine *U.S. Report and World News?*

—How come you always slap the sticker with the subscriber's address on it right over some important word on the cover? Do you do this on purpose, or is it just careless? Which would you rather we believed?

This is the way you go after one of our Presidents. Now how do you like it? Let me ask you some other questions:

—How come your magazine is dated September 7 if I read it September 1? Don't you have a calendar over there in your editorial offices, or are you just trying to make your magazine seem up-to-date by putting an advance day on it? No comment?

—One of the stories you have headlined on your cover says "An Expert Tells: Which Diet is Best for You?" You're *U.S. News and World Report* and you're doing *diet* stories? Doesn't that sound more like *Reader's Digest* or *Cosmopolitan* magazine to you? Do you also run recipes and advice on how to have a satisfactory sex life? Is that considered U.S. News or a World Report?

—And one more question before I let you go. You don't exactly put out a magazine that would appeal to teenagers. How many of your subscribers are seventy years old or older? Of those subscribers seventy years old, how many of them don't have gray hair?

Those are just a few of the questions I'd like to ask *U.S. News and World Report*. If I make a story out of it, maybe I'll run it with pictures of what the editors' wives wore at their last party.

The Presidential Breakfast

THE President had breakfast the other morning with a group of influential congressmen.

Isn't that job tough enough without scheduling breakfast with a lot of people you probably don't even want to talk to during the day? When did he shave? When did he read the paper? When did he do his thinking if he had breakfast with a lot of people and had to start talking first thing in the morning?

There are a few moments in each of our lives that should be preserved for ourselves alone, and breakfast is one of them. I don't want to talk to anyone at breakfast, and I'll bet the President doesn't either. Breakfast is not a social or even a family occasion on a weekday. Saturday or Sunday may be a different matter, but if I'm going to work, I don't want to diffuse my already limited ability to solve the problems I face at the office by getting into an argument about whether to paint the back bedroom or not.

Why would anyone ever schedule a business breakfast? Who can be gregarious over grapefruit? I can't help wondering, too, if it was a fake breakfast or a real one. Hadn't the President already had a little something before he sat down with all those people? I'll bet he had. I'll bet most of the congressmen had eaten, too. You couldn't get up in the morning knowing you were going to meet with the President of the United States, shower, shave or put your makeup on, drive half an hour to the White House, wait for the crowd to assemble and keep clearly in mind what you wanted to say without first having started up your system with a fast-breaker.

If the people who came to the breakfast had, indeed, already had breakfast, this gets an important meeting off to a start already tainted with falseness.

There are so many reasons why a breakfast meeting is wrong. The things we eat for breakfast don't lend themselves to conversation the way lunch or dinner items do. Dinner comes to us on a plate and we go at it in an established way. Breakfast is different. Someone ought to watch the toast, for example. You can't make toast in the kitchen and bring it out because it's cold by the time it gets to the table. The toastmaster not only has to make certain the toast doesn't burn, he has to anticipate who will want toast next and how much he should make because the average appliance makes only two slices at a time. Does the President make the toast? If so, how can he think about world affairs?

A lot of Americans eat cereal for breakfast. There are hundreds of kinds of cereal, but people who eat it regularly don't want anything else but what they're used to. Does the White House stock Grape Nuts if that's what the senator from Pennsylvania wants? He's not going to be happy with Post Toasties if he likes Grape Nuts or Cheerios. A Shredded Wheat person will simply not take Wheaties as a substitute.

Even if the White House kitchen can provide the cereals everyone wants, the problem isn't over. You can't discuss foreign affairs and eat cereal. No one wants soggy corn flakes, so once you pour the milk on, you have to stick at it until it's gone.

I suppose we don't know as much about each other's breakfast habits as we know about other eating habits. We all have lunch or dinner with other people quite often, but we seldom have breakfast except alone or with the family.

I think most Americans are grab-it-and-run breakfast eaters. The people who sit down to bacon and eggs, grits or fried potatoes and apple pie are rare now. Pancakes and sausage are Sunday morning. Even within a family, eating habits differ. When our family eats breakfast together, I gulp down my fresh orange juice while my wife dawdles—it seems to me she dawdles—over half a grapefruit. My mother wants coffee first. Brian sits there and stares a lot. Emily wants cereal, Martha toast. Ellen sits there asking how we can eat at that hour.

I don't know how the White House could possibly handle all the breakfast idiosyncrasies a bunch of congressmen would have.

I just hope the people who make up the President's schedule don't arrange any more breakfast meetings for him. He deserves his preserves in peace. The best breakfast advice I ever heard was very simple, and the President can have it: "Never work before breakfast and if you have to work before breakfast, have a little breakfast first."

Inside the White House

Considering how hard a man works to get himself into the White House, it's funny that once he gets there he can't wait to leave. I felt sort of sorry for the President when it looked as though he and Nancy weren't going to be able to get away to their ranch in California for Thanksgiving, but they finally made it.

Just about everyone who goes to work has a little trip to make to get there and then to get back home at the end of the day. We don't think of the process of getting ourselves to our place of work as a wonderful experience every day, but I suspect the President would like the White House better if he didn't have to live where he works. A trip back and forth to the office or the plant adds a little drama and punctuation to the day. When you get there, you're at work, and when you leave, you're off. There's nothing that definite for a President living upstairs over his office. They can always call him and ask him to drop down for a minute. As a result, I think all our Presidents have felt confined by the White House and they've all been anxious to take off for someplace else.

I wish I had a key to the White House so I could get in there and snoop around when the President and Nancy are away. I'd head straight for the private living quarters on the second floor. The public rooms for tourists don't interest me.

It's none of my business, mind you, I know that, but you can't hate me for being curious. There are all sorts of little things I'd like to know. I'd look at the edge of the coffee table in front of the television set to see if there was any evidence that the President props his cowboy boots up on it nights when he's watching the news broadcasts or an old movie.

What do they keep on the night table next to the bed? Any favorite book, or the crossword puzzle maybe? They don't strike me as crossword puzzle types, but you can't ever tell. What's in the drawer of the night table by the bed? A couple of letters from the kids? Or is the presidential bedroom a sterile affair without the personal junk lying around that gives all our bedrooms their special personality? Do they have so many people cleaning up after them that there's none of the typical bedroom debris at all? That's probably the case and that's why they can't wait to get away from it.

I wonder if the President's valet always lays out his clothes for him or does it only on state occasions? I'd like to look in the President's closet or his bureau drawers, just to see if he has some special old shirts in there that he wears on Saturday when he's lying around the house. The President often wears a sports shirt on unexpected occasions, and I'll bet he picks them out himself. No valet can pick out a sports shirt for anyone. (I don't actually *have* a valet myself, but I wouldn't think he could, anyway.)

I'd look in the refrigerator, too. I wonder what a President and his wife keep in their own private refrigerator. I've always thought the jelly bean thing was mostly for public consumption, but they've both probably got something special they like stashed away in the icebox. I can't imagine getting so important that I wouldn't want my own soft drinks there. What does the President eat Sunday afternoons when he's watching the game on television? That's the kind of information I'd be after if I could get into the White House and look around while Ron and Nancy are away.

I just think a look backstage at the White House would give me a better idea of whether Reaganomics will work or not. I wouldn't take anything.

Questions for the President

THERE are some things about any President of the United States we never get to know. Partly it's because it's none of our business, but partly it's because no one ever asks the President those questions. If I could have a fifteen-minute interview with Ronald Reagan, here are some of the things I'd ask him:

—First, Mr. President, what are the three things you'd least like to talk about?

—Is being President as good as you thought it would be?

—What do you hate most about it?

—Do you think you could ever go back to making movies?

—If one of the big studios offered you ten million dollars and a piece

of the action to make a film in 1985, would you be tempted to accept the offer instead of running for reelection? Twenty million dollars?
—Have you sneaked out of the White House at all without any protection?
—Who's the biggest jerk you've met in government? Democrat or Republican?
—How's the lung, still hurt? Not even when you laugh about it? You remember that joke?
—How much money do you carry on you? Ever have a chance to spend any of it?
—Could we just have a look at what you carry in your pockets and in your wallet?
—You like the water on the warm or on the cool side when you take a shower?
—I'm tired of this jelly bean thing. How do you feel about it?
—You dress beautifully except for your shirt collars. You have a fifteen-and-a-half neck, but you wear a size seventeen collar. How come?
—How many suits do you own? Do you know? How many pairs of shoes, or have you lost track of this sort of thing since you've been President? Does a President ever wear out a piece of clothing?
—You often read without glasses. Do you wear contacts?
—Would you just briefly explain the difference between Afghanistan and Pakistan?
—How do you handle your mail? Don't you miss going to the front door for it? Is it embarrassing not to have time to read letters from old friends? Do you ever sit down and write a letter to an old friend who hasn't written you, just for the hell of it?
—How's your spelling? Your arithmetic?
—I mean this as a general question. I'm not suggesting you're dumb, but how do you account for the fact that the smartest person in the United States doesn't get elected President? What do *you* have that the smartest person doesn't have that makes us all want you for the job?
—Tell me what you think of when I mention the following names:

> John Dean
> Henry Kissinger
> Billy Martin
> Jesus Christ
> Jean Harlow. She would have been exactly your age.
> Jacqueline Kennedy Onassis. Ever met her?
> Picasso

Linda Ronstadt
Mike Wallace

Thank you, Mr. President!

The First Lady

THERE are two things I wouldn't want to be in this life. I wouldn't want to be the Queen of England's husband and I wouldn't want to be the President of the United States' wife. Other than that, I'd be willing to try anything.

Both of them are really terrible jobs, even though I imagine you get all you want to eat. Prince Philip seems to handle his position with a casual charm that keeps the press off his back, but our First Lady, no matter who she is, always gets it from reporters. Mamie Eisenhower, for example, was considered to be nice but a dud as a First Lady, because she never had any strong opinions or did anything that stirred up controversy. Rosalynn Carter, on the other hand, was accused of having too many opinions because she sat in on Cabinet meetings sometimes.

Our First Ladies are asked to be the impossible. Broadcast reporters and newspaper people expect them to be busy saints. They're expected to have strong opinions but not express them. They're expected to be good hostesses in the White House without spending any money. They're expected to be beautifully dressed without buying any new clothes.

Nancy Reagan is currently getting the same kind of criticism that Jacqueline Kennedy got when she was in the White House. You can tell from the way Mrs. Reagan keeps herself that she's used to having things right. She has good and expensive taste in clothes, furnishings, food and decorations. It's not a serious defect in her character.

It is my opinion that reporters write stories picking on First Ladies because they think people *like* hating our First Lady. They think the public will object to the President's wife buying the best dinner settings available for the White House if they cost six hundred dollars each. The reporters are probably wrong. It's a strange thing about Americans, but even the ones living on food stamps don't resent rich people and they especially don't resent the President and his wife living well.

I'm soft on First Ladies. I don't know what's wrong with me, but I've liked just about all of them that I can remember. I even like Ronald Reagan better now than I did before I knew he and Nancy like each other as much as they seem to. It's nice.

If I'm ever elected President, the nation is going to be in for a shock with its new First Lady. If reporters think they have something to write about with Nancy Reagan, wait until my Marge moves in. She just isn't the type who'd make a lot of adjustments in her life-style, and the press is going to love it.

If I ever made a speech in front of the fireplace the way Franklin Roosevelt and Jimmy Carter did, my wife would be apt to walk in right in the middle of it and tell me to go out and get more wood. If I made some important policy statement she disagreed with, she certainly wouldn't hesitate to tell anyone who asked that I was out of my mind.

I know darn well she wouldn't spend half her day in the White House Rose Garden greeting Girl Scout troops, because she plays tennis three days a week, has French Club on Tuesdays, bridge on Wednesdays and she comes into New York to go to the Philharmonic every Friday. She does our bookkeeping nights. There's just no way she's going to hang around the White House to shake hands to get me in good with foreign dignitaries if she's got something she wants to do. And if she's ever First Lady and does what she did last week, the press will have a field day. She paid $350 for four tiger maple chairs that aren't even new.

As I anticipate the kind of First Lady my wife would make, I know how President Reagan must feel when they get after Nancy.

Shortsightedness

THERE are days when I wouldn't get out of bed if I started thinking about long-term, serious problems. Fortunately I have the ability to worry about the small things that I might be able to handle if I get up. Instead of worrying about whether I'll ever save enough money to die on, I'll worry about whether there'll be enough hot water for a shower or enough coffee left in the can for breakfast. These are the kind of worries I can handle.

Our political leaders do the same thing with their problems. The President of the United States, for example, has only a very short time to pay off on his campaign promises so, when he gets up in the morning, he goes to work on trying to get the economy off the ground by Christmas. He doesn't worry about whether the world we know on earth may come to an end in the year 2000 through a series of nuclear explosions.

The mayors of our cities have to worry about feeding and housing the poor this winter and paying the police more money for the fight against crime. The mayor can't get up worrying about how to raise fifty million dollars to completely reconstruct the sewer system that engineers tell him will be totally inadequate in 1995.

It's a good thing and a bad thing that we're so shortsighted personally and publicly. It would be wise but depressing if we spent all our time worrying about problems in their order of real importance.

This occurs to me today because some recent news stories have forced me to think about a lot of long-term problems I don't like to think about. Some of them are national problems, some local. Some will have to be solved with public money, others, if they're solved at all, with private money. Like what? Like these:

—The cost of making all public facilities available to handicapped people in wheelchairs has been found to be so expensive in some American cities that programs to build kneeling buses and ramps everywhere where there are now stairs have been abandoned. Where do I stand on this issue? Why, I'm in favor of doing everything possible for the handicapped, of course. If it costs every American five thousand dollars in additional taxes? One thousand dollars? A hundred dollars? If it comes to hard cash, how much of it am I willing to give to support my sentiment? Very tough question and anyway, I've got to take a shower.

—The General Accounting Office says that forty percent of all our 514,000 bridges are in need of repair. Most of them were built in the 1920s and 1930s, right after we got the automobile, and naturally they're getting old and rickety. The General Accounting Office says we could spend forty-one billion dollars fixing our bridges. Am I for safe bridges? You bet I am. Would I increase taxes to get that much or reduce, say, Social Security benefits by twenty-five percent to get the bridge-fixing money? Before I answer that question, I think I'll make the coffee.

—Chemical dumps all across the country are slowly polluting basic underground water sources, and it could cost billions to clean them up.

—Real safety for nuclear plants could make them so expensive that they'd be economically impractical.

We know how to solve these tough, long-term problems, but either we don't have the money to pay for them or we're not willing to sacrifice any of life's pleasures today for our safety and security tomorrow.

But before I worry anymore about these important matters, I think I'll go out and make sure I can get the car started.

Why No "Good" News?

L AST week I spoke to a group of people in San Diego, and by any standard you'd have to say they were above average. They were asking me questions about things I didn't know a whole lot about, but they didn't seem to mind and we were all having fun until one fellow got up and asked me the question that people in the news business are asked most often:

"How come you never report any of the good things that happen in this country?"

I say it's a question, but it's usually asked of news people in such a manner as to suggest they are the agents of a foreign government trying to bring down the United States of America.

There's something that people who ask that question don't understand, and I don't suppose anything I say here is going to help, but I'm going to say it anyway.

In the first place, news by its very nature is often negative. News is change, a deviation from what's normal or the way things have been. Mount St. Helens in repose is normal, and when it doesn't erupt you won't find pictures of it on page one. When it erupts it is a news story because it's an abrupt change that has a negative effect on the lives of a lot of people. You could say the same of a shipwreck or Congress. Congressmen are honest, for the most part, and it is only news when one of them steals and is caught.

My questioner in this case went so far as to suggest newspapers and television journalism ought to seek out stories that show America in a good light. In other words, he thinks we should put news to work creating an effect. We should choose our stories not for their news value, but for the impression they will have on readers.

I'm sure this man is good to his wife and children and works hard at his job, but he doesn't know a damned thing about what makes this country great and free. Who would he suggest choose these "good" stories about America? Could anything so important be left to editors? Wouldn't it be better to have a government agency oversee the choice? There's plenty of precedent for this around the world. Our government agency could take a trip to the Soviet Union to see how they do it there. It isn't as oppressive as we think. They just don't let the journalists create a lot of negative ideas in people's heads by letting them report "bad" stories. For instance, Russian readers never have to read about an airplane crash. Aeroflot, the Soviet airline, is run by the government, and why undermine confidence in the government—right, Ivan? Russians didn't have to worry about wheat production falling twenty percent below predictions in the Soviet Union this year either, because that bad news wasn't reported in the papers. They'll find out about it soon enough when there's not enough bread to go around this winter.

It's difficult for anyone in the news business to understand how anyone can think news ought to be used for any purpose but to inform. As soon as it is used to promote one good cause, such as patriotism, by having positive allusions to that cause inserted in its news columns, that's the end of a free press, and first thing you know Spiro Agnew is running against George Wallace for President.

There's no doubt about it, news is tough to take here sometimes. In a single day's paper, you can read of one politician calling another a liar, you can read of murder, drug busts, bribery of elected officials, dishonest police and twelve percent inflation, but if some Americans find it more difficult to believe this is a great country because of the negative stories they read about it, that's their problem. It's right for us all to love America because you have to love your own in the world, but we ought to love it enough and believe in it enough to know that it will stand up in open competition with any country in the world, even when all the unpleasant facts about it are known.

War Games

No coach of a professional team ever tells his players or the owners of the team that the opposition is going to be easy this year. That's not the way to motivate the players or the way to get the owners to spend more money on the team.

That's why our Army and Navy people are always telling us how dangerous and well armed the Soviet Union is. They figure the best way to get their budget raised is to scare us to death.

Every American probably ought to go to the toilet just once in Moscow. It would put the whole threat Russia poses for us in better perspective. When I see one of their tanks or one of those giant weapons they have rolling over the cobblestones in Red Square, I always wonder whether they're any better made than their toilets. Plumbing is one of the many modern inventions the Russians have not mastered. I am hard put to explain how they ever got a man in space and can only conclude that they still have enough German scientists left over from World War II to help them accomplish it.

Everyone who has ridden in a car made in the Soviet Union, raise his hand! What did you think? Would you compare it to a prewar Pontiac? How about a late model Hupmobile? Their best car, the Zev, is most like a cheap imitation of the last Packard, made in 1958.

It is simply impossible to be impressed with Russian technology if you go there. Almost everything that's impressive is impressive for its size—like the Russian army—not its excellence. With the possible exception of vodka, I can't think of a single thing they do better than anyone else in the world.

I don't suppose the military men on either side would like the idea, but what we ought to do is stage a sort of military Olympics with the Russians. I've drawn up a tentative schedule of events. The networks would be allowed to bid for the rights to televise the games and that income would be used to help defray defense costs.

—One-hundred-meter dash for tanks. This would be a test of speed.
—Combination marathon and steeplechase for tanks. This race of 26 miles 385 yards would be over an obstacle course. The unmanned tanks would be shot at periodically to judge their resistance to at-

tack. They'd also be judged on their gas mileage, endurance and how they looked under parade conditions.

—Guided missiles. Each nation would designate a target area somewhere in a deserted part of its country where no further damage could be done. We might indicate the Russians' target could be the South Bronx. Each country would see how close their missile with a small warhead on board could come to the target.

—Nuclear submarines. In this contest the competition organizers would put an empty freighter in the middle of the Pacific. We and the Russians would each start a nuclear sub from a neutral corner of the ocean. The first one to torpedo the freighter and leave the scene without looking for survivors would be the winner.

—The spy contest. Each country would be given twenty-four hours in which to hide a top secret document. The whereabouts of the document would be known by just ten people, and each contestant would be given a set of clues. Five spies from each country would be provided with false passports and American Express cards. They could try to buy one of the ten people or offer them sexual favors according to the sexual preference of their choice. The first spy team to find the other country's documents would be the victor.

These military Olympics might be held between any two countries when war between them became inevitable. Syria and Israel could save themselves time, money and bloodshed by having one now. Instead of attacking each other, nations would hold a contest to determine who would have won if they'd fought each other for real.

I'd love to see us take on the Russians in a contest like this. I've been to the bathroom in Russia.

The Russians

THERE are certain things in each of our lives that we look on with pride. Four years ago I was refused permission to enter the Soviet Union with a film crew for the purpose of making a television documentary. How's that for a feather in my cap? How many of my friends can say they were refused admission to Russia? I find ways to drop it into conversations all the time.

But I am deeply puzzled by the Russians. I can't make out what I think of them or decide what kind of people they are. My first contact with them was towards the end of World War II when the Allies were driving east and the Russians west, across Germany. On April 25, 1945, the armored division with which I was traveling as a reporter met the Russians coming from the opposite direction at the town of Torgau on the Elbe River.

For me the significance of seeing the beginning of the end of the war was overshadowed by the drama of the meeting of Russian and American soldiers, and by something that made Torgau a very special town. Torgau, it turned out, was the site of the huge Hohner harmonica and accordion factory, and that accident of wartime geography influenced my first impression of the Russians in an unreasonably favorable way.

Russian soldiers, free for the first time in years of having an enemy in front of them, went berserk. They smashed their way into the Hohner factory and took thousands of harmonicas and accordions. There was nothing exceptional about this. American soldiers often did the same thing. What made this exceptional was that half the soldiers in the Red Army seemed to know how to play an instrument.

Russian refugees who had been caught in Germany followed along behind the U.S. forces as they advanced, and when these displaced persons, many of them women, met the Russian soldiers it was a monumentally emotional moment. It was comparable, in many ways, to our entrance into Paris eight months earlier.

One of the refugee women must certainly have been a prominent soprano before the war, because the impromptu concert that began in the streets of Torgau with her great voice rising above the chorus of a thousand harmonicas and accordions was the most memorable musical experience of my lifetime.

The Russian soldiers seemed wonderfully free-spirited and uninhibited to me at first. The following day a small contingent of us crossed the Elbe to where the bulk of the Red Army was bivouacked, and it was a sobering experience. The Russian soldiers were free-spirited there, too. They just didn't seem to give a damn about life—theirs or anyone else's.

Many had acquired bicycles in their long drive across Germany, and they were riding them aimlessly around their camp. Each of them carried a short, badly made but effective little automatic rifle slung over his shoulder. I saw one Russian soldier grab a bike from another and start across a field with it. The one from whom the bike had been taken dropped to one knee, unslung his weapon and started firing close to the ground at the tires of the bike. They were wildly, irresponsibly, dangerously free-spirited. That was the first time I ever saw that element of the Russian character, but I've seen it on every level a lot of times since then. It is always chilling.

It may not sound, from what I've said, as though I'm puzzled at all about the Russians, but I am. I have met so many of them I liked and have so often been struck by the fact that, of all other nationals I know, they are most like Americans. They have produced great music and great literature which all of us enjoy and understand. Why can't we talk to them?

And there is another paradoxical side to the Russian character that provides me with some comfort when I watch their May Day parade of weapons cross the cobblestone Kremlin Square. When you pass a convoy of Russian vehicles, twenty percent of them have pulled over to the side of the road, broken down.

I have a sneaking suspicion the average Russian soldier knows more about harmonicas than engines.

The Coldback Problem

IMAGINE this:

The Soviet Ambassador to the United Nations comes before the General Assembly to plead for help with a special problem. It seems people from other countries keep sneaking across the border into the Soviet Union. Russia is such a wonderfully prosperous country, with Liberty and Freedom for all, that everyone wants to go there.

The problem is especially acute where Little Diomede Island, part of Alaska, is within two miles of Siberia across the Bering Strait. Americans keep paddling out from Nome in their kayaks and then swimming the last two miles to Russia in the middle of the night. In Russia, these illegal immigrants from the U.S. are known as "cold-backs."

Day after day, there are newspaper stories detailing the harrowing exploits of Swedish boat people who set out from Stockholm to cross the stormy waters of the Baltic Sea. Once in Poland, the

Swedes make their way on foot through Lithuania to freedom in the land of milk and honey, Russia.

In Moscow, a committee has been formed to try to help free Bob Hope, who has been placed in a detention camp in a remote section of Wyoming because of the bad jokes he's been making about the President of the United States. Hope has gone on strike, refusing to tell any more jokes at all until he's free to make bad ones.

The Free Hope Committee in Moscow has invited Bob to come to Afghanistan to entertain Soviet troops for Christmas, but U.S. authorities are afraid to grant him a visa because of the possibility he'd defect.

The U.S. doesn't want to be embarrassed again the way it was immediately after the World Series, when the New York Yankees went to Murmansk to play an exhibition game. At that time Dave Winfield, Ron Guidry, owner George Steinbrenner and two utility infielders to be named later chose to stay in Murmansk. They said they got better publicity in the newspapers there.

In Kansas, farmers are complaining because Russia is dumping cheap, high-quality wheat on the American market. Russian farmers, whose crops exceeded expectations again for the sixth straight year because of technological advances, are being encouraged by their government with price support programs that have enabled many of them to become multimillionaires.

In the case of many of the poorer Third World countries, the Russians have been giving their grain to help feed the hungry there, out of the goodness of their Communist hearts.

President Reagan decides that after a couple of years in office, he deserves a good vacation. He and Nancy go to Sochi, the Russian resort on the Black Sea. The President says the trip will be half work, half play. While he's in the Soviet Union, he hopes to be able to learn something about the way the Russian economy works so that he can apply some of those successful principles to our economy here at home when he returns . . . *if* he returns. Pictures show Brezhnev and Reagan lying around on the beach having some good laughs together.

In Israel, Menachem Begin makes a special plea to the nation, in an attempt to stem the flow of Jews leaving to seek freedom in the Soviet Union. Meanwhile, along the border separating Mexico and the United States, all customs officials and border police have been removed from their posts. Mexicans who used to come here as illegal aliens no longer wish to gain entry to the U.S. Their dream is to save enough money to make it to Moscow.

When these events come to pass, I'll believe we have a serious problem with the Soviet Union, but while everyone is trying to get out of there and into here, I'll continue believing they have more of a problem with us than we have with them.

VI:

OCCASIONS

Memorial Day

So far, it looks as though we're all going to die someday.

That goes for you young people reading this, too. Don't think for a minute that you're going to get out of it, because you aren't.

It doesn't give us much to look forward to, and the Memorial Day weekend isn't much help. If we're all remembered after we go the way those who have gone before are remembered by us now, things don't look too good.

Like everything else you can think of—and for better or for worse—Memorial Day isn't what it used to be. A lot of Americans are vague about its origin and purpose, because the federal government has jiggered the day around in order to make it more convenient for the living. The hell with the dead.

It was originally called Decoration Day and was established specifically in 1868 to honor the soldiers who died in the Civil War. Friends, relatives and patriots used to decorate their graves with flowers. (The word used in the books I looked this up in is "strew." They used to "strew" flowers on the graves. That appeals to me. Flowers are very often too carefully organized in vases for my taste. It is presumptuous of anyone to try to improve on nature's natural and random arrangement of flowers.)

As years went by, the day became one on which everyone made a specific point of remembering their dead by visiting the cemeteries where they were buried and often putting flowers on the graves.

Uncle Bill always put flowers on Auntie Belle's grave every Decoration Day. Then he'd stand there and tears would come to his eyes.

Not many of us put flowers on the graves of our dead friends anymore, and with the price of flowers what it is, certainly no one strews them.

I'm always touched when I see someone doing it or when I pass a cemetery and see evidence that they have done it, but I'd like to make an announcement: I'd prefer that no one put flowers on my grave if I have one. I don't like the idea of flowers dying on top of me.

Visiting a cemetery on Memorial Day is an intense experience. It's a good thing to do, but it's hard to bring yourself to do it because, for most of us, cemeteries are just too sad to contemplate. They bring to mind thoughts we'd prefer not to think.

I've talked myself out of visiting cemeteries, and I hope it isn't because I find it so sad. I say to myself I don't go because I find it's meaningless. You're no closer to the person you loved (I say to myself) when you're there by their grave than you are when you're anywhere else. If you wish to honor them by thinking about them, you can do that anywhere.

A visit to a cemetery on Memorial Day or any other day does force the memory, though, and sometimes that's a good thing to do. I don't care about the flowers, but I'd like very much to have someone remember me long and often. Each of us hopes for this. We have some kind of dream of immortality, but we know in our hearts that at best we'll only be remembered for a generation or two.

I remember my father and mother, of course, and I remember their fathers and mothers. But who remembers my grandfathers' and grandmothers' grandfathers and grandmothers? Or theirs? Not me, and in the long hard history of the world, that isn't much time.

It's all too much to consider—and too depressing.

I suspect the best thoughts of old friends come not on specific days set aside for remembering them, but from the things we used to do with them and from the special way we do things because that was the way *they* did them. The life they lived is now part of our own.

It's about the only kind of memorial that means much.

The Summer List

Y ou can complain a lot about how bad things are and about all the changes we've made for the worse, but there's just no doubt about it, we've moved summer up by a month in the last twenty-five years and that's not all bad.

I use the word "summer" loosely. By summer I mean the beginning of the time of year when you're more apt to knock off a little early on Friday and be a little later getting at things Monday. You start watching less television, you put more miles on the car, and you take some time off work to plan your vacation. I mean, let's face it, friends. Who are we kidding? *Everyone* is cheating on vacation days now. If you get three weeks, you somehow manage to connect it to a long weekend, two sick days, one plain goof-off day and you make it into a month. Everyone's doing it.

Summer used to start on July Fourth, but those days are long gone. We're a month into summer by the time the Fourth of July comes along now. That may be the time we *officially* start our vacation, but usually we've been stealing a day here and a day there from the boss long before that. It probably accounts for why the Japanese took the car business away from Detroit, but I don't want to get nasty just when we're all about to enjoy ourselves.

I was relaxing over the Memorial Day weekend making plans for some jobs I want to do around the house this summer. It's a good list:

—The windowsills on the back side of the house where the sun hits are in bad shape. I ought to scrape and sand them down to bare wood and put two coats of paint on them.

—This would be a good time to go through those closets and throw out the stuff I don't want. I particularly want to get at the closets where we keep the suitcases.

—The lock on the kitchen door doesn't work very well. Maybe I better replace that or fix the one that's there.

—We really need another bookshelf downstairs. I'll make that and put it in. If I put it in the room with the television set, I guess I better take everything out of there first and paint the room before I make the bookshelves.

—One of the cars has been dripping grease or something on the garage floor all winter. They have a kind of detergent that cleans it up. I'll clean up the garage floor. While I'm out there, I'll clean out the garage, too. I don't think anyone's ever going to use that cheap plastic toboggan. I'll keep the two Flexible Flyers in case we ever have grandchildren and snow the same year.

—This would be a good time to go through those boxes of old newspapers I've kept. That takes a while, of course, because when I look at the paper I usually can't remember why I kept it and I have to read the whole thing.

—That strap holding the television aerial on the roof looks loose, and the aerial is facing a little more south than it used to. We don't get as good a picture as we did. I'll get the ladder out and get up there and straighten it out.

—Some of those bushes around the house have gotten out of hand.

I'll clean them out of there. I'll pile the branches and junk from the garage out back, and then maybe I'll rent a small truck and take it all to the dump someday.

—One of the first things I guess I'll do is feed the lawn. Lime and fertilizer. Before I do that, I've got to take the one wheel that doesn't work off the spreader and oil or grease the bearing. As a matter of fact, before I fix the wheel or fertilize the lawn, I really ought to feed the maple trees. I'll pound a crowbar about a foot deep into the lawn around the perimeter of the trees and pour tree food in them.

I've had a tough winter and I deserve a little time off, so I don't want to rush into these things. Maybe the first thing I'll do is lie down and take some weight off my feet. After all, that list was good enough for last year and the year before. It'll be good enough for next year, too.

Thanksgiving

WE need a good, quiet, low-key holiday once in a while, and that's what Thanksgiving is.

It's unfortunate that we've diminished the importance of the word "thanks" by using it so often when we don't really mean it. We say it so many times during the average day that there isn't much left to say when you really appreciate something someone has done for you, and want to thank him or her with a word of appreciation.

What we've done is to invent a lot of superlative forms of the word. We say "Thank you very much," "thanks a lot," "how can I ever thank you" and "thanks a million." A million what is not clear.

For the most part, polite people use these phrases as a matter of common courtesy. We can't hate people for being courteous but, the fact is, we're filling the air with junk phrases. When the man who fills my tank with gas for $19.75 gives me my quarter change and says, "Thank you very much. Have a nice day," my inclination is to say, "I'd trade your kind words in for a windshield wash."

The sign over the pump in one gas station I've been to several times says, "No charge if we fail to smile and say thank you." That's fine, but they no longer have an air pump. What I want is less thanks for my patronage and more service.

The junk phrase that has begun to irritate me is the one being uttered as a matter of course by checkout cashiers. You lug a load of groceries to their counter, unpack your cart, put it on the moving belt and they say "Will that be it?"

What do they mean "Will that be it?" Of course that'll be it. If it wasn't it, I'd have picked up what was "it" and put it in front of them with everything else.

Yesterday I bought about fourteen items in a supermarket, and the cashier gave me the inevitable four words. I said, "Yes." I gave her a twenty and a ten to pay the $26.50 I owed. She carefully doled out my change of $3.50, and when she finished I just stood there with the change in the palm of my hand and said, "Will that be it?"

The cashier looked at me as if I'd said, "This is a stickup."

"Will that be it?" I repeated.

"What do you mean?" she asked.

"I mean," I said, "will that be it? Just like when you ask me 'Will that be it?'"

The cashier just shook her head, relieved that I was just crazy, not violent.

"Have a nice day," she said nervously and looked at the next customer.

When it comes to the "Thanks" in Thanksgiving, I hope we don't use it without any thought the way we so often use the word. I've often thought it ought to be called "Appreciation Day," but I realize that just doesn't have the same fine sound to it that "Thanksgiving" does.

Most of us go through the average days and weeks of our lives using those meaningless junk phrases that have no real thought behind them. It takes a toothache, the loss of a job or a death in the family to make us recall how good things were when our teeth didn't ache, when we were employed and when everyone in the family was healthy.

The trick to being happy is to stop and think occasionally, during normal times, how good things are going. At this very moment at Thanksgiving, my teeth don't hurt, I'm making a living and my family is fine. I'm just going to take the day off and sit around appreciating how lucky I am, and I hope you can do the same.

Have a nice day.

The Christmas Holidays Limitation Act

F OR everything there is a season and a time for every purpose under heaven," it says in the Bible.

That was obviously written by some ancient sage who didn't anticipate that there would be so much money to be made off professional football in July and January. Money seems to be the only thing that affects the seasons anymore.

There may once have been "a time to plant and a time to harvest that which is planted," but now the natural season for things is ignored. The seasons are becoming a blur on the calendar. Between rushing into the next season too soon, the way they do with fashions in store windows, staying with the last season too long, the way the professional sports teams do, and completely ignoring the seasons, the way the fruit and vegetable purveyors try to, we're losing the four-season definition of our years.

Last weekend I went into the department store over on the highway nearest our home looking for a leaf rake. (We don't burn leaves any longer and I approve, but it makes fall a less clearly defined season of the year, too.) It turned out the store didn't have any leaf rakes, because they'd cleared out their garden department to make room for Christmas tree ornaments.

In order to help preserve the Christmas season, I propose a Christmas seasons law. It would be called the Christmas Holidays Limitation Act. Here are some of its provisions:

—Capital punishment would be mandatory for anyone caught selling Christmas ornaments before Thanksgiving.

—Magazines would be precluded from issuing three Christmas editions, the first in October. No magazine dated "December" or calling itself "Christmas Edition" could be made available before December 1.

—Mail order houses would have their mail boxes taken away from them if they sent out brochures offering Christmas gifts before Labor Day.

—Every Christmas tree sold would have to be dated, like a quart of milk. The tree would be tagged with the exact day on which it was cut down.

—It would henceforth be illegal for any store to have a sale sooner than two weeks following Christmas Day.

—There would be stiff penalties for any individual caught mailing out Christmas cards before the tenth of December.

—Insurance companies, funeral homes, hardware stores and real estate operators would be forbidden from mailing out anything to anyone that said "Merry Christmas" on it.

If this Christmas Holidays Limitation Act is made into law, it could be expanded at a later date to include provisions that might help preserve the integrity of all our seasons.

If we can't make this a law, perhaps the following item should be added to an updated Ecclesiastes: "There's a time for Christmas holiday celebration and a time when it's too early to celebrate the Christmas holidays."

Christmas Trees

THE people who think Christmas is too commercial are the people who find something wrong with everything. They say, for instance, that store decorations and Christmas trees in shopping areas are just a trick of business.

Well, I'm not inclined to think of them that way, and if there are people whose first thought of Christmas is money, that's too bad for them, not for the rest of us.

If a store that spends money to decorate its windows has commerce in mind, it doesn't ruin my Christmas. If I pay nine cents more for a pair of gloves from one of the good stores that spent that much decorating its windows to attract me inside to buy them, I'm pleased with that arrangement. It was good for their gross and my Christmas spirit. I stay away from the places that pretend they're saving me money by looking drab.

I like Christmas above any time of the year. It turns gray winter into bright colors and the world with it.

I like the lights and the crowds of people who are not sad at all.

They're hurrying to do something for someone because they love them and want to please them and want to be loved and pleased in return.

In New York City, the big, lighted Christmas trees put up along Park Avenue for three weeks every year produce one of the great sights on earth.

There is a kind of glory to a lighted Christmas tree. It can give you the feeling that everything is not low and rotten and dishonest, but that people are good and capable of being elated just at the thought of being alive this year.

When I'm looking at a well-decorated Christmas tree, no amount of adverse experience can convince me that people are anything but good. If people were bad, they wouldn't go to all that trouble to display that much affection for each other and the world they live in.

The Christmas tree is a symbol of love, not money. There's a kind of glory to them when they're all lit up that exceeds anything all the money in the world could buy.

The trees in our homes do not look like the ones in public places and they ought not to. They look more the way we look, and we are all different. They reflect our personalities, and if someone is able to read palms or tea leaves and know what a person is like, they ought to be able to tell a great deal about a family by studying the Christmas tree it puts up in the living room.

Christmas trees should be real trees except where fire laws prohibit them from being real. It is better if they are fir or balsam, but Scotch pines are pretty, often more symmetrical and sometimes cheaper.

Nothing that is blue, gold, silver, pink or any color other than green is a Christmas tree.

A lot of people are ignoring the Christmas tree tradition, but just to review it, it goes like this:

You put up the Christmas tree Christmas Eve. You do not put it up three weeks in advance or three days in advance.

If you have young children, you put them to bed first.

As the children get older, you let them help decorate the tree.

As they get even older, you *make* them help decorate the tree.

When the tree is decorated, you put the presents around it.

You do not open presents Christmas Eve.

The first one down in the morning turns on the Christmas tree lights.

The best Christmas trees come very close to exceeding nature.

If some of our great decorated trees had grown in a remote forest area with lights that came on every evening as it grew dark, the whole world would come to look at them and marvel at the mystery of their great beauty.

So, don't tell me Christmas is too commercial.

Christmas Thoughts

SOME Christmas thoughts:

—A Tuesday is the ideal day for Christmas. It gives us Sunday to sit back and think about what last-minute things we have to do Monday.

—You know you've left your shopping until too late when the clerks and the shopkeepers are in the back of the store drinking eggnog when you come in.

—If your Christmas tree fits in the living room easily, it isn't big enough.

—One person in a household is almost always a better wrapper and string tier than anyone else. It's usually a woman, and the presents she receives don't look as good because someone else wrapped them.

—When children grow up, leave home and marry, parents often think about moving to a smaller house. The fact is they need a bigger house when sons and daughters start coming home for Christmas with wives, husbands, and children of their own.

—There are always fleeting moments of depression at Christmas. If they're only fleeting, you're lucky.

—The perfume counters in stores seem bigger than ever this Christmas. I assume we can count on people smelling better in the near future.

—One of the most glorious messes in the world is the mess created in a living room where eight or ten people have just opened their Christmas presents. It should not be cleaned up too quickly.

—It's difficult to know when to put the turkey in.

—There are always a few presents that resist being wrapped at all. It is impossible to wrap a bicycle.

—Lunch doesn't fit very well into the Christmas Day schedule.

—Sometime during the afternoon of Christmas Day, the people in our house divide themselves between those who feel they need exercise and those who think they'll take a little nap. I personally like to get some exercise and then take a nap.

—I'd hate to be President on Christmas Day.

—Someone always leaves one gift upstairs or in a drawer somewhere and forgets to give it until late in the day.

—None of the tricks they tell you about helps keep the needles on a tree. You either have a good tree that was cut recently or a dry tree that was cut last month.

—Christmas trees stacked for sale are one of the happiest Christmas sights. The same trees, still there, unsold, the day after Christmas are one of the saddest.

—Dogs seem to love Christmas.

—Kids don't get electric trains as much as they used to.

—We always get at least three Christmas cards with names we don't recognize.

—Last year I read Charles Dickens' "A Christmas Carol" and couldn't get over how good it was. I guess everyone else knew but me.

—It's too bad that anyone has to go anywhere at all on Christmas, but there's usually some little bit of business to be done, even if it's only picking up someone at the station or getting the newspaper.

—Someone always thinks something has been thrown out with the wrappings, but it turns out not to be true. It was under something else.

—I have always ignored advice on how to carve a turkey, but last year I read where you could remove the whole breast and then slice it down, across the grain. Pretty good idea. Now if they'd produce a turkey with less white meat and more dark, my family would be pleased.

—I'd hate to work in a department store the day after Christmas, even more than I'd hate to be President Christmas Day.

—Is there an American alive who can put something back in its original wrapping and package if it was originally put there by a Japanese?

—Every year there are a few people for whom I see dozens of things but then there's someone else on my list for whom I can find nothing satisfactory.

Favorite Presents

Wحат are the best Christmas presents you ever got?

I was trying to recall my favorites.

My parents gave me a Buddy-L truck that was strong enough for me to sit on when I was five or six and I can still remember everything about it. That was certainly one of my best presents ever.

A year or two later they gave me a little steam engine that actually worked. It ran from a boiler that was heated with a can of Sterno. The steam made the wheels go round, but I'm a little vague about what the wheels did once you got them going. It was a wonderful little toy, but in retrospect I think my uncle, who was there that Christmas, had more fun with it than I did. It certainly didn't compare with my Buddy-L.

Another uncle used to give me some dumb thing he found in his attic. I never liked whatever it was, but he usually gave me a five-dollar bill and a twenty-dollar gold piece too. At the age of ten or so I preferred the cold cash to the gold piece because, of course, my mother never let me spend that. I don't know what ever happened to all those gold pieces he gave me. I suspect my mother might have cashed them in one of those years they were having a tough time. Mom wasn't very sentimental about things like Indian head pennies or gold pieces that I'd saved.

Considering that I got dozens of presents every Christmas, it's not very nice of me to have forgotten all but a few. I remember the year I got an Iver Johnson bicycle and the year I got a pair of high leather boots with a jackknife in a little pocket on the side of the right one.

Once you get over being a kid, there's no telling what Christmas presents are going to strike you as exceptional. I have a cashmere scarf a friend gave me about twelve years ago. It looked just like any other scarf when I got it, but I've never lost it and I've worn it a lot on very cold days. Scarves don't normally turn me on when I get one as a present, but this one has been special.

My four kids, grown now, have been great gift-givers. There's no reason I should be surprised, but I always am at how intimately they know me. It's fun to get a present you weren't expecting that indicates that the person who gave it to you knows you thoroughly well. (Most of us are modest enough to be grateful to be liked by anyone who knows us well.)

Brian gave me a Japanese dovetail saw last year that must have been hard to find. I still use the pasta maker Emily got for me five years ago, and I love the wood-identification book that Ellen found. It has little samples of more than a hundred different kinds of wood, describing their properties. Martha and Leo gave me a whole *case* of tennis balls. I love anything in wholesale amounts, but it had never occurred to me to buy a case of tennis balls.

One of my great all-time presents was given to me by Arthur Godfrey in about 1954, when I was working for him. He gave me a woodworking tool called a Shopsmith. It must have cost about two hundred and fifty dollars at that time, and I couldn't have been happier if I'd been six again getting that Buddy-L. I still have it and use it every single weekend of my life and often on a week night.

I realize how personal all this is. I even understand that a reader wouldn't care specifically about my scarf or my Buddy-L. When you write something like this, you hope it will be understood that the specific examples represent something more universal. By which I mean, I'm sure you've all had your own equivalent of my Buddy-Ls, tennis balls and five-dollar bills.

Whoopie!

THE compulsion people feel to have fun New Year's Eve has always irritated me, because I'm not any good at it. A little fun goes a long way in my life, and very often *fun* isn't what I most feel like having. Fun means to me gay, lighthearted, thoughtless activity. There are other ways I prefer to spend my time, and before you decide I sound pretentious, I'll tell you that I'd include sleeping as one of the other ways.

We have gone to the same New Year's Eve party with the same people for twenty-five years now. I always enjoy seeing those old friends; it's the fun part of the evening that I hate. Someone always feels obliged to break balloons and blow horns, and I have a terrible time trying to act as though I am having a good time. I always have this strong urge to go home and go down cellar with a good piece of wood and see what I can make of it. Unfortunately for me, my wife is able to throw herself into the fun in a genuine way, so I can hardly leave or even act as though I'm not having a good time.

I don't kid myself that hating New Year's Eve is any virtue I have. I'm envious of people who like it. Hating it has nothing to do with brains either, because I notice that some of the smartest people are capable of acting like the biggest idiots New Year's Eve.

People who like New Year's Eve are usually good dancers. They learn new steps easily because they aren't afraid of making fools of themselves by trying them. (This is the same ability that enables some people to pick up a foreign language quicker than others. I am a very slow learner of both new dance steps and foreign languages.)

New Year's Eve rings a false bell in my brain because it seems contrived. The best kind of fun is the kind that comes unexpectedly. As soon as you plan to have fun or set out to go somewhere and pay money for it, you're usually disappointed. Fun, like love, is something you either fall into, or you don't. It can't be arranged. And that's the trouble with the New Year's Eve kind of fun. It's phony. There's nothing spontaneous about it. The noisemakers were bought at the five-and-ten. The confetti was cut by machine and sold in boxes. The fun is compulsory, and if you aren't having any, you're a bad sport and a party-pooper.

It is fitting that the traditional New Year's Eve drink is champagne, because if there's anything I hate worse than compulsory fun, it's bad champagne, and I think it's all bad; some of it is just worse than others. I am uneducable when it comes to champagne. By the time it is served, I've usually had two drinks of bourbon, and when I put a glass of bubbling white wine down on top of those, it assures me an uncertain tomorrow. It is not the way to start the New Year.

There are always people who are left out of the New Year's Eve festivities. I suspect there are almost as many people who sit home alone as there are revelers (I think the word is). I wish I could convey to these people how lucky I think they are. They are able to view the whole idiotic ritual on television, thinking their own thoughts, feeling melancholy or lonely if they wish, but at least they are in command of their own situation. They can go to the icebox;

they can sit there staring; they can go to bed at 11:47 and forget the whole thing.

That's what I'd like to do some New Year's Eve. Whoopie!

Proverbs for the New Year

AT the beginning of a new year, I tend to get philosophical. When I get philosophical it's usually in a very minor way. I don't review Spinoza, Plato or Aristotle. I get thinking about proverbs and truisms, the philosophy of nonintellectuals.

This year I got thinking that some of those old sayings aren't true.

Take, for example, the saying "Beauty is in the eye of the beholder."

I happen to think that is not true at all. Some things are beautiful and some are not. If you don't know which is which, that is your shortcoming, or mine, but the quality of the object is unchanged. We all have different experiences that influence our attitude toward something, but the fact is that the world's most knowledgeable art experts would not disagree very much on which are the best paintings. You can say "Beauty is in the eye of the beholder" or you can say "That's your opinion," but once two people know all about a subject, they almost always agree. We disagree on things when one person knows more than the other.

"A penny saved is a penny earned." There's another truism that isn't true anymore. A penny saved won't be worth as much next year as it is this year. That's one reason why the government is going to let savings banks pay higher interest rates.

"You can't judge a book by its cover." Says who? Have you spent much time in a bookstore lately? If you see a book jacket with the title *Weekend Date*, bearing a picture of a buxom young woman wearing a dress with a neckline ending at her navel, you are not apt to mistake the book for an instruction manual on how to solve Rubik's Cube.

Of course you can tell a book by its cover.

"Haste makes waste." Baloney. Haste usually saves time. Most of us move too slowly. The fastest workers are the people who know how to do the job best. I can fuss with a little job of carpentry for days, but if we get a professional carpenter in to make some china closets in the dining room, he's finished before I'd have figured out where to put them. Haste only makes waste if you don't know what you're doing.

"To the victors go the spoils." I guess that used to be true in ancient times when one nation invaded another and took what it wanted, but it doesn't seem true any longer. The Germans and the Japanese lost the last great war, but they're doing better than the winners. "To the victors go the headaches" is more like it.

"You can't teach an old dog new tricks." It may be conceit on my part, but I think I've learned some things about writing that I didn't know ten years ago. And I wasn't a kid ten years ago, either. We all get set in our ways, but some of the ways we get set in are right. We refuse to learn new tricks sometimes because we're satisfied with the old ones we know. You *can* teach an old dog a new trick if you want to. Here's one old dog who is still learning some new ways to roll over.

"Seek and thou shalt find." Not in the bottom drawer of my dresser you won't find. I've looked and it isn't there.

"Don't put all your eggs in one basket." This may be good advice, but I've never been able to take it. I don't like to spread anything too thin, not my time, my money or my interest. I like to know where all the eggs are. I just try hard not to drop the basket.

"Crime doesn't pay." We all hope this one is true, but sometimes we have to wonder.

"Two can live as cheaply as one." How about that for a dated proverb? Even if two could live for the same amount of money as one, you'd hardly call it cheap. Two *can't* live as cheaply as one, either. Two can live for about twice what one can. Maybe even a little more.

I don't mean to put you off proverbs. There are still a lot that are true. We just ought to weed out the ones that aren't and stop saying them.

Resolutions

THE holidays are over and I assume we're all ready to stop goofing off and get down to work. I was so busy watching football over the long New Year's weekend that I never did get at making any resolutions for this year, but they're ready now. I hereby resolve:

—Not to try to lose weight or go on any diets. I know the diets don't work and there's no sense pretending they might.

—That trying to balance my bank statement is a waste of time. If there's a swindler in the bookkeeping department at the bank, I doubt if he's going to pick my account to steal from. In the future I'm going to assume the bank is right.

—To forget about trying to be in bed by 11 PM every night. I've worried about it for years and I'm not ging to worry about it anymore. On the average night I miss by twenty minutes. Many nights I miss by half an hour, and occasionally I don't get to bed until 12:30. In the future when that happens, I'm just going to enjoy it and find someplace to sleep on the job the next day.

—That the cellar and garage are fine the way they are. And so is the attic. Every Saturday morning for years I've awakened and started to make plans to clean them out. I hereby resolve not to suffer through another year of guilt about the mess in the basement, the garage and the attic. I like them the way they are and I'm going to leave them that way.

—Not to try and keep either a diary or careful income tax records. I've started both of these half a dozen times in the past ten years and never got past March with them, so what I did keep was a waste of time, because three months of records gets you you-know-where with the IRS. Next year I'll fake the whole twelve months.

I further resolve that:

—I'm not going to try to stand up any straighter in 1982 than I naturally stand, which is a little bent over. People have been nagging at me to "stand up straight" for as long as I can remember. My mother started at me when I was nine. I'm tired of worrying about it. Take me as I am, a little stoop-shouldered, or don't take me at all.

—There are books that I've always thought I should read and I never have. I'm not going to read them this year, either. *The Brothers Karamazov, The Grapes of Wrath, Moby Dick* and *A Farewell to Arms* will have to wait.

—There may be a day I miss reading the newspaper, too, and I'm not going to kid myself this year by leaving it on the coffee table as if I was going to get at it tomorrow or the next day. I know damn well I'm not going to read it then either, so if I haven't read today's paper by the time tomorrow comes, I'm throwing it out this year . . . whether it has my column in it or not.

—I'm not going to worry about never having been to Spain. I didn't go to Spain last year, I didn't go to Spain ten years ago and I'm not going to Spain next year, either. There are just too many places I've never been to to start worrying about one.

—No matter what time I go to bed, I'm not going to resist falling asleep on the couch at 9:30 PM in front of the television set. I've spent hundreds of miserable hours trying not to fall asleep watching terrible television shows, and I'm not going to do it anymore. If I feel like taking a little nap before going to bed, I'm going to take it.

—I'm not going to try to improve my tennis game. My tennis game is just fine the way it is, and any attempts I've ever made to make it better have failed.

At long last I have become convinced we are what we are. I am what I am and no amount of resolve will change me.

VII:

RICH AND FAMOUS

A Cat Story

THERE are certain things writers don't say about themselves, even if they're relatively honest, because they feel there's no sense going out of their way to lose friends.

It is for this reason that I've never revealed that I don't love cats, and I wouldn't be telling you now except that last weekend I had an experience with a cat that I can't get out of my mind.

It is necessary to say that I spend time in my woodworking shop only on Saturdays and Sundays, and the shop is half barn and half garage. When I finish working, I have to move a lot of wood and tools to the back and sides to get my car in. Early Saturday morning I took the car out and started moving my tools into place, when a full-grown gray cat scampered past me and out the door. It startled me, but there are mice in the rafters so I assumed it had been back there trying to kill one. A cat's idea of a good time is to kill something.

As I started to work, I heard the barest suggestion of a meow from behind a pile of lumber. I stopped and stood absolutely still until I heard it again. I may not like cats but I'm not stupid about them, and I realized that the cat had not been back there killing mice but having kittens.

I carefully moved some lumber and uncovered a grocery store–sized box that I'd left old clothes in. For a minute in the shadow I saw nothing but an old wool jacket, but then something small and white moved. It was four inches long, pure white and had a cocoonlike look. It was a kitten a few minutes old.

I instantly forgot that I hated cats. I felt terrible. For an instant I froze as the whole terrible truth dawned on me. There was only *one* kitten! I had interrupted the mother in the process of having a litter. No one hates cats so much that they wouldn't feel bad under these circumstances.

My enthusiasm for woodworking was gone, and I withdrew from the barn to think about what to do. It was cold and obviously the kitten wouldn't survive without its mother. I left the door open and went down to the house to call a neighbor who is not really a farmer but lives as one. She's a kindly person, but she's been around animals a lot and I think it makes you less sentimental about them. She said the best thing to do was to put the kitten in a plastic bag with a rock tied to it and drop it in the lake down the road. She was only thinking of the kitten, she said. She didn't want it to suffer.

I guess you have to face things like that if you live on a farm, but I don't live on one and I don't have to. I knew if I did that I'd never get it out of my mind as long as I lived.

For the next half hour I puttered around the house, with just an occasional glance up toward the barn, until my wife came home from the store. I told her I wanted to show her something and explained that I had a big problem without telling her what it was.

We tiptoed into the barn and crept up on the box. The kitten was gone!

The mother cat had gone somewhere else to have the rest of her litter and then sneaked back into the grocery box in the barn for the white one and carried it to safety.

I'm still not crazy about cats, but I'm sure mighty grateful to that one, and if I ever see that little white kitten around and can get close to it, I'm going to tell it what a good mother it has.

An Address to My Family on Economics

(Following is a transcript of Mr. Rooney's comments to his family at the dinner table the other evening.)

I AM speaking to you tonight, following your mother's beef stew, to give you a report on our family's economy. You won't like it and I don't like it. As a matter of fact, I hate it. Let's face it, we're just about broke.

The economic lesson I wish to make clear to you tonight is that we're putting out too much and taking in too little. I'm not going to subject you to my checkbook. Take my word for it, I was overdrawn twice last month. We're in worse shape than at any time since the operation on Brian's appendix.

So much for the details. Now I want to draw up the broad outlines of our new program for you. First let me say that it is with great reluctance that I am raising my own allowance. In order to do that, I am increasing the self-imposed debt limit of what I borrow from the bank, from the $21,000 I now owe on mortgages, car payments and miscellaneous emergency loans, to a new ceiling of $30,000. This will give me the necessary capital I need to accomplish the programs that I feel are necessary if this family is to survive. Also, I want to pay my dues at the club with some of it.

There is no quick fix, to borrow an expression from one of our economy's most successful businesses. We're going to have to start by cutting the least important programs we now maintain in this family. Money for education is going to be eliminated. I'm certain none of you wishes to be the product of a welfare society, and I am therefore giving each of you the opportunity to become self-made men and women. It's time to recognize, too, that it would be foolish for the women in the house to go out and get a lot of education that would qualify you for jobs you can't get. I am therefore asking you girls to limit yourselves to a high school education.

It's time to recognize we've come to a turning point. For too long we've overlooked the fact that the family, any family, has a built-in tendency to grow. We've come to the end of that, too. The population of this family is six now. It seems like just a few short years ago it was two. This is an increase of three hundred percent, during which time my income has increased eleven percent.

What happened to the family dream of owning this house without the bank being in on it with us? I'm sure you're getting the idea that things are going to be a lot tougher around here. For many years now, you have complained about the regulations that have been imposed on you by me. That's all a thing of the past. You can go anywhere you want when you want to. Just don't ask me for any money to get there on. And don't go there in the Joneses' Rabbit diesel, either.

For too long now, we've been falling behind the Joneses. We're inflated and they're not. We have three cars, they have two. We put an addition on this house, they closed off their attic and den. No man is prouder of his family's capacity for work than I am but, frankly, you're all lousy workers. We are no longer competing effectively with the Joneses. In the winter, we're pouring gasoline into our snow blower, they're out there shoveling whether it snows or not.

In two weeks, I'll be talking to you again about the specifics of how you've got to cut back on what you spend and how I've got to spend money to make money.

Travelers Checks

EVERY night on television, we're faced with these people in the commercials who have gone somewhere without any real money and are in a panic because they can't find the imitation money they took with them instead.

My question is this: Why do people keep losing their travelers checks? It seems to me there can be only two reasons: (1) The people who buy travelers checks tend to be more careless about things than the rest of us, or (2) there is something basically wrong with the way travelers checks themselves are designed that makes them easy to lose.

I should think all this scare talk about losing them would be very bad for the people in the travelers check business, because the basic idea I get from the television commercials is that, while you may be able to get your money back, it would probably have been easier if you'd just taken money in the first place and been damned careful what you did with it.

On television, when the person or persons who lost the checks comes up to the tour guide or the hotel manager, the person in a position of authority always says, "What kind were they?"

They almost always seem to be American Express. Now, American Express always seemed like a pretty good company to me and I think it's high time top management looked into the reason for so many losses. When American Express goes to the trouble of returning money to the loser, it must take a lot of man-hours and machinery. This must add to what they have to charge for the travelers checks in the first place. If they could get to the bottom of this problem of why all these people are losing them, they could charge less.

Losing something is one of the least pleasant experiences in life. It's frustrating because you can't strike out at it. The thing is just gone, that's all, and you don't know where. There's often something traumatic about an unnecessary loss that you don't get over. I don't buy travelers checks because I'd rather just lose the money if that's what's going to happen. Money would be less personal than checks with my name on them.

Maybe it would be a good idea if American Express gave a course on where to hide things in a hotel room. That could cut down on thefts. Putting money in the pages of the Bible is one way to hide it in a hotel room. I have a friend who carries a waterproof plastic container. He puts his money in that and hides it in the water closet behind the toilet, if the room has one. Sometimes I put my extra money in with the clean towels. There are a lot of good hiding places in a hotel room.

There are two ways to lose something, of course. You can lose it through your own carelessness, by forgetting where you put it, or someone can steal it. Neither way is any fun, but if it's stolen, at least you have the pleasure of hating someone anonymously. If you lose it yourself, it's hard to find anyone to blame.

I've lost a lot of things in my life. The things I lose most often that don't worry me very much are sunglasses, gloves and umbrellas. I often wonder who has ended up with all those gloves I've lost. Somewhere I suppose there is someone as good at finding things as I am at losing them.

The first thing I remember losing was a Boy Scout knife my father bought me when I was about eight. It was a bitter day. There was no American Express office near our summer camp, and they wouldn't have replaced my Boy Scout knife anyway.

The most dramatic loss I ever suffered was when I fell asleep in a helicopter while photographing the *Queen Mary*. My arm hit the lever that opened the door. The door flew open and my camera and tape recorder dropped into the water below. A jacket with my money and credit cards drifted down the freeway nearby. We landed, and a watchman for the *Queen Mary* said he knew of a diver who might find my camera. I said I guessed it wasn't worth it and I was more worried about the jacket anyway. Within minutes a Richfield Oil truck pulled up and the driver waved at me. "Saw the whole thing," he laughed. "Here's your jacket."

If American Express sold jackets instead of travelers checks, it would have made a beautiful commercial.

The Rich

THERE are always things in the newspaper that I can't understand in terms of how they affect me, personally. For instance, the
other day I was reading about the tax cut. The reporter said that
some people were complaining that it helped the rich and hurt the
poor. Naturally I was trying to figure out, reading the story,
which category the writer thought I was in.

I got thinking about how to tell the rich from the poor. It's
harder than it used to be. It used to be anyone making over $18,000
was rich, but these days I suppose you're eligible for food stamps
if you're only making $18,000.

There are some dependable ways you can tell when someone is
rich. If someone doesn't carry any money, the chances are he's
loaded. I'm not sure about rich women, but I know rich men
don't usually have a nickel with them. Years ago I had a friend
named Steve Schlesinger who had made a bundle on the Red Ryder
comic strip by selling it to newspapers and to Hollywood for
Grade B movies. Steve would go into any restaurant in the world,
order drinks and dinner for a party of ten, and then worry about
what to do about money when the check came, because he never
carried credit cards or cash.

Another way to tell a rich person from a poor person is one I
learned years ago when I worked for a morning news broadcast.
We often had important people on it as guests, and I began to
notice one thing that the rich men had in common. They never
wore overcoats.

Nelson Rockefeller must have been on the show five times on
different winter days, and he never wore an overcoat or carried
one. It was a long while before I realized he was so rich he didn't
need one. He was never out in the cold, because all he ever did
was walk the ten feet from his chauffeur-driven limousine to the
building, and anyone can stand that much cold. For all I know,
Rockefeller didn't even own a raincoat or an umbrella. Most of the
restaurants a rich person would eat in would have canopies that
extended to the street.

Bankruptcy seems to be another sign of great wealth. You never hear of any poor people going bankrupt. It's always the rich.

There are dozens of ways to tell when someone is rich . . . they keep the same car for ten years, they're slow to pay their bills, they're bad tippers and all they read in the newspaper is the stock market report and the sports page. In France you're considered rich when the company starts mailing your check to you twice a month instead of paying you in cash every week. That still leaves me uncertain about whether I'm rich or poor. My check is mailed but it's mailed every week and it's a darn good thing, too, because I need the money.

An Equerry

THE royal family doesn't carry any money in its pockets. That's the single most interesting piece of information I know about British royalty. When Prince Charles goes someplace, he doesn't have a shilling on him because he has someone who takes care of money for him.

He can complain all he wants about his lack of privacy, but he has to admit that never having to worry about money makes up for a lot. Kings, princes and even presidents have valets who lay out their clothes and butlers who bring fruit, toast and coffee to their bedrooms in the morning. I know they all have chauffeurs who drive them where they want to go and a lot of places they don't want to go. Those are all things I don't mind doing for myself. I don't need any help reaching in the bottom drawer for my underwear or putting sliced bread in the toaster, but I sure would like to have one of those guys follow me around and take care of paying for everything.

The prince has something called equerries. Equerries used to just take care of the royal horses, but now they do a lot of odd jobs around the palace for a prince, and one of them is taking care of the cash.

Can't you imagine how handy it would be to have someone like that? You go to the supermarket, load up the cart with everything that strikes your fancy, including several expensive gourmet items you'll probably never use. You trundle your cart up to the line at the checkout counter, then you just drop it and squeeze past the other customers. When the cashier looks up at you, you motion over your shoulder with a jerk of your thumb and say, "My equerry will take care of this. Put the eggs in a separate bag, please."

Not having to carry money would make life so much easier. Just not having to decide what to do with the pennies, nickels and dimes that collect on top of the dresser would be a relief.

I often make a forty-mile drive from New York City to Connecticut. There is a one-dollar toll bridge, one forty-cent road toll and another thirty-five-cent one. You can use the automatic toll gates only if you have the exact change. That means to go through all of them without waiting in line at the manned gates, you have to plan in advance to have six quarters, two dimes and a nickel or some comparable combination. That takes a lot of planning. If I were a prince, I'd have no problem. My equerry would have change coming out his ears.

My equerry would be an expert on tipping, too. I've traveled a lot and eaten in a great many restaurants, but I'm never sure what I should tip anyone. My equerry would know. I'd never worry about whether I'd tipped the right amount again. My moneyman would know exactly what he ought to give the bellboy, the porter at the airport and the waiter in the restaurant. When I went to a fancy restaurant with a waiter, a captain and a headwaiter, he'd know what to give each of them. I never have. On those occasions, I'd start to leave the restaurant and as I passed the outstretched palms, I'd just smile and say, "Thank you. It was very nice. My equerry will grease that."

The idea of a money handler appeals to me especially this week, because Tuesday I did what I haven't done in years. I actually got stranded in a small town in upstate New York without enough money to buy gas to get home. I asked several gas stations if they'd take a check or one of my credit cards. They gave me the kind of look that made me feel half my size. I went into the branch of a bank whose president in the main office fifty miles away had been a classmate of mine in high school. If you don't want to feel like a jerk, don't try to get a teller to cash a check by explaining to him that you know the president of his bank.

The thing to do in a case like this is to get yourself an equerry, like Prince Charles.

Awards

Most of us have an award we've been given, collecting dust somewhere around the house. It may be a bronze medal for a third-place finish in a camp swimming meet or a citation of merit for having collected more than a thousand dollars for some charity, but everyone can point with pride to something he or she has won in a lifetime.

I'm as susceptible to the pleasure of being given an award as anyone, but award-giving worries me. There is often a fine line between who's being honored, the individual getting it or the organization giving it. A lot of times the presence of the recipient does more honor to the giver than the getter.

This doesn't seem to me to be the way awards were meant to be given. Something's gone wrong. During the last month of his tenure as the CBS News anchorman, Walter Cronkite attended something like eighteen dinners, lunches or special awards ceremonies in his honor.

Cronkite is too nice a man to decline when someone says they want him to show up at one of their functions so they can honor him, but he must have gotten awfully tired of it. He must also have wondered, at least once or twice, if the honor wasn't being bestowed on him principally as a means for the sponsoring organization to sell a lot of tickets to the dinner.

I'm even a little suspicious of an award I've just been offered. During my college years I belonged to a fraternity that I'm not going to name. I enjoyed being with a good group of guys, but when I left college I had no interest in maintaining any relationship with it.

It wasn't as easy to drop the association as I thought. The national group started mailing letters to me almost immediately after college. They wanted me to pay my dues so that I'd get the monthly magazine and continue as "a member in good standing." I didn't want to stand anywhere with them, but they continued to follow me with hundreds of pieces of mail over the years. They sent things like too-good-to-pass-up group insurance pitches, brochures with great buys on watches and jewelry bearing the insignia of the organization, and travel package offers.

I got so fed up with mail from the organization that I started returning everything with my name on it, marked "deceased." The mail stopped coming.

Recently, the fraternity discovered me again on television. They think I'm wonderful and they want to reward me. They want me to be an honored member and they want me to come to their annual banquet to accept an award.

One of the good things about me is that I'm not as nice a person as Cronkite. I don't *want* their award and I'm not going to their banquet to accept it, because I'm just egotistical enough to think there's some question about who'd get the most out of my being there. While I'm not exactly Walter Cronkite, the organization offering me the award isn't exactly the Nobel Prize Committee, either.

Colleges have been in the business for years of giving awards to people they think can do them the most good. If you look at the roster of people to whom any university is giving its honorary degrees, you'll notice more of them are rich than smart. College authorities always sprinkle a few legitimate academic people in their list of honorees, but they never pass up the man who flunked out after his second semester but went on to become chairman of the board of his company and a multimillionaire.

On a bookshelf in my house, there's a small, tarnished cup with most of its thin plating of silver gone now. I won it for writing an article in my school magazine when I was fourteen, and I wouldn't swap it for any award in the world. When they gave it to me, they meant it.

A Realist's Horoscope

THE astrologists who say they can predict what our day is going to be like, based on the position of the stars in relation to the date of our birth, don't usually hit it with me. For one thing, they're unrealistically optimistic. I've been doing some gazing myself recently, and I'm going to take a shot at some horoscopes. This is more apt to be the way things will go:

Aries (Mar. 21–Apr. 19) You are a wonderfully interesting, honest, hard-working person and you should make many new friends, but you won't because you've got a mean streak in you a mile wide.

Taurus (Apr. 20–May 20) Take advantage of this opportunity to get a little extra sleep, because you're going to miss the bus again today anyway. You will decide to lose weight today, just like yesterday.

Gemini (May 21–June 20) A day to take the initiative. Put the garbage out, for instance, and pick up the stuff at the dry cleaners. Watch the mail carefully, although there won't be anything good in it today, either.

Cancer (June 21–July 22) This is a good time for those of you who are rich and happy, but a poor time for those of you born under this sign who are poor and unhappy. To tell you the truth, *any* day is tough when you're poor and unhappy.

Leo (July 23–Aug. 22) Your determination and sense of humor will come to the fore. Your ability to laugh at adversity will be a blessing because you've got a day coming you wouldn't believe. As a matter of fact, if you can laugh at what happens to you today, you've got a sick sense of humor.

Virgo (Aug. 23–Sept. 22) Learn something new today, like how to spell or how to count to ten without using your fingers. Be careful dressing this morning. You may be hit by a car later in the day and you wouldn't want to be taken to the doctor's office in some of that old underwear you own.

Libra (Sept. 23–Oct. 23) Major achievements, new friends and a previously unexplored way to make a lot of money will come to a lot of people today, but unfortunately you won't be one of them. Consider not getting out of bed today.

Scorpio (Oct. 24–Nov. 21) You will receive word today that you are eligible to win a million dollars in prizes. It will be from a magazine trying to get you to subscribe, and you're just dumb enough to think you've got a chance to win. You never learn.

Sagittarius (Nov. 22–Dec. 21) Your efforts to help a little old lady cross a street will backfire when you learn that she was waiting for a bus. Subdue impulse you have to push her out into traffic.

Capricorn (Dec. 22–Jan. 19) Play your hunches. This is a day when luck will play an important part in your life. If you were smarter, you wouldn't need so much luck and you wouldn't be reading your horoscope, either. You are a suspicoius person, and it will occur to you that astrologers don't know what they're talking about any more than your Aunt Martha.

Aquarius (Jan. 20–Feb. 18) You are the type of person who never has enough money to do what you want. Don't expect things to get any better today, either. As a matter of fact they might get worse. Intensify your relationship with your bank and any friends you have who might be able to lend you a few bucks.

Pisces (Feb. 19–Mar. 20) You will get some very interesting news of a promotion today. It will go to someone in the office you dislike and will be the job you wanted. Don't lend anyone a car today. You don't have a car.

Returning to College

I F I thought I'd live to be a hundred, I'd go back to college next fall. I was drafted into the Army at the end of my junior year and, after four years in the service, had no inclination to return to finish. By then, it seemed, I knew everything.

Well, as it turns out, I *don't* know everything, and I'm ready to spend some time learning. I wouldn't want to pick up where I left off. I'd like to start all over again as a freshman. You see, it isn't just the education that appeals to me. I've visited a dozen colleges in the last two years, and college life looks extraordinarily pleasant.

The young people on campus are all gung ho to get out and get at life. They don't seem to understand they're having one of its best parts. Here they are with no responsibility to anyone but themselves, a hundred or a thousand ready-made friends, teachers trying to help them, families at home waiting for them to return for Christmas to tell all about their triumphs, three meals a day. So it isn't gourmet food. You can't have everything.

Too many students don't really have much patience with the process of being educated. They think half the teachers are idiots, and I wouldn't deny this. They think the system stinks sometimes. I wouldn't deny that. They think there aren't any nice girls around/

there aren't any nice boys around. I'd deny that. They just won't know what an idyllic time of life college can be until it's over. And don't tell me about the exceptions. I know about them.

The students are anxious to acquire the knowledge they think they need to make a buck, but they aren't really interested in education for education's sake. That's where they're wrong, and that's why I'd like to go back to college. I know now what a joy knowledge can be, independent of anything you do with it.

I'd take several courses in philosophy. I like the thinking process that goes with it. Philosophers are fairer than is absolutely necessary, but I like them, even the ones I think are wrong. Too much of what I know of the great philosophers comes secondhand or from condensations. I'd like to take a course in which I actually had to read Plato, Aristotle, Hume, Spinoza, Locke, John Dewey and the other great thinkers.

I'd like to take some calculus, too. I have absolutely no ability in that direction and not much interest, either, but there's something going on in mathematics that I don't understand, and I'd like to find out what it is. My report cards won't be mailed to my father and mother, so I won't have to worry about marks. I bet I'll do better than when they *were* mailed.

I think I'd like to take a one-semester course in reading and interpreting the Bible. I haven't known many people who have actually read the Bible all the way through in an intelligent way, and it comes up so often, I'd like to be pressed to do that. There was a course in Bible at the college I attended, but I didn't take it. It was taught by the organist, and I'd want someone better than he was.

There are some literary classics I ought to read and I never will, unless I'm forced to by a good professor, so I'll take a few courses in English literature. I took a course that featured George Gordon Byron, usually referred to now as "Lord Byron," and I'd like to take that over again. I did very well in it the first time. I actually read all of *Don Juan* and have never gotten over how great it was. I know I could get an A in that if I took it over. I'd like to have a few easy courses.

My history is very weak, and I'd want several history courses. I'm not going to break my back over them, but I'd like to be refreshed about the broad outline of history. When someone says sixteenth century to me, I'd like to be able to associate it with some names and events. This is just a little conversational conceit, but that's life.

If I can find a good teacher, I'd certainly want to go back over

English grammar and usage. He'd have to be good, because you might not think so sometimes, but I know a lot about using the language. Still, there are times when I'm stumped. I was wondering the other day what part of speech the word "please" is in the sentence, "Please don't take me seriously."

I've been asked to speak at several college graduation ceremonies. Maybe if I graduate, they'll ask me to speak at my own.

Haircuts and Frank Costello

How many times have you had your hair cut?

My hair is beginning to curl in back and obviously I have to go to the barber today. I don't like going to the barber. Having someone fooling around with my hair isn't unpleasant, but when it's over I never look the way I'd hoped to look. I want to look great and I never do.

One of the problems for most of us is that we really look best when we need a haircut the worst. When you have it cut off, it gives you a brand-new, shorn look that you don't want. Women who have just too obviously come from the hairdresser never look good to me. I'd rather have them a little rumpled and windblown.

I always tell the barber the same thing: "Don't take much off." While he's snipping away I think he's not taking enough off, but the next morning, after I've taken a shower, it looks as though he took too much. I've decided the reason for this is that when he combs it for the way he cut it, it looks fine, but after a night's sleep I go back to combing it *my* way and it doesn't look the same at all. It doesn't fit the haircut he gave me. Some of the strands of hair that I put on the right of my part were cut to go on the left of my part, and vice versa.

In spite of quite a bit of dissatisfaction, most of us are loyal to a barber. Women are a little more fickle. They get mad at their hairdresser every once in a while and move to another. Manny has been cutting my hair for about eight years now and I wouldn't think of going to anyone else, even though I pass ten barbershops to get to his. "Manny" is an unlikely name for a barber, but I'm comfortable with him, even though I don't know his last name.

It takes a while to break in a new barber, and I suppose it takes even longer to break in a hairdresser. I originally went to Manny when my former barber retired, and I was apprehensive because there was a sign in the window that said "Men's Hair Styling." I didn't want my hair "styled," I wanted it cut. I don't want to tell you how much it costs. It always costs more if the barbershop claims to style your hair instead of just giving you a haircut.

The first barber I ever had was named Kelly. Just as I don't know Manny's last name, I didn't know Mr. Kelly's first. I was young, and he was just "Mr. Kelly" to me. A haircut cost thirty-five cents then, and I hated getting one. I had to sit there in a line of chairs Saturday morning while the other kids were out playing. There were always a few kids getting their hair cut Saturday, and Mr. Kelly took us in order. We each moved up one chair when he finished the kid he was working on. Every once in a while a grown man would come in Saturday morning, and Mr. Kelly would put him right in the chair ahead of all of us kids. It never occurred to me at the time that it was wrong. In retrospect I doubt that the adult was going to do anything more important with the rest of his Saturday morning than I was going to do with mine.

The most interesting place I ever got my hair cut was in a big hotel barbershop in New York. They charged the same as everyone else, but the shop was very classy and they had twenty barbers. Every time I went there to have my hair cut, Frank Costello, the mob leader who was later gunned down but survived to die a natural death, was holding forth. He was having his shoes shined, he was getting a shave and having his nails done, all while the barber snipped lightly at the hair on his head.

About the fourth time I went there I said to my barber, "Gee, it's a coincidence but every time I've come in here, Costello has been here too."

"He comes in here every day and stays all morning," the barber told me.

Everyone who worked there liked Frank Costello. He was a great storyteller and a big tipper. He even began saying hello to me with a big smile, so I kind of liked him too.

We all have our good points and our bad points. Frank Costello was a gangster responsible for dozens of murders and half the crime in the United States during the 1940s and 1950s, but, on the other hand, he was good to his barber.

The World Affairs Test

I f you read the papers much, you read recently that according to a test given to three thousand college students on a hundred and eighty-five campuses, American young people are ignorant about world affairs.

According to the study, paid for by the federal government and Exxon, two of the richest organizations in the world, the students averaged a score of less than fifty percent correct on one hundred and one questions.

I sent for a copy of all the questions that the Educational Testing Service and the Council on Learning produced for the $630,000 it cost, and they mailed me a book two hundred and eighty-nine pages thick that included not only the questions and the answers, but a lot of high-flying conclusions by the people who gave the test.

I'd like to send the whole thing back to the Educational Testing Service with a failing mark. It may or may not be true that college students aren't very knowledgeable about world affairs ("global understanding," the testers always call it), but the testers ought to go back to the fourth grade and start all over again learning how to write a sentence in plain English.

As an example of a question that must have given some smug satisfaction to the person who wrote it, but would be considered tortured English by anyone reading it, consider Question #72:

> Each religion below is correctly matched with countries in *each* of which it either predominates or has a significant minority following EXCEPT
> 1—Christianity . . . Greece, Lebanon, the Philippines, Ethiopia.
> 2—Islam . . . Saudi Arabia, the Soviet Union, Indonesia, Nigeria.
> 3—Buddhism . . . Japan, Thailand, Vietnam, Sri Lanka (Ceylon).
> 4—Hinduism . . . India, Pakistan, Afghanistan, Kampuchea (Cambodia).

If the object of the test was to make students stop to figure out what the question was, that's a good question. If the object was to test them on their knowledge of foreign countries, it is unnecessarily complicated. I suspect if you asked Henry Kissinger that question, he'd reply "Vhat?"

How about this as a substitute: "Which religion listed below is not usually associated with all the countries after it?"

The correct answer, by the way, according to the testers, was #4. Must have something to do with Kampuchea.

Before they start the test, the students are asked a lot of personal questions. To give you some idea of how the whole thing is going to go, the first personal question is this: "1. Age (in years)."

I can't for the life of me think how the testers thought the students were going to answer that question except in years, but I suppose that's why I've never been given $630,000 to administer a test.

In an introduction, the project director begins by writing, "While the required breadth of content coverage seems to have been the surprise in development of the knowledge or cognitive area, method was unquestionably the potential stumbling block of affective measurement."

Could you play that over once more, professor, for the kids in the back of the class? The professor has about ten words he's in love with. He loves any "perception," but especially "self-perception." He prefers "replicate" to "duplicate," and he never passes up a chance to drop in "cognitive" or "component." He doesn't call the test a "test," he refers to it as "the survey instrument." He never talks about radio and television. He calls them "the electronic media."

I personally thought his most devastating criticism of American college students was when he said, "The estimates reveal deficits in knowledge and affect through comparisons with explicit criteria and reasonable implicit criteria."

You get an A in Government Grants, professor, but an F in English.

We Need More Time

THE object, I think, is to get as much living into your life as possible. Most of us live at half speed most of the time, and we lose a lot of good living that way. We goof off or don't have a plan, or for one reason or another don't do much on many of our days.

A lot of us will live more than eighty years, but say we have just eighty years. That's 29,220 days. Maybe if we had a chart with every one of those days numbered and painted on a wall in a backroom or down in the cellar, and crossed one of them off every day, we'd be more careful to live them fully.

It seems to me that science could help us. There are a lot of things that take too long. Sleeping, for instance, takes too long. The average person sleeps seven hours a day, and some need eight. Why can't scientists develop something that makes us sleep faster? Should that be so hard? They've compounded all these mind-bending drugs that do nothing but get us in trouble; isn't there something they could make that would give us a night's sleep in a couple of hours? I wouldn't want it to be any shorter than two hours, because the whole business of getting ready to go to bed and lying there thinking for a little while before you fall asleep is a very pleasant process and a good part of a full life. I'd like it if I could get it all out of the way in two hours, though, so I could wake up refreshed and get back at all the wonderful things I like to do that I can only do when I'm awake.

There are several other things that take too long, too. I'd like to be able to get some exercise faster every day. I play tennis once or twice a week, but the exercise is incidental to the fun playing tennis. I don't want to cut down on the hour and a half tennis takes me. I want to be able to give all my muscles a workout in about ten minutes on the days I don't play.

Telephone calls take too long, and that's something we can all do something about. It takes too long to get started and too long to end the average phone call. Someone should rewrite the etiquette of the phone call and eliminate all the "How are you's?", the

"What's new with you's?" and the "Have a nice day's." We could each save a week a year by shortening our phone calls.

Dressing ourselves takes too long. I don't know whether any study has ever been done or not, but I suspect that women are able to get dressed quicker than men. The average man who wears a coat and tie puts on ten pieces of clothing. They're all different and present different problems in draping them over the body. With the exception of the brassière, women's clothes are simpler and easier to put on. A man's two shoelaces alone more than make up for the time it takes a woman to hook up a brassière. A lot of women go out into the world with only five pieces of clothing on. If men are going to save time for living by cutting down dressing time, men's clothes have got to be simplified and some of them eliminated.

There are some things that take a lot of time that might seem like a waste that are not. Sitting and staring, for example, is not wasting time. We all need to do more of that and you can't speed up staring, and I wouldn't want to if I could.

It just seems to me that science hasn't always put its effort in the right direction. We all need more time for living, and if they can't work it out so we each get at least one hundred good years, then they ought to find a way for us to get more into the years we have.

Morning People and Night People

ARE you consistently dumber during some hours of the day than others? I certainly am. I'm smartest in the morning. You might not think so if you met me in the morning, but that's the fact. After about 11:30 AM, my brain begins getting progressively duller, until by late afternoon I can't remember my middle name. It is morning as I write. My middle name is Aitken.

Each of has his best hours. The people who have to have a cup of coffee to activate their brain in the morning are the slow starters. I have a cup of coffee to get my body going, but my brain starts up without it.

It's always best if what we are coincides with the way we wish we were. It doesn't happen often to most of us, but both morning people and night people seem to be pleased with themselves the way they are.

I know I'm pleased to be a morning person. I think it's best. I associate it with virtue. It works out best for me, too. Not perfect, but best. I get to work very early, taper off around noon and have a very unproductive period between about 1:30 and 4:30. Unproductive periods are important too, you know.

Somewhere around 4:30, my brain begins to stage a mild comeback, but by then it's time to quit and go home.

I feel sorry for the people who think best in the evening and I'd like to tell you why. Night people awaken grudgingly. They dread getting up but eventually drag themselves out of bed, put themselves through their morning ablutions and stumble to work hating every minute of it. By noon their metabolism is finally moving at the same speed as the current of activity that surrounds them and they begin to blend in. It is now lunchtime.

In the early evening, after the sun has gone down and the rest of the world is settling in, they're ready to go. They waste some of their smartest hours, when they should be most productive, watching some of the dumbest shows on television.

Prime time television was designed for those of us who are smartest in the morning. By 8 PM, we've lost most of our critical faculties, and "Dallas" and "Laverne and Shirley" are just perfect for our level of intellectual activity. Even if we don't like them, they don't bother us enough to make it worth our while getting up to turn them off.

The night people sit there doing the crossword puzzle or reading the paper and grumbling because there's nothing on the tube worth watching.

It seems apparent to me that we ought to rethink the whole pattern of our daily lives. We've got to make some changes.

If each of us really does need seven hours' sleep, it would probably be better if we took it in shorter periods. I often get more sleep than I need or want all in one piece during the night. Even when I go to bed at 11:30 and get up at 5:45, which is my habit, there's something wrong with just lying there in one place for six hours and fifteen minutes.

I'll bet it would be better for both our brains and our bodies if we took our seven hours in sections instead of all at once. Say we slept for three hours between 1 AM and 4 AM, two hours from noon until 2 PM and another two hours between 7 PM and 9 PM.

This would give us the same seven hours, but better distributed over the twenty-four-hour period.

There are some problems that would have to be worked out, of course. The reason all of us now try to get what is known as "a good night's rest" is not because that's the way our bodies like it, but because the whole civilized process of going to bed and getting up is such a time-consuming activity that we couldn't afford to do it three or four times a day. And, of course, if it took the night people a couple of hours to get going again after each sleep period, they'd be less help than they are now. A personal opinion, you understand.

And, of course, there are other questions that would have to be resolved. When, for instance, would we change our underwear, take a shower and make the bed?

Rules of Life

WHAT follows are some rules of life:
—Don't pin much hope on the mail, and when the phone rings, don't expect anything wonderful from that, either.
—If everyone knew the whole truth about everything, it would be a better world.
—Any line you choose to stand in during your life will usually turn out to be the one that moves the slowest.
—The best things in life are not free, they're expensive. Good health is an example.
—If you wonder what anyone thinks of you, consider what you think of them.
—Don't take a butcher's advice on how to cook meat. If he knew, he'd be a chef.
—Anything you look for in the Yellow Pages will not be listed in the category you first try to find it under. Start with the second. Keep in mind cars are under A for "automobiles."
—Not everyone has a right to his own opinion. If he doesn't know the facts, his opinion doesn't count.
—If you think you may possibly have forgotten something, there is no doubt about it. You've forgotten something.

—Happiness depends more on how life strikes you than on what happens.

—The model you own is the only one they ever had that trouble with.

—Hoping and praying are easier but do not produce as good results as hard work.

—Wherever you go for whatever reason, it will turn out you should have been there last week.

—When you buy something, it's always a seller's market. When you sell something, it's always a buyer's market.

—The same things keep happening to the same people.

—Enthusiasm on the job gets you further than education or brains.

—Money is not the root of all evil.

—Every so often you ought to do something dangerous. It doesn't have to be physical.

—Patience is a virtue. Impatience is a virtue, too.

—All men are not created equal but should be treated as though they were under the law.

—The people who write poetry are no smarter than the rest of us, and don't let them make you think they are.

—Patriotism is only an admirable trait when the person who has a lot of it lives in the same country you do.

—Apologizing for doing something wrong is nowhere near as good as doing it right in the first place.

—If you want something you can't have, it is usually best to change what you want.

—The only way to live is as though there were an answer to every problem—although there isn't.

—New developments in science and new inventions in industry don't usually improve our lives much; the most we can hope is that they'll help us stay even.

—You may be wrong.

—You should be careful about when to go to all the trouble it takes to be different.

—It is impossible to feel sorry for everyone who deserves being felt sorry for.

—One of the best things about life is that we are happy more than we are unhappy.

—Not many of us are able to change our lives on purpose; we are all permanent victims of the way we are, but we should proceed as though this were not true.

VIII:

WHAT WE DO

Don't Do It Yourself

WHAT we need is a Don't-Do-It-Yourself Movement in this country. A lot of us are sick and tired of doing it ourselves. We'd like someone else to do it for us and we're willing to pay them. In the future, the man-of-the-house, whether he be male or female, would only do the odd jobs he felt like doing. If he didn't feel like doing them, he'd call someone and they'd come. *This* is how to create employment.

I'm not any kind of economist. When they print those graphs in the business sections of the newspaper, I can't make heads or tails of them. I don't care whether the chart goes up and down in columns, sideways in bars or roller-coaster style across a sheet of graph paper. I don't understand them. But I have a basic idea of what makes money go 'round.

Money goes 'round when *you* have something that *I* want, and I work hard enough making something other people want, to pay you for what you have. It's that simple. If I make paper and you fix cars, it's silly for you to try to make your own paper or for me to try to fix my own car. Neither of us is ever going to get to Europe that way.

What we have to do is draw the line. Neither of us will any longer waste our days off botching some job we don't know how to do. We will call for help and then retire to the living room with a drink to watch television. When the job is done we will pay for it.

Each of us has to get over the notion that the other person is getting paid too much for what he does. We can no longer be surprised when an experienced carpenter asks eighteen dollars an hour and averages five hundred dollars a week. Or whatever the figures are. What we have to do is pay him and then set out just a little earlier in the morning and hope we can bring home at least five hundred dollars a week to stay ahead.

The professionals have to do their part, too, if this Don't-Do-It-Yourself Movement is going to get off the ground. Some jobs are considered too small for an expert to bother with. That's where you professionals have to swallow your pride. Even if it's only a leaky faucet, come anyway. I'm not going to suggest electricians should drop by to change a light bulb, but when the chain-pull switch goes in the closet, don't turn down the job because any idiot ought to be able to fix it. I'm the idiot and I can't fix it.

They talk about the shortage of scientists and doctors, but have the people who talk about it tried to get anyone to fix one broken windowpane? Or to fix the flue in the fireplace? These are the experts America is short of. We've put them out of business by doing it ourselves. You can get men to erect a steel and granite skyscraper and you can go to the Yellow Pages and locate someone who will install a plate-glass window, but where are the professionals who will put a new pane in the basement window?

If the law of supply and demand really works, we're going to be paying more for a bricklayer in a few years than for an atomic scientist. That's because the Do-It-Yourself Movement has had us all laying our own bricks these past twenty years and putting bricklayers out of business. Thousands of bright young people are going to MIT every year, but how many are learning to lay a brick?

Trying to get an electrical appliance fixed is harder than trying to get a brick laid. If something small is wrong with anything, you're in big trouble. If the breakdown is major, you're lucky. It has to be sent back to the factory. They don't fix it. They don't know how, either. They remove the faulty part and replace it with a new lifetime self-lubricating built-in factory-sealed unit.

We've got to encourage the small operators in our neighborhoods to fix things for us. We shouldn't have to try to do it ourselves, and we shouldn't have to send it to the factory. I'm tired of buying oil by the quart at the supermarket instead of having it changed at the gas station. I'm even tired of putting shelves in the closets in my house. I don't care how small the job is. I'm willing to Not-Do-It Myself and pay an architect $27.50 for fifteen minutes' advice on where to have the carpenter I'm going to call put the shelves.

Tony

My relationship with Tony has lasted twenty-five years now, and I don't know whether to end it next spring or not.

I got thinking about it over the weekend, when I was raking

the last of the leaves out from under the bushes. The place just doesn't look as good as it used to.

The house isn't huge and it's on about two-thirds of an acre, and when we first bought it I spent several hours every week getting the lawnmower fixed and cutting the lawn, in that order. In about the fifth year I decided cutting the grass was something I didn't want to do any more of. I found Tony. Tony had an old pickup truck, a big, battered mower, and although it seemed like a lot of money to spend just because I was too lazy to cut my own lawn, I turned the whole thing over to him.

For four years, he cut the grass at the original price, but I noticed that toward the end of that year, he had a helper with him quite often. At the beginning of the fifth year, Tony said he was going to have to charge more. I wasn't happy, but it seemed reasonable that his prices should go up like everything else, so I agreed.

It was a satisfactory arrangement for fifteen years. By then Tony was in his middle sixties and still able to work hard, but he had a brand-new truck now, a new gang mower, a lot of other equipment and three people helping him.

I wasn't usually home when the lawn was cut, so all I ever saw were the results. The lawn always looked better on Tuesdays, but I began to notice he wasn't getting as close to the trees as he used to. The grass in the slate walk was left long and weedy, and very often he wasn't cutting the grass on the other side of the hedge by the road at all.

One Tuesday I stayed home because I had an appointment with the dentist later in the morning. I was wasting time, puttering around the garage, when an old truck swept into the driveway. Three men jumped out, rolled an old mower down the ramp,

I watched from the garage window, amazed at what I saw. While one of them sped around major parts of the property on the mower, a second made a few swipes at some tall weeds on the edge of my wife's garden and the third got back into the truck and smoked a cigarette.

In twenty minutes they had the mower back up the ramp, ready to leave.

I came out of the garage and walked to the truck.

"Where's Tony?" I asked them.

"He don't come no more," the one smoking said. "He's too busy. Too much work. He's in other truck."

"You didn't do a very good job," I said. "What about the tall grass you left over by the cellar door?"

"Next time," he said. "We get it good next time. Rained Friday and we way behind. Too much work."

I offer this story because it's only my house and my lawn, but it says a lot about what has happened to America. Everyone is an entrepreneur. Figuring a way to make a buck comes ahead of thinking about how to do the job better. Tony realized that if he hired another crew, got more customers and did the job quicker and sloppier, he could make more money.

So, I don't know what to do next spring. Tony will call with another price increase, I know that. I also know the job won't be very well done. He's charging me roughly four times as much as he charged when he started cutting my lawn.

To tell you the truth, I'd tell Tony I'm going back to cutting the grass myself again next year, except for one thing. I'm making about four times as much myself as when I first hired Tony.

Waiting for the Floorsander

I SENSED something was wrong the minute I walked in the kitchen door. Two small tables from the living room were over by the refrigerator, and the big Chinese lamp from the table with the magazines on it was next to the radiator in the kitchen. There was a pile of papers and magazines on top of the radiator.

What was wrong was that my wife had made arrangements to have the living room and dining room floors sanded and she was getting ready. All I wanted to do was sit down, have a drink and watch the news. All she wanted me to do was help move the furniture out of the living room and roll up the rug. She wanted me to disconnect the television set and move that, too.

I don't like to think and lift on the same day. My days for lifting are Saturday and Sunday. During the week I try to do my thinking or, at least, worry over why I am *unable* to think. This lifting request led to a confrontation between my wife and me, the details of which I'd prefer not to talk about.

Now, two days later, we have reestablished relations because we have a common enemy. He is listed in the Yellow Pages as John the Floorsander. We are plenty mad again today, but this time not at each other. We're mad at John the Floorsander because he never showed up.

The compromise arrived at the other night was that I *did* sit down and have a drink and watch the news, but then, after dinner, I violated my rule about not *lifting* on *thinking* days by moving the furniture out of the living room.

At nine yesterday morning my wife called me at the office, something she does only in times of life's most serious emergencies. She announced that "the men" hadn't come yet. I asked if she had called John the Floorsander's number. She said she had but that she got an answering machine. The answering machine doesn't do floors.

At ten she called back to say they still hadn't arrived, but that she had reached *Mrs.* John the Floorsander, who said they'd be there shortly.

There was something ominous about the rest of the day for me. My wife never called again to say that they had come or they hadn't but I know her well. She was home, burning with anger. She was too mad and frustrated to talk at all.

When I got home my worst fears were realized. The floors were just sitting there like always, dark brown, worn, stained and unsanded. The house was a shambles, with pieces of furniture balanced on top of each other, out of their natural habitat. There was no place to sit, no place to drink, no television set to watch.

Now I'm thinking of suing John the Floorsander. I wonder what chance I'd have if I sued him for forty-eight dollars? My wife waited for him full time between 8 AM and 2 PM before she gave up and left the house the other day. That's six hours. Would eight dollars an hour be too much to ask for her waiting time? She's college-educated, a former mathematics teacher and as good at waiting as anyone else. Certainly her waiting time is worth forty-eight dollars.

Why is it that the people we call for help with jobs around the house so consistently fail to show up when they've said they would? They assume our time is worth nothing to us. Is this some kind of occupational disease that spreads from plumber to tree surgeon to television repair man to floorsander? I'm resigned to the fact that doctors don't make house calls, but do I have to bring my house to the floorsander?

And even when they come, your problem is always so difficult, highly unusual, time-consuming and hard-to-get-at that they're unable to do it until next month.

What We Do

WE know very little about each other when it comes to the work we do. I have some very good friends in the business world, but I don't really know how they spend their days. People often come up to me and ask me what I do. They know I write "those little columns in the newspaper" and they know I appear on television, but they ask what I *really* do.

The confusion comes, I think, because whatever it is we *really* do doesn't take very long. If someone digs a ditch with a steam shovel, he isn't actually digging for much of the day. A woman who takes care of a family and a home isn't usually doing anything at any specific moment that she could tell anyone about. A football player who makes half a million dollars a year as a running back probably isn't actually running in a game for an hour a year.

We all understand a writer when he's typing, a business executive when he or she is making decisions and a ditchdigger when he's digging. It's what each of us does with all the rest of our time that we don't understand about each other.

My father spent his life selling paper mill felts. The felt is vital to papermaking because it keeps the wet sheet of pulp flat while it rolls over hot steel rollers and dries, but until he took me on a trip with him through the South, I never understood why he was away for two or three weeks at a time.

He would travel for hours to get to a paper mill and then wait for hours more, as salesmen often do, to see someone important enough to make an expensive purchase. More than half the time, they didn't buy anything and that was the end of the day for him. It might take him two days to get to the next mill, and they might not buy anything either.

There's always a lot of unexplained time in any job, and if you aren't the one doing the job, you're never going to understand it. I mention all this because most of us are unfair in our assessment of the work others do. It often seems to us that we're working hard while other people are goofing off.

This lack of understanding most of us have for other people's work accounts for why we usually think our own job is pretty interesting, but that our neighbor's job is dull. It's hard to believe, but most people like what they do. They aren't just putting in their time to make a living. I have visited a lot of factories and talked with men and women doing repetitive jobs on a production line. Those of us who don't work on a production line feel sorry for those who do, but those who do don't feel sorry for themselves. More often than not it gives them a feeling of satisfaction every time they put a piece of something together.

My father loved to sit around talking to other people in the paper business. I remember spending hundreds of hours at the dinner table when he had business guests, listening to details that bored me to death. All of us do that. We like talking to people who do the same thing we do. The political conventions are great fun for anyone in the news business because there are so many other news men and women there to talk to. The great AP columnist Hal Boyle was a good friend of mine. I was standing in a group with him one day and a woman said, "You must meet a lot of interesting people in your business."

Hal had met every important person who had lived in the world between 1934 and 1974. He looked at the woman with a little smile on his face and said, "I do . . . and most of them are other newspapermen."

My father would have said the same thing, but he would have thought most of them were other papermakers.

I have a feeling that most people who don't like what they do wouldn't like anything they did, no matter what it was.

Breaking in a New Boss

I'M not looking for sympathy, but I'm breaking in a new boss, and you all know how trying that can be. He seems like a nice, bright young fellow. He's got all kinds of education and I think he shows promise. He's got a lot to learn about being my boss though. How to be my boss is not a course they teach in college.

Because being a boss is such a terrible job, I try to look at it from their point of view. One of their biggest problems is that most of us have had a lot more experience being bossed than they've had bossing, and that gives us the upper hand. I started out being bossed as a private in the Army and I've had at least one boss over me ever since, and sometimes I've had dozens. I can't tell you how many bosses I've had. Bosses come and go in my life and I keep plugging away at the same job no matter who it is. Eventually the boss gets involved in some upper-level political intrigue in the company, and he gets fired or promoted or moves into limbo in a special office they have for limbo bosses, and another boss moves in over me.

A new boss usually feels he ought to be decisive and take command. He wants to show who's boss. He doesn't really know what he's doing, though, and he doesn't want to make any serious mistakes, so he starts moving people from the third floor to the second floor and vice versa. This causes some grumbling, but is called reorganization. Often the boss will bring in a friend and appoint him his assistant. The assistant is then my boss, too.

The relationship between bosses and workers has changed. Bosses don't fire people the way they used to. Usually there's a union, a contract, a company tradition or the threat of having the firing called discrimination, so bosses don't get to do much firing anymore. For instance, this new boss of mine would have a devil of a time firing me, although if I'm fired after he reads this, you'll know I was wrong.

The trouble for my boss is that while we've just had a little disagreement, I know how to do something that makes money for the company and he wants to keep me doing it. He just wishes I was nicer to bosses. He likes me but I make his blood boil, and when he goes home at night I imagine he complains about me to his wife.

My new boss is only kind of a junior boss and that must be hard on him, too. *He* has a boss and even *his boss* has a boss, so that puts him well down the boss ladder. He's in charge of me, but his boss has been a great old friend of mine for thirty-five years, and I even have reason to believe that his boss's boss, the boss of all bosses at the company, thinks highly of my work. That's an untenable position to put a junior boss in, and my heart goes out to him.

It seems to me all of us ought to be able to hire our own bosses. Who, after all, knows more about the kind of person who would make us a good boss than we do? You can't buy the kind of experience I've had with bosses, and if you did buy it, you'd probably want your money back.

I'd choose a boss who didn't ask dumb questions, who didn't

have meetings and who protected me from making a fool of myself. I want a boss who isn't honest with me all the time. If I write something that isn't very good, I want to hear him say, "Very good!"

In spite of a little trouble here at the start, I think I'm going to like this new boss. I certainly wish him all the luck in the world with me.

Job Applicants

It's easy to mistake words for thoughts when you're writing anything. I write so much and make the mistake often enough myself that I'm very aware of it in other people's writing.

Every year at this time a lot of bad writing comes my way from recent college graduates looking for jobs. What these kids really want is *my* job, but they're smart enough to avoid actually saying that, although many of them give the impression that they really wouldn't be satisfied with my job. They'd take it just to get a start in the business.

Today I got a letter from a young man graduating from college, and he had his own stationery with his name and address embossed on it. Classy for a kid out of work, isn't it? He told me he had written for his college newspaper, majored in economics and thought "60 Minutes" was a good television show, so he'd like to work on it as a writer or producer. I don't have the heart to tell him "60 Minutes" producers don't have their own personal stationery, or he probably wouldn't want to work there.

Here's an exact quotation from another letter:

"I am interested in participating at a television station because the dynamics occurring within a communications environment are those which interest me and have a direct relation to my long-range career objective."

Another letter from a young woman graduate says, "The enclosed résumé enumerates my relevant credentials and skills, specific experiences and related interests."

Come off it, will you, kids? This is your old friend Andy. I'd like to help. I think it's great when people want to get in the same business I'm in. It means we've made it look good to you and that's flattering, but you're never going to make it with prose like that. You meant to sound important, but it came out pretentious.

Almost every letter I see refers to the job seeker's "skills and talents." Just having skill and talent doesn't sound very impressive to them, I guess, so they lay it on me and make both of them plural for added effect.

There are not many of us who don't know the desperation of not having a job. Everyone else is inside and part of something. You are outside and all alone. You feel like the only unemployed person in the world and wonder if anyone ever went through his or her whole life without being able to get a job.

Being faced with the necessity for getting a job is a frightening prospect for a young person just out of college. The chances are the graduate has been brought along under the protective financial wing of loving parents, but at the moment of graduation there is an unspoken understanding. "It would be nice if you got a job now." They aren't throwing their offspring out of the house, but there is a pressure to go to work that everyone understands. It produces a kind of terror that I am familiar with, but there is no reason it should produce so much bad writing.

One summer when I was in college, I got a job helping a rigger in a big paper mill. We did heavy odd jobs, and the man I worked with knew how to do everything, it seemed to me. One day our job called for him to run a steam shovel. He just climbed on board and went to work with it.

Later, we were sitting on a pile of bricks eating our lunch, and I asked him how he learned to operate a steam shovel. He told me, and what he said was a lesson for young job seekers who say they can't get a job because they have no experience and can't get any experience without a job.

"I read an ad in the paper," he said. "This guy was looking for someone to run a steam shovel. I got the job and climbed up there and started fooling with the pedals and the hand levers. About an hour later, the boss knew for sure I didn't know what I was doing and I got fired. A week later, I got another steam shovel job and I only lasted four days, but by this time I knew a lot about how they worked. The third job I got, I kept because I had all this experience."

Somehow that approach to a job appeals to me more than a letter from someone who enumerates his relevant credentials and skills, specific experiences and interests.

My suggestion would be that they all learn how to shovel first.

Fired

THERE's something wrong with anyone who's never been fired from a job. If I'm ever in a position to hire someone, I'm going to be very suspicious of anyone who comes in looking for work with a résumé that doesn't include the information that he or she got the ax a couple of times either for incompetence or insubordination.

What's all this resignation business? Doesn't anyone get fired anymore? You read the business pages of the paper, and presidents of corporations are always resigning. From a cushy $250,000-a-year job? Come on, fellas. We're not business tycoons, but we're not that dumb. You got canned.

The whole business of resignation is false, and it's part of a new philosophy we seem to have adopted. There aren't any losers anymore.

At children's birthday parties, they play games in the cellar or the backyard, and the parents having the party give away prizes. It doesn't matter how well or poorly a child plays a game, he'll probably get a prize anyway, because the adults don't want to damage his little psyche by making him think he might not always win in life.

Most high school teams in any sport have co-captains now. Sometimes they have more than two. No one wants to hurt the feelings of a good player by choosing someone over him for the job. Sometimes the professional football teams have six or eight men trot out on the field for the coin-tossing ceremonies. They're all co-captains. Not a loser in the crowd.

I hope we never decide not to hurt the feelings of one of the presidential candidates by electing co-Presidents. One President is plenty.

Last week I read where someone won $34,000 for finishing second in a golf tournament. Second! Imagine making $34,000 for *losing* a game of golf!

The President is always saying he's "sorry" to have to accept someone's resignation. If he was really sorry he shouldn't have accepted it. All of us are using the word "sorry" too lightly. We're always saying we're sorry when we aren't really sorry at all. It's all part of the same refusal to face things as they are.

We're excusing everyone for everything. A boy of seventeen kills the man who runs the candy store for $1.35 and a Tootsie Roll.

The boy's parents find a bloody hammer under his bed and they confront him with it.

"I'm sorry," the boy says. "I killed him, but I didn't mean to do it."

The father looks at the mother with tears in his eyes and says, "At least he's honest."

The next day the neighbors are interviewed by a television reporter. They all say he was a nice quiet boy who always went to church. They don't bother to say that he was a bully, that he'd been stealing all his life and that he was rotten through and through.

We keep letting ourselves off the hook. No one wants to judge anyone else by strict standards for fear he'll be judged by them too. No one wants to say to someone on the job, "You just aren't good enough. You're fired."

Big Business

THERE is no more interesting or important work in the world than being a reporter. That's my opinion, of course, and being at least in part a reporter myself, it's natural I'd think so.

The word "reporter" isn't quite right for the job, though, because it only describes half of it—the half where you tell the reader or the listener what you've learned. The other half of a reporter's work isn't described by that word. That's the part where he or she collects the information before telling everyone about it. That's the hard part.

A good reporter ought to be part detective, part puzzle solver and part writer. A reporter has to find the facts, piece them together so they make sense and then put them down on paper in a manner that makes them clear to everyone else.

People often complain about inaccuracies in news stories. They talk as if reporters were deliberately inaccurate or in on some conspiracy, and this is almost never the case. No reporter sets out to write a distorted or inaccurate story. They sometimes come out that way because reporting is hard and some reporters aren't good enough. They also come out that way because a lot of people are very secretive and tell the reporter what they'd like to have printed, not what the facts are.

This all comes to me now, because this morning I got a letter from a boyhood friend I haven't seen in thirty-five years. I knew him as "Bud," but now his letterhead says his first name is "Cornelius" and he's vice-chairman of a big corporation in Oregon. He was a wonderful friend when I was young, but I don't think I know him at all now. After some personal words, he went into a tirade against the news organizations.

Being attacked by businessmen isn't a new experience for most reporters. I heard Lewis Lapham, then editor of *Harper's Magazine*, attacked one evening by a Texan with huge coal interests in Montana.

"You people know nothing about business," the businessman yelled at Lapham.

"You're right," Lapham yelled back, "and it's probably a damn good thing for business."

When businessmen say newspapers and television don't cover business very well, it makes me nervous because in many cases I think it's true. It is also true that it is business's own fault. Information about any business in town is almost impossible to get. They say they have a right to privacy, and I agree with that, but they're being stupid by not being more open, and I'll bet they *won't* agree with me.

It is possible now, because of the Freedom of Information Act, to get information out of government. It has been a great thing for the American public but, of course, there is nothing like that requiring business to reveal *its* business. Some businessmen claim they are secretive so their competition won't find out what they're doing and how, but that seldom stands up to inspection. The competitor usually knows *all* about the business across town. As a matter of fact, the plant manager used to work for Acme and one member of the Board of Directors of Allied is a former vice-president of Acme.

The average business keeps its operation a deep, dark secret mostly out of habit. If the secret is not dark, at least that's the impression they give the American public. It is Mike Wallace standing in front of the locked gates saying, "They refused to talk to us." It suggests there is something evil going on in there, and nine times out of ten there is not. The average businessman in America takes as much pleasure and pride from making a good product as he does from the money, but you'd never guess it from the public image he projects.

You could take the books and the production plans of any good company in America and print them on page one of the local newspaper, and it wouldn't alter the operation one bit. That includes printing the salary of every maintenance man and executive in the place. Business is simply too secretive about everything. They don't have anything more to hide than the rest of us.

The corporate public relations people who do the best job for their company are the ones who lay it on the line. They tell you the truth, even if it hurts a little. The ones who do their companies the most damage are those who try to hide little mistakes or keep information secret that would be better made public even when there is no law demanding it.

The American public is as suspicious of Big Business as it is of Big Government, and what I'd like to say to my old friend Bud is, business would do itself a favor and get better reporting in newspapers and on television if it opened up. If the company is making a good product for an honest profit, the truth won't hurt it.

Rebels

I T used to please me to think of myself as a rebel and a nonconformist, but all the pleasure has gone out of it now. These days the nonconformists outnumber the conformists. Rebels are a dime a dozen. It's got so it's more conventional to be unconventional than it is to be conventional.

Causes are hard to come by. There is a definite shortage of them, especially for young people, and it seems to me the government ought to step in and do something about it. One of the most discontented people in the world is the rebel who wakes up in the morning and finds there isn't anything he wants to be against. This has led to a serious situation among the youth of America.

Not since the Viet Nam War has there been a cause worth getting riled up about. The no-nukes, the militant antiabortionists, the gays and the pro-marijuana groups get together and stir things up once in a while, but none of these issues has caught the public imagination on such a broad scale as long hair or the Viet Nam War did in the 1960s.

I don't know when disillusionment began to set in for me as a rebel. I guess it was back then in the sixties. Sentimentally I was on the side of the protesters, but I often argued with them. They didn't really want me on their side anyway. I was forever being suspicious that our government might just possibly have been doing the right thing, and they didn't like that in me. And, of course, I was the wrong generation.

It is only natural to defend anything of your own, and I defended my own generation. It angered me when they suggested that my generation spent all its time making money and war, and theirs did nothing but make peace and love. You can take only so much of having your generation knocked without fighting back.

There were times when I admired Jane Fonda and times when I thought she was making a fool of herself and ought to shut up. When she made me mad, I got even with her by thinking of the almost completely nude pictures of her that appeared in *Playboy* magazine years ago. It's hard to take an angry political statement seriously from a naked woman.

The rebels of the 1960s decided our school system was wrong and they forced a change; they decided our marriage convention was silly and they changed the rules; they changed our sex mores and our attitude in world affairs. You just have to hope they were right, but honestly, things don't seem a lot better than they were before they got at them.

They've dropped the whole thing now, of course. Rebels are always so preoccupied with the revolution that they don't have time to look into what's going to happen if they win.

Maybe all this soured me on being a rebel myself. I like to think that I'm really not tired of rebelling, but that I'm just smarter than I used to be about what I rebel against.

You have to decide which battles to fight, which to abandon. There are a thousand causes to whose aid I would gladly come if I had the time and the ability, but I do not have enough of either.

Conformity can be very relaxing and a great time saver. Rebellion against everything takes up a lot of your life. I've been enjoying orthodoxy in moderate amounts. Sometimes I just blend in with the crowd and let myself be carried along in the mainstream of life like a 1979 Ford doing fifty miles an hour in the right lane of a crowded highway.

Everyone Else Is Doing It

I saw the driver of a panel truck throw a paper cup and a napkin out the window onto a New York street yesterday and it angered me. I was driving myself, so I pulled up beside him at the next light and yelled, "You dropped something back there!"

He got my message and he gave me one in return.

"Whaddya want me to do, take it to the dump? This whole town's a dump."

In other words, everyone else was doing it, why shouldn't he.

"Everyone else is doing it" seems to be the single most persuasive reason most of us give ourselves for doing something we really shouldn't do. If enough people do something that's wrong, it often becomes acceptable practice.

A U.S. corporation tries to sell a few hundred million dollars' worth of its product to a foreign country with a corrupt government. It offers the potentate in charge of buying things a few million dollars to keep for himself if he'll buy the goods because, the corporation explains to itself, "that's just the way everyone does business over here."

A competitor sends a salesman overseas to the same country, and he reports back to his main office that everyone is making under-the-table deals and that it isn't considered unusual there. If they want to make a sale, he reports, they'll have to slip the potentate a few million themselves. It's the same paper cup and the napkin thrown in the street. If everyone else is doing it, why not?

The college football season is starting, and nowhere are ethical procedures more consistently violated. College teams should be made up of students who come to a school for an education and who play football for fun. The very first time one of the teams in a hot college rivalry lowered its standards just a hair to admit a high school boy who failed biology but ran the hundred-yard dash in 9.8 seconds, amateur football was done for in that league.

In the news business, the newspaper that embellishes the truth and emphasizes the stories that appeal to our lesser instincts will invariably sell the most papers. It is difficult for a competitor not to follow along on the theory that "everyone else is doing it."

There is a constant edginess among executives in network television news organizations, because if one of them ever decides to lower its journalistic standards and give people what they'd like to watch instead of what they ought to know, that network will very soon take the major part of the audience. If that happens, will the others follow? They probably will, and that will be the end of high quality television news. It has already happened in local television news in many cities.

I don't know why "everyone else is doing it" is such an attractive idea to a nation that prides itself on its individuality as ours does. We start leaning on the idea when we're kids. If our mother tells us to go to bed at eight thirty, our argument is that we ought to be able to stay up until nine because "everyone else does." Right or wrong doesn't enter into our thinking. Not only that, but if a mother learns that a lot of kids actually *do* stay up until nine, she's more apt to let hers do it too.

This isn't much of a column today, but I wanted to get one out in a hurry. I've been reading some of the other columnists and everyone else is doing it.

In Defense of Incompetence

THIS will be in defense of incompetence. There's so much of it going around, I think we have to find ways to turn it to our advantage.

Maybe as a start, we ought to stop knocking it. Incompetence has always had a bad name. People speak of it as though they alone, in all the world, were free of it, when in actual fact incompetence is a God-given gift with which all mankind is endowed. And you can throw womankind in there, too, if mankind offends you.

First we have to realize that incompetency is already a major industry in the United States. It is unlisted on the New York Stock Exchange, but certainly there's nothing we produce in such quantity.

If competency on the job replaced the slovenly, half-done work we get now, the service industry in America would shrink to nothing. Television repair shops, kitchen appliance service departments and automobile mechanics would go out of business. Unemployment figures would climb. Even incompetency in the repair business itself can't be reduced substantially without endangering the whole economy. If they fixed things right in the first place, we'd never have to come back to have them fixed again. Competency would take the bread out of their children's mouths.

If builders built houses right, if insurance agents sold the right policies the first time, and if bankers and stock brokers gave the right advice, we'd all be rich and trouble free, and there'd be no work in the world for anyone. Incompetency in every field of endeavor creates jobs.

If we were all good drivers, insurance agents would be out of work and there would be no need for auto body shops. If we were competent in caring for our own bodies, we'd need half the doctors, half the medical facilities we have now.

I'm really warming up to this defense of incompetency. Some of my best friends are incompetent. Who needs friends who make you look bad by going around doing things right all the time? I have friends whose incompetence is their most likable characteristic, and I've had bosses who were so incompetent that they were laughably lovable.

I see evidence of the advantages of my own incompetence every day of my life. A month ago, I decided to take some money I had and put it in the stock market. I kept looking at the stock charts and I asked for advice from people who know about that sort of thing, but I never got at doing anything about it. One day last week stock prices dropped an average of seventeen points and they've been going down almost every day since. Once again I was saved by my own ineptitude.

Americans have been complaining about incompetence in government for many years now. They may think things are bad, but they don't know what bad government is until they have a thoroughly efficient one that does everything it says it's going to do. If we had elected competent people for every job in Washington, this nation would be revolting now. Adolf Hitler's Third Reich was probably the most competent the world has ever known.

Do we really want an Internal Revenue Service so good and efficient that they catch every nickel and dime we deduct that we shouldn't deduct? Do we want police enforcing the letter of the law every time we drive twenty-seven mph in a twenty-five mph zone?

I contend that we do not, and I say that an efficient, thoroughly competent government is not only dangerous but un-American!

Fortunately, I don't think there's much chance that the level of incompetence in all of us will decline in the foreseeable future. In the past four months I've visited six universities, lecturing and visiting classrooms. Take my word for it, a lot of incompetent teachers are turning out large numbers of incompetent students ready to take their rightful place in our bungling world.

Voluntary Prayer

L ET's call the Town Hall Meeting of America together and discuss this question of voluntary prayer in public schools. I'll make a few prefatory remarks:

I think we're all agreed that Americans approve of prayer in our public schools. They are agreed that it is right and proper to pray to God.

Americans are also agreed, I think, that the prayers should be those from the Presbyterian prayer book. Right? Do I hear a dissenting voice from up there in Vermont? You don't think the prayers should be Presbyterian?

Well, fortunately, everyone has a right to his own opinion in America, even left-wing Commies from Vermont.

You with your hand up there in Illinois, what do you think the prayers should be? You think the prayers in public schools should be Catholic prayers? I'm not sure everyone's going to go along with you on that, sir.

I think perhaps the best thing would be if we had a kind of neutral prayer. God will understand, and that way we won't offend anyone.

I see a hand raised out there in California. Ask your question. You want to know which way the children will face when they pray? Oh, come now, sir. The children will face their teacher. What are you saying, Mecca? Mecca? Of course they won't be facing Mecca. Please sit down, sir. We will not be praying to Allah. . . . Well, there may be five hundred million Muslims in the world, but not here in the good old United States of America, and we'll be praying to the real God in our schools here. Please sit down. Give someone else a chance to speak.

Over there in Texas, yes. Who *is* the real God? Aren't we agreed that he's a white male in his middle to late sixties with a long white beard and flowing robes?

Sir, I don't think this is any time to discuss theology. Yes, over there in Ohio. Will there be religious freedom in our schools? Of course there'll be religious freedom. The children will be free to be Presbyterian, Baptist, Lutheran, Methodist, or Episcopalian.

Freedom *from* religion? I don't think the Constitution promises any such thing. Freedom *of* religion is what it says. If a child doesn't want to bow his head and pray with the others because his father and mother are troublemakers, all he has to do is raise his hand and demand his constitutional rights to be excused, and he may leave the room. If the other children make fun of him, that's something we can't control.

Church of the Latter-Day Saints? Jehovah's Witnesses? The Unification Church? We would naturally consider the rights of these sects, but I think there's such a thing as carrying freedom of religion too far.

Yes, you down there in Florida with the funny little black hat on. Jewish prayers? Of course, the Jews will be able to have their own prayers. If Jewish boys and girls don't wish to pray in the standard, proper and right way to our God with the rest of the kids, all they have to do is say so. We'll fix up a place for them to pray in Miss McClatchy's second grade room next to the gym.

Are there any other questions? Does God hear prayers if you say them silently, alone and without bowing your head? I really can't answer that question. I'm just a moderator, not a clergyman.

Just one more question, then we'll have a show of hands.

Will you repeat your question, madam? If the children pray in school, will they be taught arithmetic in church? I don't think we have time for smart-aleck questions, so I'll take one more.

What about keeping religion and government-supported schools apart? I gather what you're suggesting, if I may rephrase your question, is a separation of church and state. It's an interesting new idea, but I think we'll take it up at our next meeting.

The meeting is adjourned.

IX:

LIFE, LONG AND SHORT

Saturdays with the White House Staff

EVERY Saturday morning I make a list of Things to Do Today. I don't *do* them, I just make a list. My schedule always falls apart, and I realize that what I need is the kind of support the President gets. Here's how Saturday would go for me if I had the White House staff home with me:

7:15–7:30—I am awakened by one of the kitchen staff bringing me fresh orange juice, toast, jam and coffee.

7:30–7:45—The valet lays out my old khaki pants, a clean blue denim shirt and my old work shoes. I dress.

7:45–8:00—The newspaper is on my desk, together with a brief summary of it prepared overnight by three editors.

8:00–8:15—My mail has been sorted with only the interesting letters left for me to read. Checks for bills have been written and stamps put on envelopes. All I have to do is sign them. The Secretary of the Treasury will make sure my checks don't bounce.

8:15–8:30—Staff maintenance men have left all the right tools by the kitchen sink, together with the right size washers. I repair the leaky faucet.

8:30–8:45—While I repaired the faucet, other staff members got the ladder out of the garage and leaned it against the roof on the side of the house. While two of them hold it so I won't fall, I clean out the gutters. They put the ladder away when I finish.

8:45–9:00—Manny, my own barber, is waiting when I get down from the roof and he gives me a quick trim.

9:00–9:15—Followed by four Secret Service operatives, I drive to the car wash, where they see to it that I go to the head of the line.

9:15–9:30—On returning from the car wash, I find the staff has made a fresh pot of coffee, which I enjoy with my wife, who thanks me for having done so many of the little jobs around the house that she'd asked me to do. Two insurance salesmen, a real estate woman and a college classmate trying to raise money call during this time, but one of my secretaries tells them I'm too busy to speak to them.

Long before noon, with my White House staff, I've done everything on my list, and I can relax, read a book, take a nap or watch a ballgame on television.

I'm dreaming, of course. This is more the way my Saturdays *really* go:

6:00–7:30—I am awakened by a neighbor's barking dog. After lying there for half an hour, I get up, go down to the kitchen in my bare feet and discover we're out of orange juice and filters for the coffeemaker.

7:30–8:30—I go back upstairs to get dressed, but all my clean socks are in the cellar. They're still wet because they weren't taken out of the washing machine and put in the dryer. I wait for them to dry.

8:30–9:30—Now that I have my shoes on, I go out to the driveway to get the paper. Either the paperboy has thrown it into the bushes again or he never delivered it. I drive to the news store and get into an argument about why the Raiders beat the Eagles.

9:30–10:30—The mail has come and I sit down in the kitchen to read it. The coffee was left on too high and is undrinkable. The mail is all bills and ads. I don't know how much I have in the bank, and I don't have any stamps. I don't feel like doing anything. I just sit there, staring.

10:30–11:30—I finally get up and go down cellar but can't find the right wrench for the faucet in the kitchen sink, and I don't have any washers anyway. I try to do it with pliers and string but finally give up.

11:30–12:30—I don't feel like digging the ladder out from behind the screens so I drive to the car wash, but there are twenty-three cars in front of me. Later, at the barbershop, Manny can't take me today.

I go home, get out of the car and find the left front tire is soft. I go into the house and sit down to stare again as my wife comes in and complains that I never do anything around the house.

Waiting

Today I stood in line for seventeen minutes to cash a check for seventy-five dollars. I'd given this company, a bank, all my money to hold onto for me until I needed it, and today, when I needed some of it, it took me that long to get it back.

This is a good example of the kind of things that makes so many of us smile when we read that banks are having a hard time. We're glad. It fills us with pleasure to read about their troubles. They've made us wait so often over the years that nothing bad that happens to a bank makes us do anything but laugh. "You had it coming, bank." That's what we think.

Waiting is one of the least amusing things there is to do. Short waits are worse than long waits. If you know you're going to have to wait for four hours or six months, you can plan your time and use it and still have the pleasure of anticipating what you're waiting for. If it's a short wait of undetermined length, it's a terrible waste of time.

I've read all the proverbs about waiting and patience:

"All things come to him who waits."

"They also serve who only stand and wait."

"Patience is a virtue."

I don't happen to believe any of those old saws. *Impatience* is a virtue, that's what I think. Shifting from one foot to the other and tapping your fingers on something and getting damn mad while you stand there is the only way to behave while you're waiting. There's no sense being patient with people who make you wait, because they'll only make you wait longer the next time. The thing to do is blow up . . . hit the roof when they finally show up.

Some people seem to think they were born to get there when they're ready, while you wait. Banks are not the only big offenders in the waiting game, so are doctors. Some doctors assume their time is so much more important than anyone else's that all the rest of us ought to wait for them, "patiently," of course. What other profession or line of business routinely includes in its office setup something called "the waiting room"?

In New York City many of the parking garages have signs over their cashier windows saying, "No charge for waiting time." What a preposterous sign! What it means is that they can take their time getting your car, but you don't have to pay them anything while you wait for it. I always tell them that *I* have a charge for waiting, and I think doctors ought to start knocking ten dollars off their bill for every half hour we spend in their waiting rooms. The doctor who tells all his patients to come at nine o'clock ought to be sent back to the hospital to spend another year as a resident.

All of us admire in other people the characteristics we think we have ourselves. I don't have any patience, so it's natural, I guess, that I don't admire it in other people. Sometimes I reluctantly concede it works for them, but I still don't think of it as a virtue. I secretly think that people who wait well are too lazy to go do something. Just an opinion, mind you. I don't want a lot of patient waiters mad at me.

The funny thing about that word "waiter" is that those who make a living as waiters are about the most impatient people on earth. You can't get a waiter to wait ten seconds. You go in a restaurant, he hands you a menu eighteen inches long with fifty dishes to choose from, and in three seconds he starts tapping his pencil on his order pad to let you know how impatient he is.

I'd make a great waiter. I can't wait at all.

Some Notes

W HAT follows are some notes I made on the backs of a wide variety of pieces of paper over the past few weeks. The ideas struck me as either true or funny when I first put them down.

—They always ask you to use the revolving door, but they don't make them any easier to push.

—You can't sleep late, cut wood, watch football, eat dinner and still finish all the Sunday paper.

—Several times a year I see pictures in a magazine or items in a column from Hollywood about a round bed. Do they make round electric blankets, and where do they keep the Kleenex?

—The average American, I read, is growing three-quarters of

an inch every twenty-five years. At that rate, I'll be six feet tall when I'm 210 years old.

—I don't stay to the end of civic meetings at the town hall, because they always end up in an argument about who has the floor and what motion they're voting on. Someone usually moves to table the motion on the floor, and someone else gets up to say you can't move to table a motion, because there's already a motion on the floor. That's when I get lost and leave.

—When someone isn't watching where he's going and bumps into me and almost knocks me off my feet, I almost always say "Pardon me."

—The newspapers often referred to Kennedy as JFK, to Lyndon Johnson as LBJ, to Roosevelt as FDR and to Truman as HST, but no one ever called Jimmy Carter by the initials JEC, and now I notice no one is using RWR for Ronald Wilson Reagan. What causes this?

—There's nothing people like better than being asked an easy question. For some reason, we're flattered when a stranger asks us where Maple Street is in our own home town and we can tell him.

—It's been my experience that, despite the old saying, barking dogs *are* more apt to bite than dogs that don't bark.

—I'd give $10,000 to have had some of the money I have now back in 1956 when I was dead broke.

—The back of my closet is filled with clothes that I'll be able to wear again just as soon as I lose ten pounds. On the other side of those on the pole is another, older bunch of clothes. I'll be able to wear those again just as soon as I lose twenty pounds.

—Farmers always seem to have a lot of big expensive equipment sitting all around, rusting. Are farmers really poor? How much do those machines cost? Are they paid for? Are they still any good? Why are they out there, rusting?

—When an argument comes up, I usually repeat what I thought yesterday or ten years ago. I don't very often think it through again to decide how I feel about it now.

—If you wait until you're absolutely certain before you do something, you never do it.

—Johnny Carson is largely a rumor to me. I guess he's good, but I've almost never seen him. We usually go to bed by 11:30 week nights. I'm always surprised at the ratings they say late night television shows get.

—If you gave a calf the homogenized, ultrapasteurized product they sell to humans as milk now, I wonder if it would recognize it as something that came from its mother.

—I'm not very punctual, but I like to keep my watch exactly on time to the second. That way, I know how late I am. Watches, by the way, are better than they were twenty years ago. I hate myself for it, but I've finally given up carrying my great gold Hamilton railroad watch in favor of a battery-operated quartz watch. It keeps better time. It's nice to know something is better than it used to be.

Memory

W HAT does AWACS stand for again, do you remember? Advance Warning something. Advance Warning American Command Ship? That's not it. I'll have to ask someone or look it up. And who was Lyndon Johnson's Vice President? You ought to remember a simple thing like that and I ought to myself, but I don't. There are times when I'm overwhelmed by my vast lack of memory. The other day I forgot my home phone number, and we've had it for thirty years.

I remember reading that we all start losing brain cells that make up the memory when we reach about age twenty, but this debilitating influence the years have doesn't seem to have much to do with my problem. I couldn't remember anything when I was eighteen, either.

Being tall and being able to remember things are probably the two most desirable human characteristics I don't have. Because I am neither tall nor able to remember things, I look for ways to diminish the importance of height and memory.

Just for example, memory of the past is not nearly so much fun as anticipation of the future and it's almost always sadder. Sadness is one of the principal ingredients of memory, and there's just so much of that anyone wants to bring on himself on purpose by sitting around remembering.

Another thing, as much as I'd like to have a good memory sometimes, it seems to me that people with good memories for names, exact times and dates are dull. They're not only dull, they can be a real pain in the neck to be around.

The trouble with people with good memories is that they keep wanting to show it off to you by remembering things you don't want to hear. Everything reminds them of something they've done before. I have one old friend I hate to see, because every time we're together he starts talking about World War II. I enjoy reminiscing once in a while, but do-you-remember-the-time-we stories don't hold my attention for long. I'd rather wait until I'm all through living and *then* review my life and times. Right now, I'm busy with today.

Last week, I met a friend I used to work with when I wrote for Arthur Godfrey. He repeated a story I've heard him tell fifty times. I've seen him twice a year since 1960, and I'd heard the story eight times before that.

It looks now as though those of us who can't remember anything may be saved. They're starting to sell small computerized memory banks for personal use. That's what I want when they get them pocket-size. I want to be able to reach in my pocket and enter the question, "What do the initials AWACS stand for?" and get an instant answer. I think I'll give one to my old friend for Christmas, too. If he enters the question, "Have I ever told this story to Andy before?" he'll get back the answer, "Yes, fifty times."

You often hear people say "I'm terrible with names," as if it was something to be proud of. I'm terrible with names, but I'm embarrassed about it, because I know it means I just don't care enough to make a point of remembering. That isn't nice or anything to be proud of.

My memory of my own past gives me a strange feeling, and I suppose everyone feels the same. When I look back at what I did a long time ago, it's hard to think of it as me. I see it clearly, but it's as if someone else was doing it. It's only my memory of me that's doing those things. It's like looking at the water in a river. The river looks the same all the time, but the water is always different.

I don't feel too bad about my bad memory—although I'd be happy if I could remember who Lyndon Johnson's VP was.

Trust

Last night I was driving from Harrisburg to Lewisburg, Pa., a distance of about eighty miles. It was late, I was late and if anyone asked me how fast I was driving, I'd have to plead the Fifth Amendment to avoid self-incrimination. Several times I got stuck behind a slow-moving truck on a narrow road with a solid white line on my left, and I was clinching my fists with impatience.

At one point along an open highway, I came to a crossroads with a traffic light. I was alone on the road by now, but as I approached the light, it turned red and I braked to a halt. I looked left, right and behind me. Nothing. Not a car, no suggestion of headlights, but there I sat, waiting for the light to change, the only human being for at least a mile in any direction.

I started wondering why I refused to run the light. I was not afraid of being arrested, because there was obviously no cop anywhere around, and there certainly would have been no danger in going through it.

Much later that night, after I'd met with a group in Lewisburg and had climbed into bed near midnight, the question of why I'd stopped for that light came back to me. I think I stopped because it's part of a contract we all have with each other. It's not only the law, but it's an agreement we have, and we trust each other to honor it: we don't go through red lights. Like most of us, I'm more apt to be restrained from doing something bad by the social convention that disapproves of it than by any law against it.

It's amazing that we ever trust each other to do the right thing, isn't it? And we do, too. Trust is our first inclination. We have to make a deliberate decision to mistrust someone or to be suspicious or skeptical. Those attitudes don't come naturally to us.

It's a damn good thing too, because the whole structure of our society depends on mutual trust, not distrust. This whole thing we have going for us would fall apart if we didn't trust each other most of the time. In Italy, they have an awful time getting any money for the government, because many people just plain don't pay their income tax. Here the Internal Revenue Service makes some gestures toward enforcing the law, but mostly they just have to trust that we'll pay what we owe. There has often been talk of a tax revolt in this country, most recently among unemployed auto workers in Michigan, and our government pretty much admits if there was a widespread tax revolt here, they wouldn't be able to do anything about it.

We do what we say we'll do; we show up when we say we'll show up; we deliver when we say we'll deliver, and we pay when we say we'll pay. We trust each other in these matters, and when we don't do what we've promised, it's a deviation from the normal. It happens often that we don't act in good faith and in a trustworthy manner, but we still consider it unusual, and we're angry or disappointed with the person or organization that violates the trust we have in them. (I'm looking for something good to say about mankind today.)

I hate to see a story about a bank swindler who has jiggered the books to his own advantage, because I trust banks. I don't *like* them, but I trust them. I don't go in and demand that they show me my money all the time just to make sure they still have it.

It's the same buying a can of coffee or a quart of milk. You don't take the coffee home and weigh it to make sure it's a pound. There isn't time in life to distrust every person you meet or every company you do business with. I hated the company that started selling beer in eleven-ounce bottles years ago. One of the million things we take on trust is that a beer bottle contains twelve ounces.

It's interesting to look around and at people and compare their faith or lack of faith in other people with their success or lack of success in life. The patsies, the suckers, the people who always assume everyone else is as honest as they are, make out better in the long run than the people who distrust everyone—and they're a lot happier even if they get taken once in a while.

I was so proud of myself for stopping for that red light, and inasmuch as no one would ever have known what a good person I was on the road from Harrisburg to Lewisburg, I had to tell someone.

My Looting Career

THE story said a U.S. federal judge had ruled that two paintings worth three to five million dollars apiece had to be returned to Germany because they had been stolen from a castle there by an American soldier who was one of the occupying American forces in 1945.

The judge was probably right, but I hope he understood. The paintings weren't stolen, they were looted. The word looting didn't have the same evil sound to soldiers then as it has to civilians now. Looting was a wild, lawless, uncivilized thing to do, but I saw enough of it during World War II to understand how even a relatively civilized soldier could do it.

Here they were, fighting for their lives in a country whose people were responsible for their being there in the first place. Here was a house—call it a castle if you want—only recently occupied by the Germans whose guns had poked out its windows with the intention of killing Americans. The house was a shambles. It was not a person's house. It was the abandoned stronghold of the enemy. The former owners were gone, forever probably. Dead maybe, but certainly gone, and anyway they were Germans. Why not rummage through these rooms, this wine cellar, those drawers? If you didn't do it because of some feelings it was wrong, would the ten thousand soldiers that followed you through that house in the days to come also honor the possessions of the departed owners? Ten thousand honest, thoughtful, sympathetic soldiers without an acquisitive instinct among them? Hardly.

Of course it was not right, but you couldn't expect an American soldier under those circumstances to determine that kind of right from that kind of wrong.

I was a young correspondent for *The Stars and Stripes* at the time. Looting didn't bother me as much as the family photographs of the owners scattered on the floor by the soldiers rooting through the trunk or the bureau drawer. The people in the pictures didn't look like enemy. They looked like people.

My only looting excursion had a paradoxical ending for me. I guess no one will bring charges against me now if I tell you about it. I went into Cologne behind the tanks of the Third Armored Division and got several good firsthand stories for the paper about the fighting down by the Cathedral. I watched as our soldiers got to one of the great wine cellars in all Europe, the one in the bowels of the Excelsior Hotel. They didn't ask for the wine steward.

The following morning I headed for the rail yards just outside town. I had covered the Eighth Air Force raids from England before the invasion, and we had bombed Cologne so often I was curious about what effect the raids had had on train service.

I wandered alone among miles and miles of freight cars, some of them broken open by shells, some of them on their side and some untouched. Finally I pulled myself up into one whose middle door gaped open. It was stacked to its top with square wooden boxes. They were small, about eighteen inches on a side, but each must have weighed fifty pounds.

The stenciled marks on the side of the boxes said GUMMI SCHLAUCHE DER FAHRRADER 144. My German was terrible, but I realized that each box held 144 inner tubes for bicycle tires. I don't suppose there was a scarcer or more highly prized item in all of Belgium than the inner tube of a bicycle tire, and I was staying in a hotel in Liège, Belgium, taken over for correspondents. I got one box on my shoulder, leaving perhaps a thousand more in the freight car, and carried my pure gold up the bank to my jeep. Triumphantly, I drove back to Liège with my loot. Certainly the tubes were worth the equivalent of ten dollars each.

Well, I never found out, and I didn't have to wait for a federal judge to order me to return them. I left them in the jeep in the garage overnight and they were stolen.

So much for my looting career.

Weapons

THERE's always a lot of high level talk about how the next war will be fought. They don't talk much about *if*, but about *how*. Some people feel that if we arm ourselves with a lot of nuclear weapons, the Russians will never dare attack us. Others feel by doing that we are only asking the Russians to make more nuclear weapons themselves and eventually both countries will use them.

I just don't know. I've never owned a nuclear weapon myself. As a matter of fact, the most lethal weapon I ever had was a slingshot I sent away for when I was a kid. It was advertised in a magazine and it looked great in the ad, but when it came, I found I didn't really like it any better than the slingshot Alfie Gordon and I had made for ourselves out of some rubber bands and the crotch of a small tree.

Arming yourself as a kid is not that different from the way it is for a nation. If the kids on the next block have a new weapon, you've got to get one like it.

I didn't live in a tough area of town and we didn't have gang wars, but still, we were aware of weapons. In the spring we all had water pistols. Water pistols may be the best weapons ever made, because they're accurate, inexpensive and ammunition is readily available. It isn't like having to get yourself heavy plutonium or whatever it is they arm nuclear warheads with. All you need is a puddle.

They have that new nuclear weapon now that kills all the people in the area but doesn't damage the buildings. This must certainly rank with the greatest inventions of all time, but I still think that a shot right in the face or down the back of the neck with a well-aimed water pistol would be more help to mankind in the long run.

We had cap pistols, too, and there must be a mandatory death penalty now for carrying a cap pistol, because I haven't seen one for sale in years. I was lucky enough to have been born during the era that saw the introduction of the repeater, a cap pistol that could be loaded with a roll of caps. Up until that time, you had to insert a cap in front of the hammer for each shot. This, too, was considered a great advance in weaponry when I was young.

I don't know what position the National Rifle Association takes on bean blowers. Water pistols were our spring weapons, cap pistols our summer guns, but in the fall we switched to bean blowers. A bean blower was a metal tube about fourteen inches long with a hole through it about three-eighths of an inch in diameter. On one end it had a wood mouthpiece. You filled your mouth with white beans, positioned one in front of the mouthpiece with your tongue and then exhausted your lungs in an explosive puff. The bean shot out the tube and hurtled toward the target.

For several years this seemed like the ultimate weapon to us. It hurt more than the water pistol and it had a range of up to fifty feet, whereas even the most expert marksman couldn't hit anything with a water pistol at more than fifteen feet.

The weapons makers, perfectionists that they are, wouldn't quit with the bean blower though. By the time I was nine, the bean blower was obsolete, replaced by a more accurate weapon with greater range and greater hurt power. It was, of course, the pea shooter. It may not seem like much to those of you who don't comprehend weaponry, but the pea shooter represented a great step forward in our arms race on Partridge Street. The opening in the pea shooter was only half the size of the opening in the bean blower, so it not only hurtled the projectile faster, but the projectile itself, a small, hard green pea put fear in the hearts of the enemy over on Western Avenue.

There was only one weapon so fearful we hardly dared talk about it. For us it was as though they had made an atomic bomb encased in a cannister of bubonic plague. It was the dreaded BB gun. So armed, I might have conquered the world bounded by Madison, Western, Partridge and Maine. Unfortunately, my mother would never let me have one, and it has led to the greatly weakened position I find myself in today.

Joe McCarthy

No one is ever satisfied with the obituary notice printed on the occasion of the death of a friend or relative. It isn't good enough or complete enough. I suppose it is because, in the death notices of our friends, we see our own.

Joe McCarthy died recently, and the notices in the two papers I read were not right.

"Joseph W. McCarthy," one of them said, "was known for his books on the Kennedy family." Joe wrote two books about the Kennedys, but that isn't what he was known for at all. He was known to millions of soldiers during World War II as the editor of *Yank*, the best and most literate publication any army ever had.

Joe was working for the Boston *Post* as a sports reporter when he was drafted in 1941. He was assigned to the last mule pack artillery outfit in the Army, and by reporting his experiences with the animals, the guns and the people he met, he set the tone for the lighthearted literary tradition that emerged from the war.

I was a reporter for *The Stars and Stripes* when I first met Joe. He had come to London to see how things were going with the biggest of the twenty-one editions of *Yank* that he supervised. After the war he became editor of *Cosmopolitan*, vastly different then from now, and at one point hired me and my coauthor Bud Hutton to return to Europe as correspondents for the magazine.

Every writer needs an editor, and Joe was perfect. We turned in material another editor might have thrown in the waste basket, but Joe never lost patience. He talked it over with us, pointed out what was wrong and how it could be fixed. It always looked good when it was finally printed with our names on it, but by then it was as much Joe's piece as it was ours.

During the 1950s, when I was struggling to make a living as a free-lance writer, I used to drink with Joe in Toots Shor's. By then he was a free-lance writer himself and doing very well, although he was somewhat disillusioned with the magazine business. He gave me some advice about free-lance writing that I've never forgotten.

"Making a living as a free-lance writer isn't very hard," he said. "Find out what the editor wants, how long he wants it and get it to him the day he has to have it. It doesn't have to be any good."

Joe's writing was always good. He had an easy grace about himself that came through in anything he wrote.

There are stories I heard yesterday I can't remember at all, but Joe used to tell stories twenty years ago that I'll always remember.

He never got over his Irish youth in Cambridge, the town so dominated by Harvard and its sister college, Radcliffe. During his freshman year at the less well-known Boston College, Joe fell in love with a Radcliffe girl who came from a wealthy, social background. He took her out several times and left her with the impression that he was a Harvard student.

It is necessary to say, for those of you who don't know, that Harvard and Radcliffe share a campus and that Hasty Pudding is the name of a prestigious Harvard club known then for its inventive initiation rites.

In an effort to help himself through college and, incidentally, to scrape together a few dollars for another date with his Radcliffe friend, Joe took a Saturday job as a helper collecting trash in Cambridge.

One Saturday in the spring, his truck route took him along the fringe of the Harvard campus. Who should come bouncing along the street, as Joe was heaving a full can of garbage onto the truck, but the Radcliffe girl he had been trying to impress.

She saw him and Joe knew it. He didn't avoid her. He looked her right in the eye, smiled, gave her a big wink and said, "Hasty Pudding!"

The late A. J. Liebling, the journalist's journalist, often spoke of the advantage to a person of dying at the peak of his obituary value. Joe McCarthy, though only sixty-four, had not been in good health and had not written much for several years. If Joe had died at the end of World War II, he would have been on page one of every paper in the country.

It is very sad for those of us who knew him, but even if his obituary today were bigger and better, it wouldn't have said what we all thought about him. He was such a sweet guy.

Planning Ahead

WOULD you like a calendar that runs from January 1, 1981, to December 31, 1990? Someone has just sent me one and I'm throwing it out. I do not wish to contemplate that distant future. I am not going to plan my life so far ahead, and I don't care to think about where I'll be when I'm ten years older than I am today.

The passing of time is depressing to me, and planning for something six months in advance makes time pass even faster. I have no interest in rushing through the 1980s in order to get to some event I've put on my ten-year calendar for the year 1990.

The best thing that's happened to me in this regard is to have had a President elected who is nine years older than I am. It makes me feel great and gives me reason to hope I haven't even reached my peak yet. Ronald Reagan isn't going to be doing a lot of talking about the year 2000, because he'll be eighty-nine then. He's not going to be initiating programs that come to fruition in fifteen years because he'll want to see the programs he starts finished. I'd be surprised if Reagan has one of these ten-year calendars I'm throwing out.

This feeling I have is nothing new to me. I had it when I was twenty-five. Insurance salesmen were always talking to me about what I'd need when I was fifty and sixty, and I didn't want to hear what they said. I bought some insurance from them, but I did it more because I thought that's what everyone was supposed to do than because I really wanted it. I guess it pays off in the feeling of security it gives me, though. If I were to die tomorrow, my wife wouldn't have to worry. She'd be taken care of. Between the $1.35 a month she'd get for the rest of her life and some money her parents left her, she'd be comfortable.

All of us have to plan ahead as though our lives were going to proceed according to plan, but they never do. It's a good thing, too, because one of the best things about life is how unpredictable it is. No calendar, no digital watch that shows the time in three zones and goes off at 6:30 every morning can make the course of our lives any more certain. The certainty of uncertainty is the only thing that keeps us out of the hands of the computers.

My rule is not to plan on being anywhere more than three months in advance, and at that distance only when the circumstances are unusual.

I know people who have planned their whole lives in advance. They've stayed with the same company for twenty-five years in jobs they hated, just waiting for the day they were eligible for a pension. That's what I'd call planning your life away. Spending the best years of your life gritting your teeth and just getting through one day after another waiting for the time you can retire to nothing seems like an awful waste of life. It would serve one of these people right if, the day after they retired, a rich distant relative died and left them a million dollars and their pension meant nothing to them.

I know in my heart and mind that I'm wrong not planning my life more carefully, but I lack the ability to do it, so I take my pleasure from being disorganized. I delight in long distance plans that go wrong for other people, because it reduces them to my level. I don't like insurance companies or the people who take polls or the smart-money people on Wall Street whose businesses are based on statistical evidence that this or that will happen. We are all somewhat defeated by the evidence of our own predictability, but I refuse to accept defeat gracefully.

Life, Long and Short

I CHANGE my mind a lot about whether life is long or short. Looking back at how quickly a son or daughter grew up or at how many years I've been out of high school, life seems to be passing frighteningly fast. Then I look around me at the evidence of the day-to-day things I've done and life seems long. Just looking at the coffee cans I've saved makes life look like practically forever. We only use eight or ten tablespoons of coffee a day. Those cans sure represent a lot of days.

Used coffee cans are the kind of statistics on life that we don't keep. Maybe if we kept them, it would help give a feeling of longevity. Maybe when each of us has his own computer at home, we'll be able to save the kinds of statistics the announcers use during baseball games.

It's always fun, for instance, to try to remember how many cars you've owned. Think back to your first car, and it makes life seem longer. If you're fifty years old, you've probably owned so many cars you can't even remember all of them in order. I've also wondered how many miles I've driven. That's a statistic most people could probably make a fair guess at. If you've put roughly seventy-five thousand miles on twenty cars, you've driven a million and a half miles. You've probably spent something like twenty-five thousand dollars on gas.

It's more difficult to estimate the number of miles you've walked. Is there any chance you've walked as far as you've driven in a car? I'm not sure. You don't go out on a weekend and walk four hundred miles the way you'd drive a car. On the other hand, every time you cross a street or walk across the room, you're adding to the steps you've taken. All those little walks every day must add up to a lot of miles, even if you aren't a hiker.

And how much have you climbed? I must have lifted myself ten thousand miles straight up with all the stairs I've negotiated in my life. There are seventeen nine-inch steps in our front hallway and I often climb them twenty times a day, so I've lifted my two hundred pounds two hundred and fifty feet on the stairs in the house in one day alone. That doesn't include the day I climbed the Washington Monument with the kids or the time my uncle took me up the Statue of Liberty.

And how many pairs of shoes have I worn out walking and climbing all that distance? I'm always looking for the perfect pair of shoes and I've never found them yet, so I buy more shoes than I wear. There must be six old pairs of sneaks of mine in closets around the house. All in all, I'll bet I've had two hundred fifty pairs of shoes in my life. Easy, two hundred fifty.

How long would your hair be if you'd never cut it? Everyone has wondered about that at some time. What length would my beard be if I hadn't shaved every morning? And, it's a repulsive thought, but I suppose my fingernails would be several feet long if I hadn't hacked them off about every ten days. I don't know. Does hair stop growing once it gets a few feet long? I don't ever recall seeing anyone with hair ten feet long. My hair must grow at least an inch a month. That's a foot a year. I've certainly never seen anyone my age with hair sixty feet long.

This is the kind of thinking that helps make life seem longer to me. When I think of how many times I've been to the barber or even to the dentist, life seems to stretch back practically forever.

The one statistic I hate to think about is how many pounds of food I've consumed. Pounds would be an unmanageably large number. I'd have to estimate it in tons. I must have eaten ten tons of ice cream alone in my lifetime.

It makes life seem long and lovely just thinking about every bite of it.

Age

I AM sixty now. I hate it and I constantly inspect my brain and my body for signs of decline. I don't see it yet, but I suppose others do. There must be some. I played three sets of tennis today and I never played better. As a matter of fact, I never played that well.

Oh, I notice a little falling apart in the face when I look in the mirror to shave, but it's no worse a look than I had when I looked too young at twenty-five. The only really disturbing thing about that is that to detect the deterioration in the face, I need my glasses now.

I am most surprised at my physical stamina. I played a lot of football in high school and college and, watching games on television, I dream of what it would be like to get in for a few plays. I think I could, but I guess I'd be in for an awful surprise—still, I tend to run up a flight of stairs two at a time. I don't walk. I feel in shape. People haven't started saying how good I look for my age yet. That's a good sign.

It surprises me to consider how long the body lasts. I've been doing all these things I do with it for a long time now. And without much servicing, either.

I suppose I'll be the last one to know, but I haven't detected any deterioration in my ability to do what I do for a living, either. I write, of course. It still bothers me to look at something I wrote five years ago. I don't usually like it. I have a feeling I've learned a lot since then and wouldn't say it that way now. Is the time ever going to come when I read something I wrote a few years ago and say to myself, "I couldn't write it that well today"?

This is a recurring thought I've had for as long as I've written for a living. The things I wrote last year never seem very good, but that thought doesn't usually occur to me as I'm writing them. Some kind of protective thing that goes on in the brain, no doubt.

My hands look older. There are some veins showing through now and a few brown spots. I hadn't noticed them until I heard the commercials on television telling me about some salve that gets rid of them. I can't believe the salve is very good for you if it makes brown spots in your skin go away. The salve certainly doesn't make you any younger, and youth is the only thing that would really help. If they ever make a jar of that, I'll have some.

Even though my feeling that I haven't deteriorated much mentally or physically in the last forty years may be an illusion, I am convinced that there is enough truth to it to be cause for rejoicing. Forty adult years of full strength and mental capacity isn't bad.

What worries me is that physical deterioration is a lot more apparent than mental deterioration. There's no mirror I'm going to be able to look in, even with glasses, and be able to determine that my brain has brown spots.

I still expect Ben Hogan or Sam Snead or at least Arnold Palmer to win the U.S. Open again, but of course none of them will. There is too, too solid evidence that the body can't do at forty what it did at thirty. Let alone seventy. The evidence of what the brain can and cannot do with added age is not so clear.

My hero as a writer is E. B. White. He's eighty-two now and living in Maine. I know him some, not well, and I'd like to ask why he isn't writing much anymore. Has he said what he wants to say, or does he feel he can't say it as well anymore? Or is it just that he wrote to make a living and doesn't have to do that now?

When I'm eighty-two, I hope I can read what I wrote when I was sixty and think it wasn't very good.

The Body

THE only consolation you can find when you look in the mirror at yourself is that everyone is funny-looking, lopsided, blemished or seriously flawed in appearance, one way or the other. What makes us nervous, of course, is that we see in ourselves our own special flaws, and we inspect them so carefully and think about them so much that they often seem worse than other people's.

I often look at a body other than my own and wish I could swap. The trouble is, if I got myself the perfect body today, the chances are that in a few months I'd have it looking like the one I have now. The way we look has some connection with the way we are. It goes further than "you are what you eat." I suspect "we are what we think," too. The way we think affects our eating, our walking and every move we make, and this shapes the body much as the genes we were born with. Of course, the genes we were born with affect the way we think, so we're all trapped with being the way we are. It's hard to get out of it.

I'm not complaining about the body I got in the deal. If I did the right things with it, it wouldn't be bad at all. Even abusing it the way I have, it seems to be standing up pretty well. Yesterday I stacked a pile of lumber that must have weighed a total of five thousand pounds. I can play three sets of singles without dropping dead on a tennis court, and my wife still asks me to take the tops off jars. I don't notice much I can't do at sixty that I could at forty. Someone else might, but I don't, and with this body, I'm the one that counts.

The worst thing that's happened to me is that I now weigh more than two hundred pounds. My mother always called me "sturdy." At 5'9", two hundred pounds is too much. "Big bones," my mother said. I used to believe my mother, but for the last thirty-five years I've faced the fact that I'm overweight. I still avoid thinking of myself as fat. I suspect there are some people who *don't* avoid thinking of me that way, but they keep it from me.

The best thing that's happened to me, as far as appearance goes, is that I still have most of my hair. I suppose if I got bald I might try and lose some weight, so having hair may shorten my life. I'm telling you all these things about myself not because I think you care about *my* problems, but it might interest you to translate them in terms of your own.

Almost everyone has some physical handicap. It might be one they were born with or one they acquired along the way. My biggest handicap is an ankle I tore up skiing fifteen years ago. I don't have much strength left in the right ankle or the foot because of torn ligaments that never reattached themselves to the bone. (That's correct, isn't it, doctor?) Three years ago I went to Joe Namath's doctor with it. He measured my thigh and calf, and pointed out that my right leg was substantially smaller than my left because I wasn't using the muscles in my right leg. I couldn't, because if I did, my foot and ankle collapsed.

But we're all in this thing together. If you get to know someone well enough or talk to him or her long enough, they get talking about what's wrong with their body. The marvel is that we're all so different with so many different things wrong with us, but nonetheless we manage to drag ourselves out of bed mornings.

The real question we all face is this: How much time do we want to spend taking care of our bodies as compared to the time we spend using them? The body seems to work pretty well if we just go about our business without paying a lot of attention to it. If I play tennis, I play to win at tennis, I play to win at tennis, not to exercise. That's a byproduct. I find joggers, as a group, nice people, but a little intense and more consumed with attention to their own bodies than is absolutely necessary.

Body Building

THE smartest people I've ever known were always excessively interested in their own bodies. They were right, of course, but they were often a pain in the neck to other people. I remember when someone accused the brilliant Eric Sevareid of being a hypochondriac. Eric just looked up slowly and said, "Hypochondriacs get sick too, you know."

The only time my body attracts my attention, other than those times when it's sick, is when a muscle is sore from overuse. That's the case today. The muscle in my right thigh is sore because I was trying to do deep knee bends yesterday on one leg. It's a good feeling in a way because it reminds me that I have muscles.

I've never really known what to do about my muscles. I'd like to look and be more muscular than I am, but there are so many of them I never know which ones to try to build up. Those body-building people go after all of them, but that's a full-time job and they end up looking like freaks in their perfection. The thing that's wrong with them is that they have developed those muscles with no intention of doing anything with them except showing them off.

The muscles that look best are the ones that have developed because of some natural activity the person engages in, not the ones built up by exercises designed for the purpose. I admire the muscular forearm of Billie Jean King and the biceps of the man who picks up our garbage twice a week. (I wish he didn't spill so much, but that's another matter.)

I've often set out on some body-building program of my own, but except for one three-year period when I was in school and did a hundred pushups a day, it's never lasted long. Each of us has good and bad body parts, and one temptation with muscles is to work on the ones that are already your best. I have strong shoulders and legs but weak feet and hands, but it's a lot more interesting to me to work on my legs than my feet, even though my leg muscles would be a lot more use to me if I had the feet to go with them.

Two years ago I bought a ten-pound dumbbell and started

lifting it to my shoulder one hundred times with each hand to strengthen my arm muscle. I brought it to the office and was doing it there, but someone stole the dumbbell about a year ago and I haven't given those muscles any attention since. You really can't, that's the trouble. It's easy enough to say, "It only takes fifteen minutes a day," but it takes more than that. It takes having your mind more on your muscle than on your brain.

I like natural exercise. I wish it was illegal for people to build up muscles deliberately, because they start beating you at whatever you're doing and you have to start building yours. I think of jogging as a natural exercise. I hate doing it myself and don't, but I love to see others jogging. On the days when I drive in to work in New York City, I always see a hundred great-looking women trotting along the drive by the East River. They look great not because they are necessarily beautiful, but because they look so alive and so determined to do the right thing. I'm moved by their muscles.

The real question is, how much time can we spend on our bodies? We all know they're important, but my feeling is we should use them and not fuss with them so much. I play tennis twice a week and usually run up any flight of stairs I'm faced with, but that's all the exercise I get in a normal week. Any week I try to do one-legged knee bends is not normal for me. If I'd spent more time on my muscles, I'd look better, but I'd have spent a lot less time writing, woodworking, cooking, reading and napping. Much as I yearn to look more muscular, it's not worth it.

Self-improvement

WE have chairs in the house no one has sat on in years. We have beds no one has slept in, except at Christmas, since the kids went away to college. We have dishes no one eats off and glasses no one drinks from. I can understand all that, but why we still have that piano in the living room, I'll never understand.

The piano itself must have forgotten what music sounds like by now. It's a magnificent piece of wood, but it hasn't been played in ten years, and then only for one night when an old school friend was at the house. He was the one who always played the piano when we were in high school, too.

Last weekend I got staring at the piano, and I walked over and picked up the lid of the piano bench and started looking at the sheet music and books stored in the compartment. There, yellow with age, was Schirmer's *Beginner's Piano Lesson Book* with my name on it.

I remember that whole sorry incident. When I was a freshman in college and playing a lot of football, I got worried about the lack of culture in my life, so I started paying a history teacher's wife two dollars an hour to teach me how to play the piano. She was very nice and patient, but I could tell she didn't think she had another Horowitz on her hands.

On the third Saturday of the football season, I broke my left index finger and that was the end of my musical career.

All this flashed through my mind over the weekend and, as I stood staring at that unused piano, I got thinking of all the other little gestures I'd made in an effort to improve myself one way or another over the years.

The number of times I have silently vowed to lose weight is too depressing a statistic to recall. I don't have to eat all bananas or all carbohydrates at one meal, all sugars or all fats at others. I pass through Scarsdale on the train every day and *that* hasn't helped. I don't need any calorie-counting charts or a plan for every meal. All I need to do to lose weight is to stop overeating. If I knocked off with the ice cream alone, it wouldn't do any harm.

Then I noticed about a year ago that the bulge at the back of the upper part of my arm was getting almost as big as the bicep muscle in front, except the bulge in back was mostly fat. I went to a sports store at lunchtime and bought two ten-pound dumb-bells. For three weeks I got up from the chair at my desk several times a day, walked to the table under which I kept the dumbbells and lifted them from down by my knees up to my shoulders as many times as I could. Then I'd rest a minute and do it again. I thought I'd begun to notice some firming up of my arm muscles, front and back, but I came in one morning and the dumbbells were gone, stolen probably by someone with plenty of muscle.

That was the end of that exercise in self-improvement.

I type with three fingers, one on my left hand and two on my right. This is ridiculous for someone who makes his living writing, so something like fifteen years ago I decided to correct this professional shortcoming of mine. I set out to take a typing course. It was too late. You can't teach an old dog a new way to type. I still have the books and I went to one class, but I'm resigned now to the three-finger school.

Years ago I lived in California for eight months and worked at MGM. None of the people I was involved with put in an eight-hour day, but I don't play golf and I hate lying on a beach, so I decided to learn how to fly a plane. I still have my logbook. I put in eight hours before something more pressing came along and I gave up my dream of expanding my world by learning to fly.

It's got so I hate to poke through old boxes of papers. Every time I do, I come on some bit of evidence of some plan I once had for making myself a better person. And look at me.

Simple Sensations

Every once in a while, I'm reminded of some way I used to feel or some simple sensation I used to have that I don't have anymore because I no longer do whatever it was that brought it on.

I was trying to recall some of them:

—The last time I was out of work was twenty-five years ago, but being out of work and unwanted by anyone is a feeling you never forget. Everyone else is inside with a place to go and be, and you're outside with nothing.

—I suppose there are people with outboard motors equipped with electric starters who have never wrapped that rope around the flywheel and yanked on it until the engine started.

—It's been a long while since I toasted a marshmallow on a stick over an open fire and even longer since I melted one in a cup of hot cocoa.

—We haven't had a power failure in our house in six years now and I miss them. If it didn't last too long, it was sort of adventurous to live by candlelight and find ways to improvise dinner.

—When you walk up to someone's front door and ring the bell and wait for someone to come, it's an uncomfortable few minutes. You don't know what they're doing in there. You don't know who is going to come to the door. You aren't sure anyone will. I haven't been in that position in years. When I go to someone's house now, I either know them so well I just walk in, or they're having a big party and the door is already open, so I don't ring.

—Filling a fountain pen from a bottle of ink was satisfying.

—In the last three years, half a dozen quick car wash places have opened for business in our area. Every time the car gets dirty now, my wife takes it over there and has it washed, and I'm left with nothing easy to do Saturday morning. Washing a car gives me a sense of accomplishment without demanding much from me.

—The way I used to save money was a lot more satisfying than the way I save it now. Every night I used to empty my pockets and put all the loose change in a big jar in my closet. Now the company takes money out of my check every week. I never see the money and don't get anywhere near the pleasure from saving that I did with the jar. I guess I'm saving more now but it isn't money, it's just a number.

—There is no more secure feeling than being inside a tent that doesn't leak when it's pouring outside.

—Nothing was ever more uncomfortable than riding on the crossbar or the handlebars of a friend's bicycle.

—It's been years since I've heard the sound or had the satisfaction that comes from slamming a genuine wooden frame screen door. Aluminum screen doors are just not the same.

—There was something special about running a stick along an iron picket fence.

—Not once this winter have I had to shovel the snow from my sidewalk, but I haven't forgotten the unpleasant feeling you get when you're sliding the shovel along to scoop up the snow and hit a crack.

—When I delivered newspapers, they were usually thin enough so I could fold them into a square. You folded them once longways and then you folded them in three equal parts and tucked one part into the other. This way you could throw them on a porch from a moving bicycle. Or *near* the porch, anyway. Mrs. Potter wouldn't pay one week because she said I put too many in the bushes.

—Cakes of ice are all an inch square now and that's too bad, because getting a fifty-pound cake to break cleanly in two with an icepick was an art.

Small Pleasures

I<small>T'S</small> too bad all of us don't have some way to remind ourselves
how good life is when life is going well. We are more apt to think
of it as merely average and normal.

When I was fifteen, I had an appendectomy. There was some
minor complication, and I was in the hospital for almost three
weeks. (It's always surprising how serious a minor operation seems
when you're the one who has had it.) But I recall then appreciating
the colors and the action of everyday life when I got out of the
hospital. My perception of many things I had always taken for
granted was razor sharp. The grass looked greener, our house
looked better and my mother's cooking tasted great.

The fact is, any time we or someone we love isn't dying, it should
be considered a great time in life.

Just now, in the course of writing this, I was trying to remind
myself of small pleasures I enjoy almost daily:

—My shower first thing in the morning is a wonderfully pleasant
and exhilarating way to start the day. I like the warmth, I like a
good cake of soap, and I like the idea that I'm part of a civilization
that has organized itself to get water to my house and have it warm
and waiting for me when I get up. It's difficult to remember to be
amazed every day, but it is amazing.

—The morning newspaper and that first cup of coffee are two
things I'm sure they have in heaven if there is one. I always pick up
any newspaper with a great sense of anticipation. I'm a newspaper
nut. There are times when I don't find much in it that interests me,
but that never dampens my enthusiasm for getting at it again the
following day.

—I love my work. I love writing. I even like the physical process of
hitting the keys of the typewriter with my fingers, although I only
use three of them. I enjoy thinking of things to write, and there is
always a vague sense of excitement about whether I can do it or
not; this heightens my interest. And to finish a piece of writing is
a great satisfaction. It's as good as getting a sliver out of your finger.

—By noon I'm getting hungry and feeling desk-bound. I know a hundred good little restaurants, and it is a wonderfully civilized pleasure to find a friend and go to one of them for lunch.

—In the afternoons I'm not nearly so smart as I am in the shower eight hours earlier, but if I'm not pressed to do something for a deadline, I'm just as happy. It's pleasant to browse through the mail and the debris on my desk, looking for a job easy enough for my brain to handle at that hour. Perhaps I call one of my four kids working in Boston, Washington, New York and Providence.

—By late afternoon I can't wait to get home—the same home I couldn't wait to leave that morning. It's a pleasant place. My wife is glad to see me, I'm glad to see her, and we sit down and have a drink while we watch the evening news on television.

—On Saturdays I have fresh orange juice, one of the great luxuries of my life. As I sit there sipping it, I think how lucky I am to be able to make enough money to squeeze three oranges for a drink. After a great time with coffee, toast and the newspaper, I go down to my cellar filled with tools and good wood. I've had some of the pieces of wood for twenty years. I sit and consider for the hundredth time what I might make of a wide piece of walnut. I feel it and enjoy it and decide to save it.

I am not sick or dying at all right now, and I'm determined to remind myself how good life is.

X:

ENDINGS

John Lennon

A young man I like came into the office the other morning, and I happened to be walking past the coat rack when he was fumbling with a hanger.

"Good morning," I said.

As if I had asked him how he felt, he said, "I feel terrible about this thing."

His eyes were red and tears came to them again as he turned and hung his coat. What had moved him was the murder of John Lennon.

I walked back to my office and got thinking about how little it had moved me; I felt no real sadness, only interest in it as a news story and anger over its violent nature.

I had closed my mind to the Beatles. They were a phenomenon I had been exposed to a thousand times, but they never interested me much. I liked some of their music, but I'm a musical ignoramus and didn't really appreciate how technically good they were. Nor did I get much meaning from the words of their songs. I thought they confused obscurity with depth.

Part of my negative feeling about the Beatles came not so much because I never bothered to appreciate their music, but because I thought they had made drugs look attractive to a whole generation. Many of their songs seemed to me to be invitations to go fly with them. The "Yellow Submarine" was made to look like an attractive trip for young people to take.

My young office friend's genuine sorrow made it clear to me that I'd missed something, and in the days since John Lennon's death, I've read and heard a lot more about him. I feel a lot worse now than I did the night I heard he'd been shot. No amount of reading about or listening to Elvis Presley would make me feel anything different about him, but Lennon was out of Presley's class as a musician and as a human being.

It is apparent that Lennon had been trying desperately and with a lot of success to live his way out of what he got himself into by being a Beatle. He wasn't rejecting everything that had meant to him; he was just saying it was over and he wanted to move on to something else. It was something he didn't want to be anymore, and a lot of people weren't satisfied to let him stop being it. The man who killed him was one of those.

Whatever Lennon was as a Beatle, he'd obviously been something different for the last five years. He said he liked to stay home and bake bread and take care of his five-year-old son. It is obvious that he was sincere. He said it not to create an effect on the minds of readers of that statement, but because that's honestly what he wanted to do. He had had all the fame anyone could ever wish for, and he didn't want it anymore. It's easier to be an iconoclast, of course, if you've made your two hundred million dollars, but you can't fault him for that.

We make such fools of ourselves with our heroes, that's what irritates me the most about the kind of idiotic adulation the Beatles got. Wouldn't it have been possible for that whole sixties generation to have loved the Beatles' music without chasing them up and down the streets of the world?

Almost everyone who becomes famous ends up acting the way famous people act. It isn't so much that famous people *want* to act that way; they are forced into certain patterns of behavior. John Lennon was trying to act some way other than the way famous people act, and people wouldn't let him. Most of all, his murderer wouldn't let him.

It's very sad, and I understand now my friend's tears.

Herbert Hahn

He lived only a thirty-five-cent phone call away, but I never called him. No one influenced my life more than he did. Now he's gone and I don't think I ever told him.

I worked late yesterday and didn't get home until after eight. We had a quick dinner and it was too late to start anything else, so at ten I got into bed with the newspaper I'd never taken the time to read. The economic news was bad and the Giants' coach said he wasn't discouraged. I leafed through to the obituary page and my eye caught the little headline in boldface type:

HERBERT HAHN, 75
ENGLISH TEACHER

I dropped the paper to the floor next to the bed and stared at the ceiling. Mr. Hahn was dead. *Why* hadn't I called him? I was surprised to find myself crying. I hadn't really seen Mr. Hahn for forty years, didn't even know he was "Dr. Hahn" now, but I had thought of him on almost every one of the days of those forty years.

My memory of exactly what he was like in school was incredibly clear to me. I remember every mannerism, the way he pulled at the crease at the knee of his pants when he sat on the edge of his desk. I even remember that he only had two suits in 1936. One was his old suit and one was his good suit. He wore the old one for two days every other week when the good one was at the cleaners. He only made twenty-seven hundred dollars a year teaching history in Albany, N.Y., then and clothes were not a top priority of his.

He left Albany in about 1945 to teach at a good private school in New Jersey, and I wasn't surprised that the obituary called him an English teacher. It didn't really matter what Mr. Hahn's class was called. He taught life and his subject was of secondary importance. When we were fourteen and fifteen, he talked to us as though we were human beings, not children. He talked about everything in class, and just to make sure we knew he didn't think he was omnipotent, he often followed some pronouncement he'd made about government or politics by saying, "And don't forget you heard it from the same teacher who predicted in 1932 that Hitler would get nowhere in Germany."

How many teachers do you have in your life? I lay there wondering last night. Between grade school, high school and college, if you're lucky enough to go to college, I suppose you have about fifty teachers. Is that about right?

I don't remember much about some of mine, and nothing about what they were trying to teach me, but of those fifty, I had five who were very good and two who were great. Mr. Hahn was one of those.

He didn't do a lot of extra talking, but when he talked he was direct and often brilliant. He was the only genuine philosopher I ever knew. He wasn't a teacher of philosophy, but a living, breathing philosophizer. He exuded wisdom, concern for the world and quite often a bad temper. Idiots irritated him, and it annoyed him when teenagers acted younger than he was treating them.

I went to the service for him today. I don't know why, really. There was no one there I knew, and one phone call over the years would have meant more to him. A minister spoke, but it was standard stuff, and Mr. Hahn was not what most people would call a religious person, even though he wrote a book called *The Great Religions: Interpretations*.

A young woman who taught with him spoke, and she brought the tears back to my eyes. He had touched her life in the 1970s as he had touched mine in the 1930s.

Mr. Hahn could have taught at any college in the country, but he chose to stay at the secondary level. He didn't think teaching college-age people was any more important than teaching boys and girls fourteen to eighteen. He was the kind of person who gave teachers the right to be proud to be teachers.

I just wish I'd called or written to tell him how much he meant to my life.

Mother

MY mother died today.

She was a great mom and I am typing with tears in my eyes. There were a lot of things she wasn't so good at, but no one was ever better at being a mother.

She never wanted to be anything *but* a good mother. It would not satisfy many women today. If I were a woman it would not satisfy me, but there was something good about her being one that exceeded any good I will ever do.

I think I know why she was a world champion mother. She had unlimited love and forgiveness in her heart for those close to her. Neither my sister nor I ever did anything so wrong in her eyes that she couldn't explain it in terms of right. She assumed our goodness, and no amount of badness in either of us could change her mind. It made us better.

Mother gave the same love to our four children and even had enough left for our family bulldog, Gifford. One summer afternoon at her cottage in a wooded area with a lot of wildlife, some food was left on the table on the front patio. When we came back later, part of it had been eaten, and everyone but Mother suspected our bulldog.

"It couldn't have been Gifford," Mother said. "It must have been some animal."

From the day she went into the hospital, there was never any question about her living. The doctor treated her as though she might recover, but he knew she would not. I hope he is treated as well on his deathbed.

Something has to be done about the way we die, though. Too often it is not good enough. Some of the people who have heard of Mother's death at age ninety-three and knew of her protracted illness said, "It's a blessing," but there was nothing blessed about it.

For seven terrible weeks after a stroke, Mother held on to life with a determination she would not have had if she hadn't wanted to live.

Visiting her, at first, I was pleased that she seemed unaware of anything and not suffering. I would bend over, stroke her hair, and whisper in her ear, "It's Andrew, Mom." It would not seem as though she heard, but her hand, which had been picking at the blanket in a manner distinctively her own, groped for mine. She did hear. She did know. She was in a terrible half-dream from which she could not arouse herself. She was suffering and in fear of death, and I could not console myself that she was not.

My wife stood on the other side of the bed. They got along during the twenty years Mother lived with us. Mother lifted her other hand vaguely toward her. Dying, she wished to include my wife, who had been so good to her, in her affection.

Something is wrong, though. She has something in her throat, or one of her legs is caught in an uncomfortable position. You don't dare touch anything for fear of disconnecting one of the tubes leading from the bottles hanging overhead into her. The nurses are busy with their bookwork, or they are down the hall working routinely toward Mother's room. Other patients there are caught or choking, too. The nurses know Mother will probably not choke before they get there. They've done it all before.

The nurses are very good, but without apparent compassion, and you realize it has to be that way. They could not possibly work as nurses without some protective coating against tragedy. We all have it. In those seven weeks Mother lay dying, I visited the hospital fifty times, but when I left, it was impossible not to lose some of the sense of her suffering. I knew she was still lying there picking vaguely at the blankets in that sad, familiar way, but it didn't hurt as much as when I was there, watching.

I wondered—if she was the President of the United States, what extraordinary measures would they be taking for her? How could I get them for her? She is not President, she is only my mother. The doctors and nurses cannot know that this frail, dying old woman did a million kindnesses for me. They wouldn't know or care that she was girls' high-jump champion of Ballston Spa in 1902 or that she often got up early Sunday morning to make hot popovers for us or that she drove her old Packard too fast and too close to the righthand side of the road. No stranger would have guessed any of those things looking at her there and perhaps would not have cared.

There is no time for each of us to weep for the whole world. We each weep for our own.

Andrew Rooney writes a column three days a week for the Tribune Company Syndicate that appears in over 250 newspapers nationwide. In addition, his television essays have won him three Emmys, six Writers Guild Awards, the Peabody Award, and a host of other honors.

He began his writing career as a correspondent for *The Stars and Stripes* during World War II, and went on to become a radio and television writer for Arthur Godfrey, Garry Moore, and others, before joining Harry Reasoner in a collaboration—Rooney writing and producing, Reasoner narrating—that produced notable essays on chairs, hotels, bridges and the English language. In 1971, he began reading his own material with "An Essay on War" on NET's "The Great American Dream Machine," and since then has produced such acclaimed specials as "Mr. Rooney Goes to Washington" (1975), "Mr. Rooney Goes to Dinner" (1976) and "Mr. Rooney Goes to Work" (1977), as well as his weekly "A Few Minutes with Andy Rooney" on "60 Minutes."

Andrew Rooney is the author of five previous books, including *The Story of The Stars and Stripes, Air Gunner,* and *Conqueror's Peace* (all with Bud Hutton), *The Fortunes of War*, and the best seller *A Few Minutes with Andy Rooney.*